Teaching Information Literacy Skills to Social Sciences Students and Practitioners: A Casebook of Applications

edited by
Douglas Cook and Natasha Cooper

Association of College and Research Libraries
A division of the American Library Association

Chicago 2006

The paper used in this publication meets the minimum requirements of American National Standard for Information Sciences–Permanence of Paper for Printed Library Materials, ANSI Z39.48-1992. ∞

Teaching information literacy skills to social sciences students and practitioners : a casebook of applications / Douglas Cook and Natasha Cooper, editors.
    p. cm.
Includes bibliographical references and index.
ISBN 0-8389-8389-8 (alk. paper)
1. Information literacy--Study and teaching--Case studies.
2. Electronic information resource literacy--Study and teaching
--Case studies. 3. Social sciences--Information resources--Case
studies. 4. Research--Methodology--Study and teaching--Case
studies. 5. Academic libraries--Relations with faculty and curricu-
lum--Case studies. 6. Information literacy--Standards--United
States--Case studies. I. Cook, Douglas. II. Cooper, Natasha,
1955- .
ZA3075.T43 2006
028.7071--dc22
2006019905

Printed on recycled paper.

Printed in the United States of America.

10 09 08 07 06 5 4 3 2 1

Table of Contents

Foreword

Patricia O'Brien Libutti

This book has deep roots.
This casebook can trace its origins to work undertaken over a period of almost thirty years. The first edition, *Teaching Information Retrieval and Evaluation Skills to Education Students and Practitioners: A Casebook of Applications*[1] was published in the mid-1990s, when the Association of College and Research Libraries (ACRL), Education and Behavioral Sciences Section (EBSS) committees were addressing increasing concerns about standards and their application in instruction via articles, programming, first Internet sites, and books.

Social sciences librarians affiliated with EBSS discussed and wrote about instruction almost as soon as the section was established. In 1978, a simple "Worksheet on How to Use Resources in Education"[2] was published in *C&RL News*, produced by the EBSS Bibliographic Instruction for Educators (BIE) Committee. The next step, preparing instructional guidelines, was displayed in the first "Bibliographic Competencies for Education Students," in 1981.[3] The second rewriting, in 1992,[4] extended guidelines into suggested subject information standards. The outgrowth was a careful look at the actual instructional practice in library sessions.

This author, and others involved in EBSS during that time period, felt that the 1992 "Competencies" needed practical application. During 1993–1995, the EBSS BIE Committee developed and worked as a group on *Teaching Information Retrieval and Evaluation Skills to Education Students and Practitioners,*[5] the inspiration for the current work. The intention of the first casebook was to share real-world examples of librarians in action as they instructed students at various levels. The focus that united all the chapters was a template based on Gagne's work.[6] The template included a lesson plan, a narrative of the actual session, and lessons learned; helping others see the often not-quite-perfect, nonairbrushed sessions for what they were.

The library profession has had major developments since publication of the 1995 casebook. The ACRL *Information Literacy Competency Standards for Higher Education,*[7] although emerging at the time of the publication, did not have the impact on instructional practice and publication that they do now. Indeed, infusion of these standards into the basic construction of planning and case reporting is what separates the second casebook from the first. Instead of the subject-specific standards seen in the earlier works, information literacy standards cross all disciplines and inform this volume.

Also notable was the sparseness of collaboration in the first casebook between librarian and teaching faculty. However, the Web site developed for the ACRL/EBSS national program in 1996, Strategic Academic Partnerships: Leading the Development of Interactive Learning Environments,[8] showed the beginnings of the shift in collaborative thinking, as did *The Collaborative Imperative,* one of the most referenced books in the academic instruction library field.[9]

The development of collaboration and instructional standards across disciplines in library instruction mandated that a second casebook be published. Also supporting the second edition were inquiries from library and information science faculty to this author: "When will you start the second edition?" The answer to that was clear: both editors for the first edition had progressed in research agendas and believed that others involved in EBSS could now address this concern. Doug Cook and Tasha Cooper took on the challenge of creating this second casebook. Although the basic format of this casebook and the first remain the same, the outpouring of interest and the resulting chapter proposals demanded a reshaping of the schema of presentation and reflection.

Teaching Information Literacy Skills to Social Sciences Students and Practitioners: A Casebook of Applications retains an emphasis on narrative cases, reflections, and plans but is anchored solidly in the ACRL *Information Literacy Competency Standards for Higher Education,*[10] as the title change notes. This book presents the reader with images of current practice and interests across the social sciences beyond, but including, education. Chapters reflect the practice of collaboration between teaching faculty and librarians commonly seen in academic libraries with information literacy initiatives. There is a richness of content in specific topic examinations developed from information and practice combined in this book. Both new and veteran social sciences librarians will gain much from a thoughtful reading of the diversity of applications of information literacy instruction across the disciplines.

Enjoy!

Patricia O'Brien Libutti, PhD
March 15, 2006

Notes

1. Patricia O'Brien Libutti and Bonnie Gratch-Lindauer, *Teaching Information Retrieval and Evaluation Skills to Education Students and Practitioners: A Casebook of Applications* (Chicago: ACRL, 1995).

2. "Worksheet on How to Use Resources in Education." *College & Research Libraries News* (Oct. 1978): 286–87.

3. "Bibliographic Competencies for Education Students," *College & Research Libraries News* (July–Aug. 1981): 209–10.

4. Bonnie Gratch, et al., "Information Retrieval and Evaluation Skills for Education Students," *College & Research Libraries News* (Oct. 1992): 583–88.

5. Libutti and Gratch-Lindauer, *Teaching Information Retrieval and Evaluation Skills to Education Students and Practitioners*

6. See, for example, Robert Gagne, *Essentials of Learning for Instruction.* (Englewood Cliffs, NJ: Prentice Hall, 1988).

7. Association of College and Research Libraries, *Information Literacy Competency Standards for Higher Education* (Chicago: ACRL, 2000). Available online from http://www.ala.org/ala/acrl/acrlstandards/inform ationliteracycompetency.htm.

8. Kim Kelley, "Welcome to the W.E.B.B.: Working Educator's Bulletin Board." Available online from http://nova.umuc.edu/~kelley/webb/ webb.html. This Web site archives information from the 1996 ACRL, EBSS Annual Program in New York. It was also chronicled in *College & Research Libraries News* (June 1996): 357–58.

9. The *Encyclopedia of Library and Information Science, 2nd ed., ed. Miriam A. Drake (New York:* Marcel Dekker, *2003), s.v. "Education Librarians," (by S. Sowell),* named Richard Raspa and Dane Ward, eds. *The Collaborative Imperative: Librarians and Faculty Working Together in the Information Universe* (Chicago: ACRL, 2000) and O'Brien Libutti and Gratch-Lindauer, *Teaching Information Retrieval and Evaluation Skills to Education Students and Practitioners,* as two of the three most referenced books in the academic instruction library field.

10. ACRL, *Information Literacy Competency Standards.*

Acknowledgements

The authors wish to thank all those who responded to our call for chapters for their interest and cooperation as we moved this project forward. Thanks are also due to those who worked on the previous edition and who set up the format; and to EBSS members generally, who contributed to discussions about instruction in these subject areas. Hugh Thompson, Dawn Mueller, and other editorial staff members at ACRL deserve thanks for their editorial assistance. Special thanks go to our project mentor—Patricia O'Brien Libutti—who encouraged us to create this second Casebook, and also cheered us on throughout the process.

Introduction

Teaching Information Literacy Skills to Social Sciences Students and Practitioners: A Casebook of Applications expands and builds on the first edition, *Teaching Information Retrieval and Evaluation Skills to Education Students and Practitioners: A Casebook of Applications.*[1] This second *Casebook* follows much the same format as the first, incorporating an established chapter template that includes an analysis of the learning situation, description of "what happened," and reflection on how the experience might be improved next time around. The second edition is also broadened by the inclusion of Association of College and Research Libraries (ACRL) Information Literacy Competency Standards[2] correlated to each session.

Because of recent changes in our profession, the scope of this edition is wider than the first. The ACRL Education and Behavioral Sciences Section (EBSS) has recently gone through an expansion of its emphases to include more of the social sciences in its programming; and as the editors are members of EBSS we felt it important to reflect this positive change. So in addition to chapters on education, a range of social sciences and practitioner instruction sessions are presented, including communication studies, management, political science, psychology, and social work.

A second change in the field of academic librarianship has been the wide-spread acceptance of the ACRL Information Literacy Competency Standards. These Standards have provided a rallying point for academic instruction librarians of all stripes. As members of EBSS, we realize that more than any other document in recent memory, the ACRL Standards have provided the necessity and the shared terminology for librarians from all subject areas to discuss instruction and student outcomes. Furthermore, these Standards have helped academic librarians to share with their classroom faculty colleagues their passion to impart to students the skills of lifelong learning. The ACRL Standards are at the heart of this book. Each chapter is aligned to particular student outcomes. In fact, one way to make use of this *Casebook* is to think about it as a practical study of the applications of each of the five ACRL standards.

Themes

A number of themes emerge from the chapters of this edition. One of the strongest themes—collaboration—was just beginning to become a topic of interest to academic librarians when the first *Casebook* was published. Collaboration between faculty and librarians; librarians and librarians; and librarians, faculty, and students is a recurring theme, reflecting the complexity of the learning process and the need to understand the expertise and experience of all participants in the instructional setting. At the most basic level of collaboration, fourteen of our cases were written by two or more authors. Of those chapters, Barrett and Parker; Charoenpanitkul and Sittler; Faix and Hughes; Laverty and Reed; and Yu and Shrimplin are examples of librarians who are teaching in teams. On a more complex level, eight of the chapters were written by a librarian (or librarians) and a faculty member working together—Bielat and Bhavnagri; Cast and Pasco; Childers and Renne; Duke and Brown; Kearns, Stockham, and Westman; Koehn and Hurlbert; Leigh, Gibbon, and Wertzberger; and Warner and Templeton. Such collaborative efforts require significant planning time, but can only make our instruction richer for its contextualization.

The complexity of the research process is also a theme. Ariew encourages students to learn about the challenges of the research process from each other; and Childers and Renne explore ways to approach the challenges of literature reviews. Numerous chapters—for example, Barrett and Parker; Cast and Pasco; Daugherty; Duke and Brown; and Koehn and Hurlbert—describe settings in which the instructors provide structure to students, helping them organize their searches and results, using worksheets and matrices. During a time when such a large quantity of information is readily available to student researchers, these authors offer models for helping students structure their work.

Many of the authors used ACRL Information Literacy Competency Standards One through Three as a framework for their instruction: 1) determining information needs, 2) acquiring information, and 3) evaluating information. Standards One through Three seem to be at the heart of what we do as librarians. These information-gathering skill sets make a lot of common sense in the context of lifelong learning. Several authors, however, go beyond Standards One through Three. Kearns, Stockham, and Westman used Standard Four as a framework to assist students in small groups to find and validate information to use in the creation of Web sites. And Caravello was fortunate enough to be asked to discuss plagiarism with large groups of graduate students, thus focusing entirely on Standard Five. Various authors stretched our thinking about the ACRL Standards. Xu (Social Work); Bielat and Bhavnagri (Teacher Education); Warner and Templeton (Early Childhood); and Leigh, Gibbons, and Wertzberger (Management), for example, extended their instruction with standards and competencies from their specific disciplines. Barrett and Parker redefined literacy to include critical thinking about images. And Yu and Shrimplin further developed the concept of information literacy to include data literacy.

In viewing the chapters together it becomes obvious that learning occurs in a variety of settings, ranging from traditional face-to-face classroom formats to individualized, or group, online distance settings. Cast and Pasco; Duke and Brown; and Xu work with students at a distance. Xu describes the creation of a tutorial used by graduate students to asynchronously learn information literacy skills. Distance settings often bring about specialized circumstances which require different instructional methodologies. Charoenpanitkul and Sittler; Koehn and Hurlbert; and Leigh, Gibbon, and Wertzberger teach in a more traditional setting allowing active and face-to-face engagement with students. The chapters in this edition also point out that instruction occurs in individual, as well as group settings, and may even be incorporated into the reference consultation. For example, Oldenkamp found that his instructional engagement and work at the reference desk were closely linked. Dreyer, Jordan, and Wassertzug note that one-to-one consultations often meet the needs of students in their professional graduate programs better than would a group session. And Osa uses a step-by-step, tailored and personalized, instructional approach as a successful strategy.

This book also reflects a variety of approaches to teaching. Many authors incorporate active learning. Warner and Templeton are strong advocates for this approach. Faix and Hughes; and Kearns, Stockham, and Westman have built their instruction around small group exercises or projects. Some chapters reflect the use of more traditional demonstration methods. Daugherty; Smith; and Yu and Shrimplin use lecture and demonstration quite effectively in some very specialized situations.

Many of these authors make use of technology in various ways. PowerPoint, online databases, and the Internet, of course, were utilized by a number of librarians. Several chapters describe the use of Blackboard course-management software in hybrid, face-to-face instruction—Bielet and Bhavnagri; Cox; Leigh, Gibbon, Wertzberger; and Xu. Duke and Brown also used course-management software with their distance education graduate students and expanded their use of stand-alone PowerPoint tutorials by using Macromedia Breeze to add an audio track. Kearns, Stockham, and Westman used a Web site about a children's author as a final project. Leigh, Gibbon, and Wertzberger used TurningPoint "clickers" for immediate student feedback during their instruction session. And perhaps one of the most contextual uses of technology was that of Warner and Templeton, who had pre-service teachers use Kid Pix Deluxe software to create lessons, and Intel Teach to the Future software which is designed to help teachers integrate technology into classrooms to enhance student learning. Librarians are often willing to try new instructional software and it seems that many of these "early-adapters" are represented here.

Another theme which has recently become quite important to most academic instruction librarians is assessment. Several authors in this edition describe assessment efforts, ranging from programmatic to class-specific, reflecting initiatives to evaluate the overall effectiveness of curricula and individual teaching methods. Ariew presents a simple assessment tool which can be used with graduate students at the beginning of a session to discover the depth of their knowledge. Bielat and Bhavnagri; and Leigh, Gibbon, and Wertzberger use ACRL Standards as a basis for an objective pretest and posttest. And Laverty and Reed describe a tailored, instructional initiative that grew out of a survey of teacher candidates.

Overall, these chapters reveal the challenges of information literacy instruction, if we understand that to mean instruction beyond a basic "how to" and an effort to incorporate the ACRL standards. Each librarian (or group of librarians) describes a unique setting, into which instruction is incorporated. Each librarian also brings his or her own interests and level of experience to the situation, describing and sharing successes and less-than-successful experiences. All authors show an interest in learning from each instructional experience, working to improve, in a continuous process of growth, creativity, and development.

We hope that readers of this *Casebook* will learn from the ideas presented, share ideas in the future, and continue to explore ways to understand our surroundings and improve our practice. Whether used as a casebook of lesson plans for new or pre-practice academic librarians, or used as an idea book for experienced instruction librarians in the social sciences, the editors hope that you, the reader, find this book informative and challenging in its range of instructional settings. We trust that you learn as much from each of these authors about the current practice of information literacy instruction in the social sciences as we did.

Notes regarding format

Standards. Each author was asked to indicate which ACRL Information Literacy Competency Standards were addressed in their instruction. In order to eliminate repetition of standards throughout, we include the complete *Standards, Performance Indicators, and Outcomes* of the *Information Literacy Competency Standards for Higher Education*, as an Appendix A, and will, in some cases refer to the performance indicator or outcome by number only.

Chapter format. In order to make it possible for the reader to quickly find related portions across chapters, all authors were asked to follow a specific outline:

- Introduction
- Analysis of the Learning Situation
- Information Literacy Standards

- Lesson Plan
- Description of the Instruction Session: What Actually Happened?
- Reflection on the Instruction Session: Lessons Learned
- Notes
- Teaching Resources

Teaching resources. Handouts and accompanying materials used as teaching resources are included in the *Teaching Resources* section of each chapter, unless they are online resources, in which case URLs are provided in the *Notes* section, as appropriate.

Doug Cook
Tasha Cooper
April 15, 2006

Notes

1. Patricia O'Brien Libutti and Bonnie Gratch-Lindauer, *Teaching Information Retrieval and Evaluation Skills to Education Students and Practitioners: A Casebook of Applications.* (Chicago: Association of College and Research Libraries, 1995).

2. Association of College and Research Libraries, *Information Literacy Competency Standards for Higher Education* (Chicago: Association of College and Research Libraries, 2000), http://www.ala.org/ala/acrl/acrlstandards/informationliteracycompetency.htm.

Chapter 1

A Picture Worth a Thousand Words: Visual Literacy Through Critical Inquiry

Laura Barrett and Suzan Parker

Introduction

Visual literacy, defined here as the ability to recognize, interpret, evaluate, and create visual messages, is increasingly important for navigating daily life and for conducting effective research. Visual literacy enables us to critically assess the wide array of images that infuse our daily lives through such diverse media contexts as advertising, the Web, television, video games, books, magazines, and museums.

The need for information literacy instruction to target not only textual but also visual artifacts is growing rapidly. Since student projects increasingly involve multimedia presentations and require non-textual research sources, this increased demand for visual literacy has outpaced the development of lessons and classes to teach those skills.

This chapter addresses an information literacy session that we, a media studies and a social science librarian, facilitated together for a community college learning community focusing on gender and the media. The instruction session emphasized the critical thinking skills necessary to interpret and evaluate images, skills that we hope students will continue to utilize as they encounter images, text, and other forms of information.

Analysis of the Learning Situation

The Bothell Campus Library and Media Center, part of the University of Washington Libraries system, serves the University of Washington, Bothell (UWB) and Cascadia Community College (CCC). UWB and CCC are unique in Washington; they comprise the only fully co-located campus in the state and one of only a handful in the nation. Integrated Studies, an academic transfer program, is currently Cascadia's largest program of study, with many CCC students choosing to continue their upper division work at UWB.

The curriculum at each institution emphasizes an interdisciplinary and active approach to learning. Information literacy instruction is prevalent and integrated into the curriculum at multiple levels; collaboration between librarians and faculty is common. This allows instruction librarians and faculty to take a developmental approach with students by reinforcing previous learning and by working with them in increasingly complex ways throughout their college careers.

This lesson plan details a visual literacy workshop conducted for a freshman/sophomore-level learning community at Cascadia. Learning communities combine two existing courses from different disciplines in one classroom. The two course instructors collaborate to teach their respective course content by focusing on the ways in which the two disciplines intersect. This learning community, taught by Stephanie Skourtes and David Ortiz, combined Sex and Gender (Sociology 131) and Media in United States Society (Communications 203). The class consisted of approximately fifty predominantly-female students representing a range of ages.

The library session occurred just after the mid-point of the quarter and aimed to prepare students for their final project. The project required students to create a media campaign that integrated concepts from the two interdisciplinary study areas of media and gender. The media campaign could take the form of a flier, brochure, Web site, poster, or video consisting of text and images addressing a topic of relevance to the course. The students' campaigns should inform, educate, or persuade the intended audience about a topic of their choosing, such as the portrayal of women in clothing advertisements, the use of unfair labor practices in the production of certain products, or gender stereotypes portrayed on television and in film. The learning community faculty encouraged students to incorporate effective visual rhetorical strategies often used by advertisers into their media campaigns. In other words, their media campaigns should not simply use images to illustrate the text, but they should use images and text in partnership with one another to convey a cohesive message.

The hour-long library session asked students to apply close reading techniques to an image-intensive print advertisement, thus reinforcing the use of detailed observation as a social science research method, as well as the practice of content analysis common in media studies research. Through this active learning exercise, we aimed to help students apply textual reading skills to non-textual materials, and to practice critical inquiry techniques to guide their subsequent research projects. Before the library instruction session, students had no formal training in this analytical process; however they had been theoretically prepped by prior class discussions focused on the ways that media messages are packaged and consumed.

We faced several challenges while preparing for the session, all of which ultimately worked to our benefit and to that of our students. First, this particular learning community had not previously been offered, and it was the first time the two faculty members involved had taught collaboratively with each other. All four of us were starting from scratch; we were developing new learning outcomes, lesson plans, and assignments that were significantly different than any we had created before. Additionally, the faculty members gave us total autonomy over the content of the library session, encouraging our creativity and innovation. Their only request was that the session should support the course's final project which, at the time of our planning meeting, was not yet fully developed. The situation was both daunting and exciting.

While tackling the obstacles/opportunities above, we were cognizant of the challenges we would be facing in the classroom. The library session occurred over halfway through the term in the early stages of the final project. Students had not yet selected their topics and, therefore, were not yet ready to begin searching in the library's catalog and databases for sources to support their campaigns' messages. It was essential that we design an engaging session that taught skills the students could begin practicing right away so that the learning would be immediately reinforced.

Our decision to focus on visual literacy was a response to all of these challenges. It was a topic we had not previously taught; and we were excited to experiment with this aspect of information literacy. We did not need to know the yet-undeveloped assignment details to feel confident that a visual literacy workshop would benefit the students in their final project and beyond. We believed that students would be interested in the subject matter and would be able to practice visual literacy skills immediately as they contemplated topics for their media campaigns and participated in class discussions.

Information Literacy Standards
(Note: A complete list of ACRL *Information Literacy Competency Standards for Higher Education* (Chicago: ACRL, 2000) appears as Appendix A.)

This session focuses primarily on Standard Three of the ACRL Information Literacy Competency Standards for Higher Education: "The information literate student evaluates information and its sources critically and incorporates selected information into his or her knowledge base and value system,"[1] and predominantly on Outcomes 3.2.c, 3.2.d, and 3.6.a.

In the exercise outlined here, students critically evaluate the intent and impact of an advertising image, using the disciplinary frameworks of media and gender studies to inform their analyses. We used the image and supporting materials to generate thinking and discussion around the image's qualities, creation, intent, and audience. We used students' impressions of and questions about the image to encourage them to think more deeply about this image than they generally think about images they encounter. By thinking critically about these and other issues surrounding the image, students practiced skills and gained insights they could then utilize in other courses and throughout their lives.

Lesson Plan
Library Instruction Objectives
In this sixty-minute workshop, our learning goals were to help students:

1. Utilize information literacy skills in a non-textual environment
2. Creatively explore visual messages through their own stories and questions about the advertisement viewed
3. Collaboratively develop and practice critical analysis of an image by applying criteria such as context, authorship, agenda, and effect
4. Increase their awareness that they encounter and interpret images and other media daily
5. Examine effective visual strategies for presenting information
6. Effectively find and use images by introducing them to research tools and digital image collections

Lesson Plan:

1. Students analyze an image, which has been chosen by the librarians and dissected into quadrants. Students individually note each detail and their impressions on the Image Analysis Worksheet.
2. Next, students analyze the full image, first without, and then with the advertisement text and corporate logo, noting changes in their reading of the image.
3. Students, faculty and librarians share their observations first in small groups and then in a large class discussion.
4. Librarians introduce research tools and digital image collections that students will use for their final project exploring the interplay of gender and media.

Description of the Instruction Session: What Actually Happened?
This was a large learning community of two combined classes (Sociology 131 and Communications 203) with two faculty instructors. In order to foster more intimate class discussions, we divided the library instruction session; half the class attended the first hour and the other half the second. Each faculty member attended one of the sessions and was an active participant in the exercise and discussion. This helped to emphasize to students the importance of the session content, and set an expectation of high participation in the class discussions.

The session was held in a computer lab. Every student had access to a computer, although the exercise could be conducted entirely offline, if necessary. We introduced ourselves as the subject librarians in our respective disciplines. We talked about the overall goals of the session, which included reminding students of their media campaign project requirements. In order to make that campaign successful, they would need to understand media techniques used to communicate their ideas effectively, and they would need to be able to find appropriate examples of digital images. Because our time with the students was limited to one hour, we decided to focus on the critical evaluation process, rather than on the mechanics of finding and manipulating digital images.

We started the exercise by asking students to view a Web page with a photographic image depicting three very thin, futuristic looking women with short cropped orange hair, wearing platform shoes, and standing together around an object. One woman is wearing pants and is straddling what appears to be either a large flat television screen or computer monitor. The other two women stand on either side of her, in profile. One wears a long, slitted skirt and the other wears tight short shorts. They appear passive and vacant, staring off to the sides; the woman in the middle straddling the television/monitor stares directly and assertively at the viewer. Of the three, she appears the most stereotypically masculine in her stance and in her manner of dress.

Students were asked to view the image on the Web page for a few minutes, form an overall impression, and then examine individual items depicted. They then looked at the same image divided into quadrants. This enabled them to focus on details that they might not otherwise have noticed when looking at the whole picture. We asked them to list all the people, objects, and activities that they observed on the Image Analysis Worksheet adapted from document analysis worksheets created by the Education Staff of the National Archives and Records Administration.[2] The worksheet prompted them to write down questions the image raised for them and to brainstorm possible places where they could find answers. They were permitted to do this in groups or individually as they preferred, and we encouraged them to discuss their observations and questions with other students.

Next, we asked them to view the image in its original context with the accompanying text, "Introducing a television so thin it will give regular TVs a complex."[3] They discussed the question prompts on the Image Analysis Worksheet, considering whether the image in its original context changed their previous inferences, and if the addition of the text raised new questions for them. We then initiated a large class discussion of the image and their written and small group responses to it.

In this exercise, we hoped to foster an atmosphere that would provide exposure to diverse perspectives, allow everyone to learn from one another, engage everyone in a lively discussion, and encourage creativity and fun while interacting with librarians.

We found the class discussion to be rich and engaging. Students, faculty and librarians participated in the discussion equally and learned from one another's ideas. In several instances, students gave interpretations that neither the librarians nor the instructors had identified. For example, some students questioned whether the models in the advertisement were human or if they were actually digitally created. Other students asked if the models were transgender, or perhaps men dressed as women. Some inferred that the creators of this advertisement were intentionally playing with gender to make a connection with both a stereotypically masculine interest in technology, and a sexually desirable object/female. One student noted that the flat-chested, thin women mirrored the flat screen television.

Without prompting, students began asking critical questions: where did this advertisement come from? Who was the intended audience? What was the advertiser's motivation in telling this visual story? These verbal responses were relatively sophisticated. We were very pleased with the results because they came from the students themselves. We did not lecture, tell them the "meaning" or otherwise encourage a particular interpretation. Faculty were also involved in the discussion, but did not dominate or lecture. It was a truly collaborative teaching/learning moment between students, librarians and faculty.

One of our main goals in this exercise was to provide students with an opportunity to successfully practice critical evaluation of sources, hopefully resulting in transferable skills they could apply to other information contexts. After students had successfully generated questions and answers to the flat-screen TV advertisement, we pointed out that the types of questions they were asking were relevant to any information source—whether it be a photograph, a TV program, a newspaper article, Web site, or lecture. They should always ask about point of view, intended audience, purpose, etc.

Several of our students became curious about where we found this advertisement. We explained that we had originally encountered it through the "About Face" organization's Web site, which combats negative stereotypes of women in the media.[4] We discussed the implication of context to the interpretation one might bring to an image. How might possible readings of an image be different if we viewed it on a library class Web page *vs.* a media advocacy group's Web site *vs.* a print ad in a magazine such as *Vanity Fair* or *Wired*? Each context promotes an agenda that is remarkably different than the others (learning about visual literacy *vs.*

combating gender stereotyping *vs.* grabbing attention to sell a product). Thinking about context helped students reveal the assumptions that influenced their interpretations of the image.

Because the image we chose was so intellectually, emotionally, and aesthetically provocative there was a high level of energy in students' responses. Everyone had fun with this activity, including the librarians. It was gratifying to work with students who were excited about the material. The exercise allowed students to take intellectual risks, without the fear of being "wrong" in their subjective interpretations. The exercise also broadened the students' view of the role of librarians and libraries in their research.

Assessment activities included gauging students' level of participation in class discussions, and reviewing their worksheet answers after class with the learning community faculty. Responses were thoughtful and indicated students were highly engaged with the session content. Students commented about the use of sex to sell products, how advertisements of unusually thin women might promote eating disorders, and how advertising often objectifies women's bodies.

One trouble spot became apparent upon reviewing the completed worksheets. After writing provocative questions in response to the image, the students provided comparatively simplistic suggestions as to where they might research their questions. Their responses indicated that they were concentrating solely on the motivations of this specific television manufacturer rather than on larger issues, such as why advertisers use gender stereotypes to sell products.

In retrospect, we realize that we asked the students to make a cognitive leap for which we had not prepared them. While the final question on the worksheet was a logical "next step" in the process, it deserved as much attention and practice as we devoted to the visual literacy skills. Ideally, we would offer a subsequent session to focus on other information literacy skills, such as generating search terms and developing effective search strategies. We could then help the students identify and use appropriate resources, such as subject encyclopedias and interdisciplinary databases, to explore their questions and make connections between the specific advertisement they viewed and the broader concepts to which it relates.

Reflection on the Instruction Session: Lessons Learned
Session Observations

1. Students were more engaged in this exercise than in previous library instruction sessions.

2. A majority of the students participated honestly, openly and thoughtfully in the discussion.

3. The level playing field gave everyone the opportunity to be an expert and a teacher as well as a learner.

4. The discussion was spontaneous and energetic (this was not a scripted session).

5. Students practiced how to think/inquire critically.

We found that this activity opened up the faculty and librarians to more innovative approaches to information literacy instruction. Faculty praised the exercise for its ability to help the students engage with the images in meaningful ways, moving beyond "obvious" interpretations. Also, they valued the ways it prompted students to devise genuine research questions to further investigate possible interpretations of the images and their implications. Faculty requested we conduct this same workshop with their faculty colleagues. They have also asked that the session be conducted in future offerings of their courses.

Since we conducted this information literacy workshop in 2004, we have had the opportunity to report on our results at an ALA poster session and in a teaching meeting with other instruction librarians.[5] While the lesson plan has been enthusiastically received, there have been those who question whether evaluation of visual information is the proper role of librarians. It is our assumption that one of the most important impacts librarians can make in students' educational careers is guiding them to consciously process the meaning, intent, and potential effects of any information, regardless of its format. This impact can persist in their lives beyond school, as members of the workforce, and as life-long learners.

Next Steps and Suggestions for Adaptation

The image analysis exercise could be a jumping off point for teaching more advanced search skills. A longer instruction session or a subsequent session focused on finding and researching images would help students move through the next steps in the research process. During these sessions, librarians could teach students how to search for images on the Web, in specialized databases, or in resources found through the library catalog. After selecting images, students could explore answers to questions that arise during the image analysis. Other activities in this session could include formulating effective research questions, brainstorming keywords, identifying primary and secondary sources, and identifying and using appropriate reference tools.

While this chapter outlines our experiences with freshmen/sophomore level students, this exercise can be adapted for use in upper-level classes as well. It already has been successfully introduced at the junior level for several University of Washington, Bothell, interdisciplinary courses that examine the depiction of race, class, and gender in art and advertising. Other instances of this activity could incorporate the following ideas and activities:

1. Research an historical image's original context; consider ways the image has been interpreted and used as its political, cultural, and physical contexts have changed. Visual artifacts could include postcards, stamps, album covers, movie posters, etc.

2. Involve students in the production of visual information through manipulating and modifying an existing image (cropping, changing colors, adding or deleting text). Explore how these manipulations affect its potential uses and interpretations.

3. Discuss the proliferation of images in today's society in order to explore issues such as copyright, consumerism, literacy, and the ethical use of information.

4. Expand on the image analysis exercise by using some of the same techniques to analyze a short text. Ask students to identify the ways in which the author uses language and form to create meaning, to express ideas, and to elicit specific responses from the reader. Explore context and audience and how changing those factors could influence the interpretation of the text. Compare and contrast the processes used in the visual and textual exercises.

Notes

1. Association of College and Research Libraries, *Information Literacy Competency Standards for Higher Education* (Chicago: Association of College and Research Libraries, 2000), http://www.ala.org/ala/acrl/acrlstandards/informationliteracycompetency.htm.

2. National Archives and Records Administration Education Staff, "Photo Analysis Worksheet," http://www.archives.gov/education/lessons/worksheets/photo_analysis_worksheet.pdf.

3. Philips Electronics North American Corporation, "Introducing a Television So Thin it will Give Regular TVs a Complex," *Vanity Fair* 33, no. 455 (1998): 75. The advertisement discussed above was printed in several popular magazines in 1998, including the issue of *Vanity Fair* cited here.

4. About-Face, "Gallery of Offenders," http://www.about-face.org/goo/. This exercise can be easily adapted for many instruction levels and in many disciplinary contexts. Because this instruction session was conducted for a learning community focused on media and gender, we chose the image discussed above from the Web site "About-Face," a San Francisco-based non-profit group that combats negative and distorted images of women in the media. We attempted but were unable to obtain permission from the TV manufacturer to reproduce the actual ad in this chapter. However you can view the image and read an analysis of the ad on the About Face Web site http://www.about-face.org/goo/newten/2/nine.shtml.

5. Laura Barrett and Suzan Parker. "A Picture Worth a Thousand Words: Visual Literacy Through Critical Inquiry" (poster session, American Library Association Annual Conference, Chicago, IL, June 23–29, 2005), http://www.uwb.edu/library/archive/visualliteracy.ppt.

Teaching Resources

The Image Analysis Worksheet for this lesson plan was adapted from "Document Analysis Worksheets" available at http://www.archives.gov/education/lessons/worksheets/.

Image Analysis Worksheet

Step 1. Observation

A. Study the image for two minutes. Form an overall impression, and then examine individual items. Next, divide the image into quadrants and study each section to see what new details become visible.

B. Use the chart below to list people, objects, and activities in the image. You can work individually or answer as a group.

People	Objects	Activities

Step 2. Inference

Based on what you have observed above, list three things you might infer from this image.

_____

_____

_____

_____

_____

Step 3. Questions

What questions does this image raise in your mind?

_____

_____

_____

Step 4. Context

View the image in its original context and read the accompanying text.

Does viewing the image in its original context change the inferences you made previously?

_____

_____

_____

Does viewing the image in its original context answer any of the questions you had in Step 3? If so, which questions were answered and what did you learn?

_____

_____

_____

What new questions does the image raise for you?

_____

_____

_____

_____

Brainstorm some possible places where could you find answers to your new questions.

Chapter 2

Introducing Undergraduates to Data Literacy: How to Find, Use, and Evaluate Numeric Data

Jen-chien Yu and Aaron K. Shrimplin

Introduction

Although there are many challenges to integrating data literacy into the curriculum of an undergraduate course, the following documents a multiyear initiative to add a data literacy component to a 200-level, interdisciplinary course. The lesson plan put forth could be modified to fit any number of instructional sessions in an effort to promote data literacy across the curriculum. Data literacy in this context refers to the process of teaching undergraduate students how to discover, manipulate, and interpret numeric data.[1]

Analysis of the Learning Situation

In 2002, the authors, librarians at Miami University, proposed adding a data literacy component to Information Studies in the Digital Age (IMS201). At that time, the course had a strong information literacy focus but neglected to introduce students to the concept of data or numeric literacy. Our proposal was accepted, and since 2002 we have been invited as guest lecturers to teach a session on data literacy in all the IMS201 classes. Each data literacy session includes a lecture, a demonstration, and hands-on exercises.

Not unlike other 200-level courses, Information Studies in the Digital Age attracts a diverse group of students with a range of skills and academic experience. Consequently, designing a lesson plan that most students could relate to is a considerable challenge.

The teaching classroom is networked and equipped with a projector and other multimedia peripherals. Twenty-four computers are loaded with professional software packages for digital media creation and equipped with dual monitors. Although it is a great facility for teaching with technology, the students are tempted by many distractions including Web surfing, chatting, and working on their homework. The instructor's station is equipped with a piece of software called NetOp School that allows instructors to take control of students' computers during a lecture or demonstration.

How to Find, Use, and Evaluate Numeric Data is a seventy-five minute instruction session that introduces undergraduates to the concept of data literacy. Our plan was to make sure that students would learn and practice data literacy skills that could be used in their classes, at work, or for personal interests. We made a conscious effort to leave as much time as possible at the end of the instruction for students to work on the hands-on exercises, with our assistance.

Information Literacy Standards
(Note: A complete list of ACRL *Information Literacy Competency Standards for Higher Education* [Chicago: ACRL, 2000] appears as appendix A.)

Lesson Goal
Teach students how to find, use, and evaluate existing numeric data.

Lesson Objectives
1. Awareness and understanding of numeric data. What are data? How are data used to support learning, research, and problem solving? (*Standard One:* "The information literate students determines the nature and extent of the information needed"; Performance Indicators 1, 2, 3, and 4)[2]

2. Steps at finding numeric data. (*Standard Two:* "The information literate student accesses needed information effectively and efficiently"; Performance Indicators 1, 2, 3, 4, and 5)[3]

3. How to evaluate data. (*Standard Three:* "The information literate student evaluates information and its sources critically and incorporates selected information into his or her knowledge base and value system:; Performance Indicators 1, 2, 3, 4, 5, 6, and 7)[4]

4. Familiarity with data resources. (*Standard One* (see above), *Two* (see above), and *Five*: "The information literate student understands many of the economic, legal, and social issues surrounding the use of information and accesses and uses information ethically and legally."[5]

Lesson Plan
Introduction and Icebreaker
Begin with a brief introduction to the value of data literacy. Encourage students to think about how "numbers" relate to their daily lives. Walk through a quick class exercise that centers on answering an entertaining data question, such as, "What is the percentage of male librarians in the United States?"

Objectives

Present learning outcomes to be realized by the students and the components of the data literacy instructional session. The concept of numeric data is clearly defined and highlighted with examples.

Presentation

PowerPoint lecture on important concepts and tools for finding, evaluating, and using numeric data, including online demonstrations. Three hands-on exercises are given to students to complete. These exercises are designed for the students to explore resources for finding numeric data for both research and personal interests.

Description of the Instruction Session: What Actually Happened?

Interactive Media Studies (IMS), a relatively new program at Miami University, offers four sections of a three-credit course entitled Information Studies in the Digital Age (IMS201). Each semester, librarians teach this course to more than a hundred undergraduates. This course explores what it means to be information literate in today's digital world and is intended for students wishing to become competent in the fields of information literacy and information technology.

The instruction session usually started with IMS201 faculty introducing the data librarians and stating the purpose of the session. Because social science numeric data are not a format of information that most undergraduate students are aware of, we began the instruction session by asking, "Does anybody know what data literacy is?" The response we usually got from the students, just as any experienced librarian would guess, was silence.

We then asked the students whether they had ever, when gathering information to write a paper, read a sentence such as "A recent research report published by *so-and-so* showed that *X* percent of respondents support *such-and-such* ..." and said to themselves "Well, this looks good for my topic." Usually, quite a few students indicated by nodding their heads in agreement that they related to this scenario.

We continued, "Then you used your highlighter to mark the entire sentence and later you used the information in your paper and cited the source." Here again, students nodded in the affirmative. Then we asked them, "Have you ever checked these sources? To see whether the research really exists? And whether the author, whose article you quoted, represented the research finding correctly?" This time, the students shook their heads no.

"We all use data all the time, for research papers, assignments, and all kinds of things," we said. "*Data* can be used as strong evidence to support your argument. *Data* are also trying to tell you stories about the world you live in." To better address the importance of data, we then asked a couple of questions the students could relate to. For example, a major strike among classified staff took place on campus in 2003. The students' daily lives were impacted by the strike because many custodial and facility maintenance staff stopped showing up to work. We asked what the students thought the hourly wage of a classified staff member was, and then we compared the hourly wage to staff employed by different state-funded institutions. We could tell by the way they were paying attention that they saw the connection between data and the "real world," and how a few numbers could reveal so much information.

Good examples, such as the strike in 2003, aren't always readily available, so we use a number of other questions to engage students in the discussion. We have asked students to guess the percentage of male librarians in the United States or the number of Asians living in Oxford, Ohio. Students usually had fun with these questions. "20 percent!" "3 percent!" They contributed answers enthusiastically. Based on their observation of the environment, they knew that the percentage of male librarians or the number of Asians living in Oxford had to be low. However, they could only guess. They were not familiar with data resources available to them for finding this type of information.

And we revealed the answers. "That is what we are going to show you today: how to find, use, and evaluate numeric data." The instruction continued by clarifying the definition of social science numeric data, different types of data (quick facts versus summary data), and their characteristics and usage. From this point a PowerPoint[6] slide presentation outlining the lecture was used.

The presentation slides showed the students how to articulate their need for numeric data and how to determine the types of data they need. We listed some research topics on the PowerPoint slides. Then, we identified the scope and purpose of different research topics and demonstrated how to use that knowledge to determine whether to use quick facts or summary data. We encouraged students to assess their needs, options, and software/hardware requirements before determining which data to use.

Although the goal of the instruction didn't include teaching students advanced statistical analysis skills, we briefly introduced statistical software packages, codebooks (metadata for numeric data), and where one can get help when working on advanced statistical analysis. We placed emphasis on the codebooks because they provide information about the source and contents of the data. The codebooks also contain valuable information on evaluating the quality of the data.

Because we didn't have time to cover every data resource in depth, during the last part of the lecture we highlighted some print resources, commercial databases, and Web sites for finding numeric data.

Then the hands-on session began. Prior to the instruction, we chose three data resources to be used in the hands-on exercises: WebUse: Scientific Research on the Internet (for the students to learn about survey data on the Web), Polls & Surveys through LexisNexis Academic Universe (public opinion poll data), and American FactFinder (US Census data). We created hands-on exercises and worksheets with instructions on how to use each data resource. We also created a Web version of the same exercises and instruction.[7]

The exercise worksheets with instructions and the URL of the Web version were given to the students. The students were required to finish the completed exercises by the end of the class. The Web version was designed with a two-frame layout: in the left frame, the exercises and instructions were listed with hyperlinks to the data resources students needed to use to complete the exercises. When the students clicked on the hyperlinks, the data resources would open in the right frame while the left frame remained the same.

We, and the IMS201 faculty, circulated around the room, answered students' questions, and made sure everybody was at the right place. If many students were having the same problem, we brought it to the group's attention. Most of time, we tried not to interfere while the students explored the data resources.

Finally, we invited students to fill out a feedback form. We ended the session by encouraging the students to visit us whenever they needed assistance regarding numeric data. On many occasions, a few students would stay after class and ask us for advice on projects they were working on that required use of numeric data. Sometimes students came to ask for clarification on notes they took during the instruction.

Reflection on the Instruction Session: Lessons Learned

Since 2002, the authors have instructed students of IMS201 in how to find, use, and evaluate numeric data. We constantly update the lesson plan and the teaching materials based on feedback from the faculty and the students.

Throughout the years we have learned the value of good icebreakers. When we asked questions such as Does anybody know what data literacy is? or What is the percentage of male librarians in the United States? at the beginning of the session, we could see that students were surprised by this different approach. The process of walking through these questions showed the students that we were attempting to establish an active and engaging learning environment rather than a traditional one-way lecture. As a result, the students felt comfortable enough to participate in the discussion or to ask questions throughout the instruction. Many students noted in their feedback that they appreciated our references to "things college kids can relate to."

However, we also learned that it is not easy to select materials to be used as icebreakers or examples for instruction. We have used numerous news stories along with visual aids such as tables or video clips; some worked out really well, but some didn't. We can only guess what *might* interest students based on our experience. Furthermore, in this "information overload" environment, students can easily forget news that happened just last month. We learned to routinely incorporate new icebreakers or examples with time-sensitive materials.

Very early on, we realized that students got confused and easily frustrated while working on the hands-on exercises. We observed several factors that caused the confusion. Technical problems such as a slow network connection, machine malfunction, or database failure were not uncommon. Unfortunately, there is not much we can do to prevent these types of problems. We learned to always check on the network and resources right before the class. If any technical problems occurred during the instruction, we gave the students the opportunity to complete the hands-on exercises after the class.

The fact that the hands-on exercises were scheduled at the end of the class when the students tended to be less focused was another problem. We also realized that teaching to different learning styles is a challenge. Some students relied on verbal instruction and were motivated mostly by the same method. On the other hand, a significant number of students were self-directed learners more comfortable discovering information from the data resources at their own pace. To address these issues, we have learned to document the instructions/steps for completing each exercise on the worksheets. Later, we enhanced our session by providing the exercises and instruction on the Web in order to help the students navigate through the data resources. We also provided verbal instruction, if necessary.

Students' confusion and frustration lessened after we revised the hands-on exercises. We observed that a lot of students in the hands-on sessions mentally wandered off to use the assigned data resources for searching topics *they* were interested in and enjoyed the wealth of numeric data they could find. One student wrote on the feedback form: "There are fourteen Native Hawaiians in Oxford" (although none of the exercises asked for demographic information about Oxford). The students also were making connections between data literacy skills and practice. Several students mentioned they could apply these skills when working on their papers or marketing projects.

From student feedback, we also learned that, although we tried to make the instruction informational and interesting, not every student found it helpful. One student wrote, "I already knew this stuff," which demonstrates the challenge of promoting data literacy in an interdisciplinary, mixed upper-class/lower-class course. "Not sure how to apply the knowledge learned today," another student wrote, which also challenges us to constantly look for ways to improve instruction, especially ways to help students make the connection between data literacy skills and practice.

The challenge of connecting data literacy learning and practice would be far less problematic if the How to Find, Use, and Evaluate Numeric Data instruction session had been conducted for all students who needed these skills to complete coursework. Consequently, we feel that data literacy needs to be integrated throughout the curriculum. In particular, it is important to include data literacy as a component of courses that address information literacy.

Notes

1. The authors would like to thank Julie Linden (Yale University). During a workshop (hosted by the International Association for Social Science Information Service & Technology, or IASSIST) on numeric data in 2002, Mrs. Linden shared many good ideas and resources on teaching data literacy.

2. Association of College and Research Libraries, *Information Literacy Competency Standards for Higher Education* (Chicago: ACRL, 2000). Available online from http://www.ala.org/ala/acrl/acrlstandards/informationliteracy competency.htm.

3. Ibid.

4. Ibid.

5. Ibid.

6. Miami University Libraries, "How to Find, Use, and Evaluate Numeric Data." Available online from http://elearn.lib.muohio.edu/ datalit/dataLiteracy.ppt.

7. Miami University Libraries, "Data Literacy—Hands-on Exercises." Available online from http://elearn.lib.muohio.edu/datalit/exercises.

Teaching Resources
Selected Sources of Data
- ICPSR (Inter-university Consortium for Political and Social Research)
- Site for Instructional Materials and Information (SIMI)
- American FactFinder by U.S. Census Bureau
- Roper Center for Public Opinion Research
- Polls & Surveys Question Database (Roper Center for Public Opinion Research)
- LexisNexis Statistical
- Health Poll Search
- Odum Institute for Research in Social Science Louis Harris Data Archive
- Data on the Net
- Social Statistics Briefing Room

In-class Exercises for "Data Literacy: How to Find, Use, and Evaluate Numeric Data"
Information for Faculty

These exercises are designed for students to practice using the tools and techniques for finding numeric data, which are taught during the "Data Literacy: How to Find, Use, and Evaluate Numeric Data" instruction. Upon completing the exercises, the students will be familiar with the tools and the types of numeric data that can be applied to academic research or personal interests. The exercises should be completed and returned to the instructor by the end of the class.

This is also an opportunity for students to think about how numeric data can be applied. Students can follow the steps of each exercise to identify possible data to answer the following questions:

- How do people use the Internet?

This question is designed for students to learn about social science surveys and documentation/codebooks

- What are people's responses toward homosexuality on television?

This question is designed for students to learn about data from public opinion polls; how these data can be used to investigate the changes of people's attitudes over a period of time

- How many people live in college dormitories in Oxford City, Ohio?

This question is designed for students to learn about how to find U.S. census data via American FactFinder

Exercises

All data archives in the exercises can be accessed via
Electronic Data Center >> Class Resources >> IMS 201 Data Literacy
[http://edc.lib.muohio.edu/datalit/]

Exercise 1: Finding a survey that includes a specific question using datasets on WebUse: Scientific Research on the Internet [http://www.webuse.umd.edu/]
Find a question that asks how people use the Internet.
1. What's the question?
2. What are the responses?

Exercise 2: Finding a survey that includes a specific question using Polls & Surveys Question Database through LexisNexis Academic Universe
Find a survey(s) that answers the following question: *"What are people's responses toward homosexuality on television?"* Please list two survey questions from the search results.
Suggested keywords—"homosexual characters" or "homosexual! and television"

Question 1
1. What is the question?
2. What are the responses?
3. When was the survey conducted?
4. What population was sampled?

Question 2
1. What is the question?
2. What are the responses?
3. When was the survey conducted?
4. What population was sampled?

Exercise 3: Using Census Data
1. Go to the American FactFinder Web site [http://factfinder.census.gov/].
2. Click on Search on the top of the page.
3. Click on the geography tab on the top of the page.
4. Enter Oxford City and then click Search.
5. Select Oxford City, Ohio and then click OK.
6. Go to Quick Tables and Demographic Profiles >> Census 2000 Summary File 1 (SF 1) 100-Percent Data.

7. Click on QT-P12. Group Quarters Population by Sex, Age, and Type of Group Quarters: 2000.

Please review the data table and answer these questions:
1. In Oxford City, Ohio, how many people live in college dormitories?
2. What's the name of the data set that you got the data from?
3. Can you download the data in Excel format from this site? List all the steps you use to download the data.

Chapter 3
Finding Historical Information to Prepare a Speech

Alice L. Daugherty

Introduction

This instructional session was requested by Danielle Vignes, a professor in the Communication Studies Department at Louisiana State University. The e-mailed request came early in the semester to reserve the physical classroom. The professor sent an attached copy of the assignment with the e-mail. The class, Public Speaking (CMST 2060), is one of the core classes in the Communication Studies program. Many students in the Communication Studies program are exposed to library instruction through one-shots in core English classes and through the required one-credit information literacy class, Library Research Methods and Materials (LIS 1001). However, there isn't a way to determine which students have had prior library instruction. Therefore, the focus of this session was designed around the parameters of a specific required assignment for which the students needed to find information about a period in United States history. Introductory library skills such as catalog searching were not included in the lesson plans.

Library instruction was given three consecutive times in one day. Each CMST 2060 class consisted of an average of twenty-two students and one faculty member. Each session was almost ninety minutes. Instruction took place in an electronic classroom in the library. The electronic classroom has twenty independent work stations plus a teacher's workstation connected to a ceiling-mounted projector.

Analysis of Learning Situation

Students are required to prepare a twenty-five-minute group speech in which they persuade their audience to travel back in time to any decade in the one hundred years from 1880 through 1980, inclusive. Each group needs to choose a different decade. Students need to quickly decide what decade they would like to visit and support their choice with a short list of reasons. Groups have to request approval for their selected decade from the professor before beginning work on their speech. Decades are approved on a first-come, first-serve basis by the professor and approval to proceed is granted based on the preliminary argument of the group as to why it chose that decade.

The students must have a list of what was going on in the years chosen: politics, world events, conflicts, popular culture (music, the arts, fashion, and entertainment), social conditions, technological and medical developments, etc. Groups consider the kinds of events and activities that might be fun to experience firsthand or witness the first time something took place. They also consider events or incidents where they might be able to go back and make a difference in what happened—things they could conceivably change in the past to improve the future. Topics should be important and interesting to the group and also to the audience.

Each group needs to submit one formal outline that encompasses the entire speech. The outline must include a thesis statement, introduction, body, conclusion, all transitions, and any works cited. Each speech must have a minimum of five references. References must be cited in the speech as well as in the works-cited page. After all the speeches are given, the class votes to choose which decade in history to travel back to in time.

One of the challenges of this assignment was introducing a number of online and traditional print resources. I wanted to provide a learning environment that supported exploration and open-ended learning coupled with some structure for organization. To help the students sort through the information they would encounter, I handed out an Historical Events Chart for them to fill in. Students cite the source they use in the left column and write in different events or developments mentioned in that resource. I didn't want students to forget where they found certain tidbits of information. Plus, I wanted to limit their feelings of disorganization and information overload.

Information Literacy Standards
(Note: A complete list of ACRL *Information Literacy Competency Standards for Higher Education* [Chicago: ACRL, 2000] appears as appendix A.)

My learning objectives for the sessions coordinate with the Information Literacy Competency Standards for Higher Education, Performance Indicators, and Outcomes[1] as follows:

1. Scan through print and electronic chronologies to increase familiarity with specific decades (1.1.c.).

2. Identify the differences between print indexes and electronic indexes (1.2.c.).

3. Gather a list of keywords and synonyms relevant to the topic (2.2.b.).

4. Explore the information gaps and limitations of using Google as a starting place for this assignment (2.2.a.).

5. Retrieve information from a variety of resources such as books, micro format, and the Internet (2.3.a.).

6. Organize information into a chart, outline, and speech (4.1.a.).

Lesson Plan

Introduction

Capture students' attention by asking, "Where should you begin to find information for this assignment?" (I am fairly certain they won't know where to begin looking for information and therefore will find my instruction worthwhile.) I ask students what they know about life between 1880 and 1890, 1890 and 1900, and so on. With this line of questioning, I show students that they can't search for 1880 on Google and find relevant information. I review the objectives of their assignment and explain how I can help them achieve those objectives.

Body

Show students that they need to know something about their selected decade before they can continue to research specifics. Look at chronologies available through the Internet and in print, showing how to pull out key phrases about events they want to research further. Gather general information about main events from general reference sources (both electronic and print reference sources). Encourage use of article indexes and newspaper indexes for further research. Encourage use of appropriate online databases. Follow the CMST 2060 Outline created for class.

Conclusion

Take the students on a tour of the Reference Department. Specifically, look through and handle appropriate print resources.

Description of the Instruction Session: What Actually Happened?

I opened with my understanding of the assignment parameters, reiterating that the students need to promote a decade from 1880 to 1980. I chose the assignment as a starting place because I wanted the students to realize that there was a purpose to their library visit. I wanted to tie together the objectives of their assignment and the instructional lecture I was about to give. I wanted the students to understand that I knew what their information needs were for this project.

Next, I wanted to capture their attention and stress the necessity of library instruction in conjunction with this particular assignment. I started by asking students a few questions, such as "What do you know about 1880?," "What do you know about 1890? 1900? 1910?" and "How far do I have to go back until you realize that you know of a major event in history?" The students remained very silent. They were unable to think of any events in history before World War One. I told the students that I wasn't trying to embarrass them by asking questions they didn't know the answers to but, rather, that I was trying to get them to see what their information needs were. I wanted the students to think about where they were going to start to look for information for this speech. I also wanted them to have a plan of attack for their information seeking.

One student suggested, "Google 1880." No one else had any idea where to start. I explained to the students that if you use 1880 as a search query in Google, you will retrieve results for everything that has the sequence of numbers 1880 in it—addresses, phone numbers, manufactured parts numbers, everything. They could be there for hours trying to find something relevant to their topic. I suggested that they use Google later in the process after they have gathered some keywords or key events.

I also asked the class several questions to get them thinking about different ways information can be formatted and categorized, such as "When did computers come into existence?" "When did computers come into everyone's homes?" "Did people of yesteryear keep a history of their events?" and "How did people of 1880 record their information?" I asked the students to think about where to find a record of modern events. I suggested that a newspaper or a magazine could record today's history. Likewise, a newspaper or a magazine from the 1880s would reflect contemporaneous thoughts and reactions relevant to given issues of that time period.

The first resource we discussed was the *Nineteenth Century Readers' Guide to Periodical Literature, 1890–1899*. I expressed that the print *Readers' Guide to Periodical Literature* was similar to the electronic indexes in the library. Using an example relevant to the time period, we found information on railroads. I also used a more contemporary example and explained to them that if they wanted to learn more about the Warner Brothers' television show *The OC,* they could look it up in a 2004 volume of *Readers' Guide* and see that the *Readers' Guide* lists an article about *The OC* published in the *TV Guide*. I emphasized that I would have to go to the *TV Guide* to get the article, stressing that full-text articles weren't available within *Readers' Guide*. I passed several withdrawn *Readers' Guide* volumes around the classroom as we talked (the library keeps these in the classroom for instruction purposes).

I gave the same basic demonstration with the *New York Times Index 1890–1893*. I looked up railroad companies in the January to June 1893 volume and then passed the book around the classroom. One student asked, "Well then, where would I go to find the *New York Times?*" This provided an excellent opportunity to briefly teach how to use the libraries' online catalog. The students found that the LSU Libraries has the *New York Times* on microfilm dating back to September 14, 1857. This discovery led to an interesting discussion about being afraid to use the microfilm reader.

I was aware that most students would likely start their research with the Internet. I wanted to guide them in their searching and enhance their skills using this valuable tool. Therefore, I had the students begin by searching in online reference Web sites. The first site I asked the students to search was Bartleby.com, explaining that this site had valuable reference materials that might aid them in other classes as well. Using the online version of the *Columbia Encyclopedia* in Bartleby.com, we found the article titled "United States,"[2] selected the first result retrieved, and scrolled through to the section subtitled "The Late Nineteenth Century." I used this source so that students could get a general idea of events occurring in U.S. history at that time. Bartleby.com does an excellent job of hyperlinking prominent events and persons to other areas within its reference collection.

The second online reference Web site I asked the students to use was Infoplease.com. Infoplease.com *Almanac* organizes various time lines under the broad categories of "World History" and "U.S. History." One example, the U.S. History time line from 1900 to 1949[3] provides a brief description of each year, specific dates of major events, and pictures of key events.

Another valuable resource within Infoplease.com *Almanac* is "Year by Year." Although the groups needing information for earlier decades would not find this useful, it is very well organized for the groups researching from 1900 to 1980. The "Year by Year" feature includes major world events, U.S. events, economic information, sports information, entertainment information, and science information. Again, all important keywords are hyperlinked to more information. As an example, the year 1970[4] includes world population statistics, life expectancy statistics, Pulitzer Prize winners, professional sports summaries, and other information.

Using the LSU Libraries Web page[5] as a springboard to finding information, I clicked through the history subject guide to HyperHistory ONLINE.[6] This online time line gives a visual display of events occurring during the times designated in the assignment. I explained to students that they needed to pull out the major events that happened during their decade of choice or find the names of famous people that were influential during that time.

The library also has a detailed Web site about Internet guides.[7] I explained to the students that the Internet consists of hundreds of billions of Web pages and that it would be easy for them to lose a great deal of time searching aimlessly for information. One specific Web site I wanted to share for this project was BUBL Information Service.[8] The BUBL Web site breaks down content according to the Dewey Decimal System. BUBL has excellent annotations that help students to select Web pages of interest and to create lists of search phrases.

The last thing I did was to bring the class into the reference stacks for a tour. I specifically went by the reference table with the *Readers' Guide* and all the newspaper indexes. This gave me a chance to stop and repeat some of the lesson. I also took them into the stacks of world history chronologies and U.S. chronologies. At this point, I pulled out several print reference books and handed them to the students. I finished by asking the students if they had any questions and handed out a sixty-seconds evaluation form for them to fill out.

Reflection on the Instruction Session: Lessons Learned

Even after the class had started looking through the print resources in the reference stacks, one student asked the professor, "You mean I can't just use Google for all of this?" Students had limited concepts of why print resources were necessary to this assignment. They were baffled that not everything was available to them online and unfamiliar with using indirect sources in order to dig deeper for further information. In addition, one of the challenges I faced was trying to present so many different resources and multiple formats of information. I tried to offer structure by providing detailed handouts.

When all three sessions were finished, I was approached near the reference stacks by a nontraditional student who thanked me tremendously for showing the class how to find the information they needed in books. The student said she felt more comfortable with print resources because she was used to print resources for work in high school. She also stated that she couldn't get over how easy it was to gather most of the information she needed in one or two reference books. This encounter was extremely encouraging to me.

I asked the students to fill out a sixty-seconds evaluation form so that I could assess how they embraced the instruction they had received. In response to the question "What is one concept in today's instruction session that you found interesting, or that you learned for the first time?" a majority of the students indicated that they did not know how to find information in reference books. One student wrote, "I was interested in the Reference Department. It seems a lot easier and faster to just look up the book instead of Googling for twenty minutes." Another student said, "None of it was really interesting but it was helpful, especially the part about the reference section in the library." The other responses included learning how to search the Internet effectively, targeting or narrowing the search, and using the library's subject guides. A few remarked that after receiving library instruction they didn't feel that Google was an appropriate or effective starting place for their research.

The student responses were very encouraging. I was afraid that too much information was being offered to them without enough hands-on experience to reinforce what I was teaching. However, several students commented that although a large amount of information was given, they felt it was very well organized and presented clearly.

I found that scheduling all of the sessions on the same day made for a very tiresome workday. By the time I was teaching the last class, I was getting bored with my own instruction and wanting to use fresh examples. I also had to make more of an effort in the later classes to remember what questions were asked by those specific students as opposed to students from an earlier class. In the future, I will try not to schedule all three classes on the same day.

Finally, I wish there was a way to actually evaluate what the students had learned from this session. I e-mailed the professor toward the end of the semester, asking if the students used any of the resources I had shown them. I also asked if there was anything I should have clarified in my instruction, but I did not receive a response (although the professor thanked me profusely at the time the instruction ended and said that I had done a wonderful job).

I want to continue to collaborate with this professor in the future. I want to discuss improvements for the following semesters and suggest a greater collaboration between us. I also want to suggest a follow-up session for the students where the students spend their time researching while I walk around the computer lab to help them with their research strategies. I want to be able to provide the students with opportunities to ask questions while keeping the "learn by doing" atmosphere.

Notes

1. Association of College and Research Libraries, *Information Literacy Competency Standards for Higher Education* (Chicago: ACRL, 2000). Available online from http://www.ala.org/ala/acrl/acrlstandards/inform ationliteracycompetency.htm.

2. *Columbia Encyclopedia,* 6th ed., s.v. "United States." Available online from http://www.bartleby.com/65/us/US.html.

3. *Infoplease Almanac,* s.v. *"1900–1949."* Available online from http://www.infoplease.com/ipa/A0903596.html.

4. *Infoplease Almanac, Year by Year, s.v.*"1970." Available online from http://www.infoplease.com/year/1970.html.

5. "LSU Libraries," Louisiana State University. Available online from http://www.lib.lsu.edu/.

6. HyperHistory ONLINE. Available online from http://www.hyperhistory.com/online_n2/History_n2/a.html.

7. "Internet Searching, Search Engines," Louisiana State University. Available online from http://www.lib.lsu.edu/general/internet_search.html.

8. BUBL Information Service. Available online from http://bubl.ac.uk/.

Teaching Resources
CMST 2060 Handout for Time Travel Speech

Readers' Guide to Periodical Literature
Reference Table 5
AI 3 R48
Reader's Guide indexes popular literature. The guide gives titles of articles, titles of journals, date of article, etc.

The New York Times Index
Reference Table 5
AI 21 N44
The NY Times Index provides the titles of the newspaper articles.

Use General Encyclopedias and General Reference Sources. General encyclopedias provide quick answers to quick questions. General reference sources (i.e., almanacs) provide a broad amount of information on general topics.

Columbia Encyclopedia
http://bartleby.com
Under Search, use the pull-down menu to select *Columbia Encyclopedia*.
Type in United States and press Enter.
Select the First Result.
Scroll through text to subtitle The Late Nineteenth Century.

http://www.infoplease.com
On Left side of screen under Home, click on United States, The Almanac United States appears. Under History & Gov't, click on Timelines
OR
Under Related Content, go to Year by Year: 1900–2005, and type in a year.

General and Subject Specific Encyclopedias are located at Reference Table 2.

Use Subject Guides. Subject Guides are various resources compiled by an information expert within that discipline.
From the Library Homepage:
Subject Guides → Social Sciences → History → Reference Sources and Maps → Hyper History Online

Use Library Internet Guides. There are hundreds of billions of Web pages out there, use the information provided carefully!
From the Library Homepage:
Internet Searching → Academic Search Engines → BUBL
   Click on 900 Geography and History
   Click on 970 History of North America
   Click on 973.9 History of the United States from 1901

Use Databases. Databases provide paid-for sources of information. When you pay for a product, the product being information, you get a higher quality.
From the Library Homepage:
Indexes and Databases → (Select a discipline of information) History (by Arts and Humanities)

Search Digital Collections
The Library of Congress,
WWW.LOC.GOV

   Search in American Memory

   Under "find it," click on "Search our Catalogs." On the right. choose Prints and Photographs Online Collection.

NEED HELP?

Use Library Tutorials!
From the Library Homepage:
Click on Tutorials
http://www.lib.lsu.edu/instruction/tutorials.html

LIVE ASSISTANCE:
From the Library Homepage:
Click on Ask a Librarian
http://www.lib.lsu.edu/virtual/
OR
Click on Live Assistance!

CALL OR E-MAIL ME!
Alice Daugherty
adaugher@lsu.edu
578-7652

Print Resources Compiled for CMST 2060 Time Travel Speech
By Alice Daugherty, adaugher@lsu.edu
Spring 2005

D21 .E578 2001
The encyclopedia of world history: ancient, medieval, and modern, chronologically arranged

E169.1 .E626 2001 V.3
Encyclopedia of the United States in the nineteenth century

D422 .B76 1996
Timelines of the 20th century: a chronology of 7500 key events, discoveries, and people that shaped our century

D421 .G63 V.1
Great events from history—worldwide twentieth century series

D11 .T83 1994
The people's chronology: a year-by-year record of human events from prehistory to the present

D11 .S83 1991
Historical tables, 58 BC-AD 1990

D11 .M39 1999 V.4
Chronology of world history

E 18 .5 T553 1996
The timetables of American history

D11 .G78 2005
The timetables of history : a horizontal linkage of people and events, based on Werner Stein's Kulturfahrplan

D11 .F75 1978B
Chronology of world history: a calendar of principal events from 3000 BC to AD 1976

D11 .C57 1997 V.1
Chronology of European history, 15,000 B.C. to 1997

E169.1 .G664 1990
American chronicle: seven decades in American life, 1920–1989

E174 .E53 2003 V.1
Encyclopedia of American history

D421 .P87 1979 V.1
20th century

Historical Events Chart

Use this chart to help you organize your information. Write down major events and activities under each topic provided. Make sure you record what resources you used in the first column.

Historical Events Chart For the years _____ to _____					
Name of Resource (book, website, newspaper, etc.)	Politics or World Events	Medical, Science, or Technological Developments	Religion or Learning or Philosophy	Popular Culture	Social Conditions or Daily Life

Sixty Seconds Response Form

Please take the next 60 seconds to respond to the following. When you are finished return it to the librarian. Thanks!

1. What is one concept in today's instruction session that you found interesting? or that you learned for the first time?

2. Was there anything you were hoping would be covered, but wasn't?

Thanks! Have a Great Day!!

Chapter 4

Using the News to Teach Reference Sources to Journalism Students

Mary Feeney

Introduction

This chapter describes information literacy instruction for two journalism courses: Reporting the News (introductory reporting) and Editing, both of which are required courses for all University of Arizona (UA) journalism majors. In the library session for the introductory reporting course, students learn what reference sources are and how to identify news article information that would come from a reference source (Part I). The library session for the Editing course (Part II) builds on students' prior knowledge of reference sources and engages them in a professionally based application of news story editing, using one type of reference source—an almanac.

Part I: Analysis of the Learning Situation
Introductory Reporting
Reporting the News is an introductory reporting course. Journalism majors must complete this course before moving on to other required reporting and writing classes, such as Advanced Reporting and Editing. The focus of the course is to provide an introduction to news reporting and writing with an emphasis on print journalism. Usually the students write stories that are local in nature (e.g., campus events, local community issues). The four to six sections of the class have been taught by a mix of full-time journalism faculty members and adjunct instructors, who are often reporters for local newspapers or former journalists.

Although most of the work in this course centers on writing news articles, the Journalism Department wants students to learn early in the program about print and online reference sources. I also teach these students about evaluating information on the Web and searching news databases, but I will focus here on teaching reference sources. The library session is held in the library's electronic classroom, with each student having access to a computer.

Information Literacy Standards
(Note: A complete list of ACRL *Information Literacy Competency Standards for Higher Education* [Chicago: ACRL, 2000] appears as appendix A.)

My objectives for the reference sources part of the library session, with the Information Literacy Competency Standards for Higher Education, Performance Indicators, and Outcomes[1] they support indicated:

   1. Students will understand that some information is organized into "reference sources" (1.2.b.).

   2. Students will understand that reference sources are available in print and online formats (1.2.c.).

   3. Students will identify what types of reference sources are used to find different kinds of information (1.2.b.).

   4. Students will be aware that reference sources often cite information such as data from primary sources and will learn they can consult the primary source (1.2.e.).

   5. Students understand the importance of accuracy and currency in news reporting (3.2.a.).

Lesson Plan

   1. Introduction and objectives of class

   2. Explanation of the need to understand how information is organized

   3. Show on flip chart different types of reference sources

   4. Show timely news article and ask students to generate questions they would investigate for their own news story on that topic

   5. Match up questions to possible types of reference sources

   6. Give examples from current news of information typically found in a reference source

   7. Emphasize importance of checking information in more than one source

   8. Show online reference sources and reference sources guide; do sample searches

Description of the Instruction Session: What Actually Happened?
I have taught a library instruction session for the introductory reporting class each semester for about six years. Because the course was often taught by adjunct faculty, I have worked with many different instructors. These two factors have led me to experiment with and modify my approach to teaching reference sources.

   I list the three major research areas we will cover in the session: reference sources, evaluating information on the Web, and searching databases for news sources. I explain that, as journalists, the students need to be able to find a variety of types of information in a wide range of sources. There are many different sources useful to journalists, even when they are assigned a specific "beat." Therefore, I explain how information is organized and what "types" of information sources exist.

I ask the students if anyone knows what reference sources are and describe them as sources "referred to" for some kind of information and not sources typically taken home to read cover to cover. I ask the students what they might use reference sources for as reporters. If the students do not raise the following points, I explain their uses for fact-checking and getting background information.

I show a list of some types of reference sources on a flip chart—almanac, atlas, biographical source, dictionary, directory, encyclopedia, and statistical source—and briefly describe what kind of information one would typically find in each. Then I show on the projection screen a recent article from one of the local newspapers. I use very current events and preferably local stories to make the examples more timely and relevant to the class. One sample article I have used is "Bloodier Sonora Drug Wars Feared."[2] I briefly summarize the article and then ask the students, "If you were assigned to write a story about how drug trafficking is affecting life for students near border towns (such as whether it's safe for university students to travel to Mexico for spring break), what kind of information would you want to find? What kinds of questions would you want your story to answer?" The class then spends a few minutes brainstorming and making suggestions. Ideas range from What is the crime rate along the Arizona–Mexico border? to How far is Rocky Point (Puerto Penasco, Mexico, a popular destination for university students) from the Arizona border?

I then ask the students where they would look to find this information. Sometimes they say they would just "look on the Web," but they often have specific suggestions, such as contacting the Mexican consulate or looking in an atlas. I also point out which questions may be answered by consulting what type of reference source.

I talk about reference sources being available in both print and online format, and tell them that, because they are in an electronic classroom, they will look at online reference sources today. However, print sources are still very important for journalists. Several of the instructors with whom I have worked frequently reinforce the importance of print resources at this point, one saying that when she worked at a newspaper, many of the reporters had copies of reference sources, such as almanacs, on their desks.

Each semester when preparing for the class, I also find examples of current news stories to demonstrate how information from reference sources is incorporated. For example, in the spring 2005 semester, I read to the class from an ABC's *World News Tonight* transcript that stated, "the most powerful earthquake in forty years cause[d] the deadliest tsunami in a century."[3] I asked the students how the reporter would know this fact and be sure it is true. I then show them the *Information Please Almanac* online. We do a search on earthquakes and find a chart showing "The Ten Largest Earthquakes Since 1900."[4] I also point out that almanacs and statistical sources often compile data from many places and usually cite a source for the data. The reporter can go to the original source to get more information or more recent data. I explain that almanacs, fact books, and statistical sources are very important to journalists because a lot of facts and other information are collected in these reference sources. Almanacs will save the reporter time when on a deadline.

I then show a resource I created, "Selected Reference Resources for Journalism Students,"[5] which is a list of print and online reference sources organized by type of reference source and briefly point out another useful resource, "Essential Reference Sources for a News Library,"[6] a Web page created by the News Division of the Special Libraries Association. I use this to reemphasize that there are many different specialized reference sources useful to journalists, relevant to various beats. Finally, I emphasize to the students that it is important for them, as journalists, to verify information in more than one source.

Reflection on the Instruction Session: Lessons Learned

I have modified how I teach this class several times over the years. The section on reference sources described here is only one-third of the library session, with evaluation of information on the Web and an introduction to news databases comprising the rest of the session. When I first started teaching the class, I only covered reference resources. I would point out certain parts of news articles and ask the students what type of reference source they would use to find that kind of information. For example, using an article about the organization Doctors Without Borders being awarded the Nobel Peace Prize in 1999,[7] I demonstrated that a directory would help them find the organization's contact information, a biographical source would have more information about the president of the organization, and an almanac would list previous Nobel Peace Prize awardees.

One of my colleagues adapted this approach for an in-house reference training session. After teaching a group of new reference desk staff about different types of reference sources, she had them read a news article, along with a list of questions to be answered about the content of the article. The exercise required that the trainees note what type of reference source would answer each question.

Formerly, I included an in-class exercise that required the students to use online reference sources. The exercise stated: "You work for a newspaper, and your editor wants you to write a story on [a current event]. Before you begin writing your story, you need to gather some background information about it." The exercise listed questions relevant to the topic. For example, following an eruption of a volcano in Japan, questions included: Where is Mount Usu? Who is the Japanese ambassador to the United States, whom you'd like to interview? What is the deadliest recorded volcanic eruption in Japan? I found the students in this introductory class were very focused on writing local stories, many of which did not require using the reference sources we covered. Now, instead of using this exercise, I have the students brainstorm what information they want to locate and what sources they would use to find it.

In addition, by also needing to teach evaluation of information on the Web and database searching, I have less time to cover reference sources. I now see this class as an introduction to the *concept* of reference sources, which the students will use in fact-checking assignments in later classes.

Two other factors have led to changes in how I present this class. The course was often taught by a different adjunct instructor each semester, making it more difficult to have continuity and ensure that all journalism students get the same basics from the start. The course is now usually taught by full-time faculty members; this facilitates consistency. In addition, I have been working closely with the Journalism Department to identify the appropriate courses in which to introduce specific skills or resources and to standardize what is taught in the different library sessions. It would be ideal to cover evaluation of information on the Web in this introductory course, reference sources in the next sequential course, and searching news databases in a later course, such as Feature Writing. Another possibility is to offer three separate sessions for the introductory reporting class throughout the semester covering these three topics.

Part II: Analysis of the Learning Situation
Editing
Editing is also a required course for all journalism majors. The introductory reporting class and the course, Law of the Press, must be completed prior to taking the editing course. Editing students also must have completed, or be concurrently enrolled in, Advanced Reporting. The Editing course involves copy editing and headline writing, as well as an introduction to layout and design. Editing is also often taught by adjunct instructors. As a result, I don't always know whether all the students have been introduced to reference sources in the earlier class.

Recently, when I was asked by an adjunct instructor to teach her editing students about reference resources, I talked to her about this situation. About half her class had been to the earlier library session, so I experimented with teaching reference sources in a different way by incorporating techniques that would be relevant to editors.

Information Literacy Standards

My objectives for the editing class are:[8]

1. Students will understand that reference sources are available in print and online formats (1.2.c.).

2. Students will explore a variety of reference sources and discuss their purposes (1.2.b.).

3. Students understand the importance of accuracy and currency in news reporting (3.2.a.).

4. Students apply their knowledge of editing and use reference sources to fact-check news articles (3.4.b.). In addition, this objective supports one of the competencies in the Accrediting Council on Education in Journalism and Mass Communications [ACEJMC] Standards for Accreditation: students should be able to "critically evaluate their own work and that of others for accuracy and fairness, clarity, appropriate style and grammatical correctness."[9]

Lesson Plan

1. Introduction

2. Discuss editing role and use of reference sources for fact-checking

3. Form groups and draw a slip of paper with the name of an online reference source: *Columbia Gazetteer, Oxford English Dictionary,* American FactFinder, World Factbook, and Arizona @ Your Service[10]

4. Have each group evaluate the resource and report back to class

5. Give out one article to each group, including a copy of the *World Almanac and Book of Facts* or *Time Almanac*

6. Students fact-check articles and then report to the class

Description of the Instruction Session: What Actually Happened?

I start the session by explaining to the class that we will be building on what they learned earlier. I do a quick review of reference sources by asking students to explain what they know about specific resources.

I then ask the students how editors use reference resources. Fact-checking is typically their first answer. I ask what an editor looks for when copyediting and record their answers on a flip chart: spelling errors, verifying dates, checking style and grammar, double-checking phone numbers and addresses, plus verifying data and statistics. I tell the class that we will focus on fact-checking in this library session and explain how reference sources (print or online) are the best way for editors to check the facts in a story. Students should not rely on what they *think* is correct, nor rely on whatever Web sites they find, unless the Web sites are reliable, accurate, authoritative sources.

The students work in groups with a reference source assigned to each: *Columbia Gazetteer*, *Oxford English Dictionary*, American FactFinder, World FactBook, Arizona @ Your Service. I selected these sources because they are not covered in the introductory reporting class and represent a variety of reference sources. Each group examines its assigned resource and reports back to the class about the content of the resource and how they might use it as an editor. This is generally meant to be a review, so we do not spend too much time on it.

At this point, I explain that one of the major sources for any journalist is an almanac. I remind them that we have looked at online almanacs in the introductory reporting class and that now they are going to use a print almanac to edit news stories. I hand out a different article to each group, along with a print copy of either the *World Almanac and Book of Facts* or the *Time Almanac*.

I gathered these news stories by searching for corrections to news articles in the Lexis-Nexis Academic, Access World News, and Academic Search Premier databases. Most news sources append a "correction" note to the original article. I identified factual errors made in news stories by searching for "correction," or "setting the record straight" (as *Time* lists corrections). I then used that information to locate the original articles. The articles follow, noting the factual errors:

• "NASA Administrator Says Space Shuttle was a Mistake," *USA Today*.[11] Stated that the space shuttle's first flight was in 1982. It was, in fact, in 1981.

• "Whatever Gets You through the Night," *The Boston Globe*.[12] Stated incorrectly that the fifteenth anniversary of John Lennon's death was approaching.

• "Verbatim," *Time*.[13] Stated, "Mark McGwire, holder of base-ball's record for most homers in a season…" As their correction noted, "McGwire's record was broken by leftfielder Barry Bonds of the San Francisco Giants in 2001."

• "We Owe Them More Than a Salute," *The Oregonian*.[14] Stated that more than 300,000 Americans died in the Civil War. The correction stated, "An estimated 498,333 Union and Confederate soldiers died in the Civil War, according to the *World Almanac*."

• "'Forgotten' War is Remembered—President Declares a National Day for Veterans of Korea," *The Washington Times*.[15] Stated, "In more than three years of fighting, 5,000 Americans died." Their correction stated that the article "gave an incorrect figure for the number of Americans who died in the Korean War. In more than three years of fighting, 36,916 Americans were killed, according to the 1998 *World Almanac and Book of Facts*."[16]

The students read through the news articles, making notes and referring to the almanacs. This usually takes about twenty minutes. I then ask each group to tell the class about its article and what kind of editing they did. Students usually are successful in finding the factual errors by verifying the information in the almanacs. However, the process raises other questions. For example, the editorial from *The Oregonian* states that since the Civil War, "400,000 more Americans have been killed in wars."[17] The *World Almanac and Book of Facts* lists separately data for battle deaths and other deaths.[18] Students "editing" that article wondered if they should count battle deaths and other deaths, and pointed out that even just counting the battle deaths, the number is more than 400,000. This led to a discussion about the importance of clarity in their own news stories. To wrap up the class, I read examples of other corrections I have found, surprising the students with how many significant, yet easily verifiable, facts are not caught in the editing process.

Reflection on the Instruction Session: Lessons Learned
This was the first time I used this method in teaching the Editing class, and I was quite impressed with the students' zeal. Many of them marked other corrections they would have made for clarity and punctuation. Some even expressed frustration that they could not check the stories more thoroughly using sources in addition to the almanacs. For example, they could not verify the date when Michael Griffin, who was quoted in the space shuttle article, became head of NASA. They also found more than I expected: the editorial from *The Oregonian* quoted Abraham Lincoln's Gettysburg Address, which one group of students found in the *World Almanac and Book of Facts*. I had forgotten how much information this source actually includes, so it really seemed like a good learning experience for all of us.

Notes
1. Association of College and Research Libraries, *Information Literacy Competency Standards for Higher Education* (Chicago: ACRL, 2000). Available online from /acrl/acrlstandards/informationliteracycompetency.htm.

2. Michael Marizco, "Bloodier Sonora Drug Wars Feared," *Arizona Daily Star*, February 21, 2005. Available online from http://infoweb.newsbank.com.

3. "World News Tonight Sunday Introduction," *World News Tonight*, ABC, December 26, 2004. Available online from http://www.lexisnexis.com.

4. Infoplease Almanac, "The Ten Largest Earthquakes Since 1900." Available online from http://www.infoplease.com/ipa/A0763403.html.

5. Mary Feeney, "Selected Reference Resources for Journalism Students," The University of Arizona Library. Available online from http://www.library. arizona.edu/search/subjects/journalism/refsources/index.html.

6. "Essential Reference Sources for a News Library," News Division of the Special Libraries Association (SLA), http://www.ibiblio.org/slanews/ reference/sources.htm.

7. Suzanne Daley, "Doctors' Group of Volunteers Awarded Nobel," *New York Times*, October 16, 1999, Late Edition-Final, Section A. Available online from http://www.lexisnexis.com.

8. ACRL, *Information Literacy Competency Standards for Higher Education*.

9. The Accrediting Council on Education in Journalism and Mass Communications, "ACEJMC Accrediting Standards." Available online from http://www.ku.edu/~acejmc/PROGRAM/STANDARDS.SHTML.

10. Arizona @ Your Service, http://az.gov/webapp/portal. Arizona @ Your Service is technically not a "reference" source, but it is the Web site for Arizona state government and includes a lot of reference-type information. The instructor specifically requested we look at this source.

11. Tracy Watson, "NASA Administrator Says Space Shuttle Was a Mistake," *USA Today*, sec. 1A, September 28 2005, Final Edition. Available online from http://www.lexisnexis.com.

12. Geoff Edgers, "Whatever Gets You through the Night," *The Boston Globe*, Living section, October 3 2005, third edition. Available online from http://www.lexisnexis.com.

13. "Verbatim," *Time*, March 28 2005. Available online from http:// epnet.com.

14. "We Owe Them More Than a Salute," *The Oregonian*, Editorial section, May 31 2004, Sunrise edition. Available online from http://www. lexisnexis.com.

15. Associated Press, "'Forgotten' War is Remembered—President Declares a National Day for Veterans of Korea," *The Washington Times*, sec. A3, July 28 1998. Available online from http://infoweb.newsbank.com.

16. "Correction," *The Washington Times*, Nation sec., A3, July 29, 1998. Available online from http://infoweb.newsbank.com.

17. "We Owe Them More Than a Salute."

18. "Casualties in Principal Wars of the U.S.," *The World Almanac and Book of Facts* (New York: World Almanac Books, 2005): 227.

Chapter 5

A Communication Capstone Project: A Developmental Model for Undergraduate Research Skills Training

Steven C. Koehn and Janet McNeil Hurlbert

Introduction

Students within the communications major at Lycoming College, a small liberal arts college, experience information assignments throughout their curriculum. The focus for the senior capstone course is a semester-long project that involves intervention and support by a communications faculty member and two librarians using multiple approaches to creating a research question, pursuing in-depth research, and completing a final major project. We operate from a heuristic, self-discovery approach. Our assumption is that students will proceed from uninformed research behaviors when confronted by constraints of time and knowledge. This fall-back position needs to be replaced with a developmental approach, enhanced by clear expectations with multiple deadlines, professional support, and frequent intervention. Our intervention is based on knowledge and observations about how students research. Students regard research as an individual occurrence that happens as close to the date due as possible. In their view, such projects tend to raise grades more than tests and quizzes because the expectations are spelled out in terms of number of pages and type font, rather than information requirements. As opposed to a decade ago, when even a small academic library and its research collection were foreign ground, now the Internet empowers students so that they feel they can quickly "research" anything.

Analysis of the Learning Situation

The completed assignment in this capstone course consists of an extensive annotated bibliography and a poster session. Approximately twenty communication majors and minors meet in the library classroom once a week for a sixty-five-minute class period to develop an annotated bibliography based on their individual research questions. A great deal of student time is devoted to this project outside class as well, but the regular class time ensures a supportive environment. To reach this goal, a concentrated period is spent developing a research topic. The resulting annotated bibliography takes the student to the point at which a researcher would conduct an actual study and write an extended undergraduate research thesis.

Given a class of students with varying abilities and limited time, an annotated bibliography is what can be managed within a semester, while still giving due attention to the research process. The use of annotations within this assignment is reinforced by the REAP concept.[1] Although there are numerous Web sites on the topic, the original concept dates to Eanet and Manzo. The Read, Encode, Annotate, and Ponder approach enhances reading and leads to annotations that exhibit analytical thinking. The annotations we require not only summarize research studies, but also add critical and comparative comments that relate to capstone research articles the students have identified in the early weeks of research. After student researchers identify their capstone articles, all other articles included in the annotated bibliography must provide information on how they relate to these capstones (for example, confirm research, illustrate a trend, or refute an accepted research). All the articles must connect through the annotations.

We also consider the practical side of annotations. Time within a semester can be allocated to a careful research process; and students can still finish with a useful written project even though it may not be an undergraduate thesis. In this case, the annotations are comparatively lengthy and contain many of the elements described as options in REAP. In addition, there is the "surprise" approach as perceived by the student. Students are confident that they know how to put a research paper together. An annotation is a different experience for students, who are then more receptive to a developmental approach.

Information Literacy Standards

(Note: A complete list of *ACRL Information Literacy Competency Standards for Higher Education* [Chicago: ACRL, 2000] appears as appendix A.)

The following Information Literacy Competency Standards for Higher Education were addressed, with Performance Indicators and Outcomes noted:

Standard One: "The information literate student determines the nature and extent of the information needed"; 1.1.c, 1.1.d, 1.1.e, 1.2.b, 1.2.d, 1.2.e, 1.3.a, 1.4.a, and 1.4.b.

Standard Two: "The information literate student accesses needed information effectively and efficiently"; 2.1.c, 2.1.d, 2.2.a, 2.2.b, 2.2.c, 2.2.d, 2.2.e, 2.2.f, 2.3.a, 2.3.b, 2.3.c, 2.4.a, and 2.5.c.

Standard Three: "The information literate student evaluates information and its sources critically and incorporates selected information into his or her knowledge base and value system"; 3.2.a, 3.2.c, 3.2.d, 3.4.e, 3.4.g, 3.7.b, and 3.7.c.

Standard Four: "The information literate student, individually or as a member of a group, uses information effectively to accomplish a specific purpose."

Standard Five: "The information literate student understands many of the economic, legal, and social issues surrounding the use of information and accesses and uses information ethically and legally"; 5.1.b. and 5.3.a.[2]

Lesson Plans
First Class
Students play *Jeopardy* to review information about library locations and basic sources. "CommBucks" are used throughout the course as incentives and may be used to raise a grade by a point or two. Three students receive free notebooks for their annotation assignment based on their high Jeopardy bucks score. The librarians have designed a booklet for students that includes information about basic resources as well as the research process and designing research questions. Key communication research resources are reviewed in a hands-on environment so that students can begin to explore research question possibilities and see what materials are available.

Second Class
Librarians complete a review of related research sources and discuss the kinds of materials that are acceptable for this study as well as the characteristics of capstone articles.

Third Class
Librarians introduce RefWorks, online software that helps students to gather references and format a bibliography. The research question is due. Librarians and the professor review and evaluate the questions and assign students to their project advisors, either the faculty member or one of the two librarians.

Later Semester Classes
Students continue meeting once a week in the library for independent work and meetings with their advisors. The beginnings of class periods are used to inform the class on observed problems or to review materials that have raised questions.

Last Week of Class

A public poster session for communication majors is followed by a banquet. The written project is submitted to the communications professor.

Description of the Instruction Session: What Actually Happened?

The communication professor designs and guides the course with active involvement from two librarians. The course begins with a review of basic library procedures and physical locations through a Jeopardy game, then moves to a thorough introduction and review of research resources, including RefWorks. We want the class as a whole to develop a general level of comfort within the physical building.

During these first few weeks, students test different research topics and begin the process of wording a research question, with several subsequent rewordings as the questions are critiqued by faculty member and librarians. The class time provides a venue for students to work individually with librarians and/or the professor to customize research techniques for their topics and to gain skill in selecting the articles and book chapters that develop their hypotheses while staying within the realm of good research materials.

As the weeks progress, we spend a few minutes at the beginning and ending of each class illustrating or summarizing research points that apply to the class in general. More time, however, is devoted to individual research and working individually with students. The research questions continue to be modified. The assessment is an evaluation form in which the students rank changes in attitudes and skills. The last week of the semester is the due date for the notebook of annotations, plus copies of all readings. A final poster session is publicized on campus, attended by communication majors and faculty and ending with a banquet.

This research class now has a reputation among majors as being demanding, even though extensive support is given by both the professor and the librarians. Each semester the course is offered, we revisit the booklet. Even though most of the students have been four years at our small college, which has an active library instruction program, increasingly, students are unfamiliar with the physical library. They also are used to selecting the first electronic articles they encounter rather than evaluating all types of resources gathered from their own library as well as through interlibrary loan.

The first sessions focus on bringing the class to a common standard. As we review resources, we need to constantly keep in mind that locations of materials may be a problem. There are usually new databases or services, so the beginning sessions are not just review. A senior librarian is paired with a junior instructional services librarian because the course is rich in so many information literacy components that it is an excellent teaching ground for the beginning librarian. Moreover, it is a true collaboration of teaching faculty and librarian. We give the students advice on revising their research questions and often revisit each question several times as the projects begin. We also frequently review the articles the students are finding, always noticing that nonacademic articles creep in and the differences have to be discussed. Our observation is that this type of an annotated bibliography, requiring evaluation and synthesis, often demands better and more critical reading on the part of students than a traditional research paper. There is always at least one student who clings to a question that is not proving fruitful and finally must surrender to another topic. No matter what steps we take to avoid this situation, we are seldom successful.

Classes vary in terms of student strengths and enthusiasm, from semester to semester and class to class. We try to change our approach and teaching style to meet these challenges as we encounter them.

Reflection on the Instruction Session: Lessons Learned

We have taught this course for three years, and each semester we keep a running list of improvements that need to be incorporated the next time the class is offered. The booklet changes and so do the timing of presentations and the active learning techniques. As stated above, we are somewhat taken back by the lack of familiarity our seniors have with the library. We have become much more experienced helping students hone their research questions and have learned that we need to eliminate certain topics that always lead to a lack of success. We have put in more check points along the way to ensure that the students understand expectations, and we give more advice about quality standards for the poster session. Students are generally pleased with the fruits of their labors, and the more successful students understand that after a semester-length project such as this they are just ready to begin "real" research, not finish it—a true sign that they are ready for a graduate research experience. We would like to eventually offer an opportunity for strong students to take their projects and sign up for another semester of an individual studies project or an honors paper.

What we do verify is that annotation assignments work. It is a terrific way to improve the reading of research material, identify leading authors in a particular area of research, and allow a more extended amount of research time in the beginning of the process without compromising the end product. We have gone on to recommend annotation projects to other professors in other disciplines.

Notes

1. Marilyn G. Eanet and Anthony V. Manzo, "REAP—A Strategy for Improving Reading/Writing/Study skills," *Journal of Reading* 19 (May 1976): 647–52.

2. Association of College and Research Libraries, *Information Literacy Competency Standards for Higher Education* (Chicago: ACRL, 2000). Available online from http://www.ala.org/ala/acrl/acrlstandards/inform ationliteracycompetency.htm.

Teaching Resources

The librarians at Lycoming have created a booklet, Formulating Your Research Question, that supports the class work and reminds students of resources. A copy of the current booklet is available from Janet Hurlbert, hurlbjan@lycoming.edu. Topics covered are:

- Due dates
- Formulating your research question
- Communication research sources, databases, and subject links
- Do I have capstone research?
- Evaluating research
- Writing annotations
- RefWorks
- Work pages for listing key words and databases
- Contact information for librarians

Following are sample pages from the booklet:

Your research question must be approved by the COMM 440 Committee. While you should choose a topic that interests you, there are some topics that are not feasible to research in a semester. Do yourself a favor; develop a question that you can live and work with for an entire semester!

What doesn't work:

- Sports topics
- Visual imagery topics
- Music topics
- Fringe communication fields

Take a look at the existing research.

If you are having trouble coming up with an idea, seeing what's already being studied can help give you direction.

If preliminary searching on the **main concepts** of a topic unearths little to no prior research, that might be a clue that there is little research on the topic and that you will have difficulty coming up with the required number of studies.

That said, don't hesitate to ask for help with search terms or techniques. Sometimes it's just a matter of coming up with the right terminology.

Remember, the idea behind this project is to do original research. If you find a study that matches your idea exactly, you will want to come up with a new twist on it or way of approaching it.

Talk to your professor and the librarians about your ideas. We have a fairly good idea about what will or won't work, so take advantage of that.

Do I Have Capstone Research?

Does the abstract or an introductory passage include phrases like the following? "This is a core article." "This is landmark research." "Many research projects have been based on this study." "This represents capstone research."

Does the material answer your research question perfectly?

Do several databases and indexes point you to the same article?

In comparing quite a few articles are there some that stand out because they are more complete? (Which ones would you choose for a research competition?)

Is the article cited by other researchers?

Is the researcher considered a leader in the field and is his/her name mentioned often in texts and other articles? Is the researcher from an institution that is noted for the particular area of research?

Is the date of the research significant in terms of the development of the topic?

Chapter 6

Faculty–Librarian–Undergraduate Collaboration for Evaluating Children's Literature Resources

Sara K. Kearns, Marcia G. Stockham, and Karin E. Westman

Introduction

Students enrolled in a children's literature course at Kansas State University researched authors and illustrators, and created Web sites that contributed to the ongoing critical conversation about children's literature. The class was designed with two intended outcomes. The first was to encourage a more collaborative relationship between undergraduate students and librarians, between students and teaching faculty, and between teaching faculty and librarians. The second was to introduce students to information literacy competencies related to synthesizing and communicating information. The project was based on a similar program at Washburn University in Topeka, Kansas, described in a presentation at the Society for Information Technology and Teacher Education 2002 conference.[1]

Analysis of the Learning Situation

Approximately forty-five students were enrolled in children's literature classes each semester from fall 2002 to fall 2003. The students were primarily preservice teachers/education majors, with a few students from other disciplines. Three faculty members from the Department of English participated; two taught sections of the course over three semesters and one served as technology coordinator. Teaching faculty provided instruction to the students in critical evaluation skills and technology, particularly Web design, as well as in critical writing skills. The class met in a computer lab classroom with access to online resources and Web design software. These resources allowed teaching faculty to model research, writing skills, and design strategies, and allowed students to practice their skills in written and visual information literacy. Three librarians participated in the collaboration: the liaison to the English Department who maintained the Juvenile Literature collection; the liaison to the College of Education; and the liaison to the College of Business who had a BA in English and an interest in children's literature.

Students worked in groups of five to six to research an author or illustrator and were matched with one of the three librarians who provided instruction in the use of relevant print and electronic resources. Librarians also provided guidance in evaluating resources, particularly free Web sites. The librarians initially met students in the classroom; subsequent meetings were held in the library in the reference collection or Juvenile Literature/Curriculum Materials collection. The librarians and teaching faculty communicated about issues that arose as the students progressed in their research.

The final product for this assignment was a Web site, written and designed by students based on research they conducted. Students researched and wrote a biography of the author or illustrator selected. Next, they generated two bibliographies, one of the selected author's work and one of the resources consulted. Finally, students synthesized their readings of the authors' works with information they located through research to write critical contexts, such as literary/artistic style, themes, or cultural connections. Teaching faculty introduced students to basic Web site design and encouraged them to study other Web sites to decide what principles worked best. The students applied these principles to their own Web sites.

All information was transferred to each group's Web site, and the groups presented their finished product, along with their observations on the process, to the class, the three instructors, and the three librarians. Because many of these students were preservice teachers, they designed their pages with K–12 teachers in mind.

Information Literacy Standards

(Note: A complete list of ACRL *Information Literacy Competency Standards for Higher Education* [Chicago: ACRL, 2000] appears as appendix A.)

The following Information Literacy Competency Standard for Higher Education was addressed: Standard Four, "The information literate student, individually or as a member of a group, uses information effectively to accomplish a specific purpose,"[2] with the following Performance Indicators and Outcomes: 4.1.c, 4.1.d, 4.3.c, and 4.3.d.

Lesson Plan

1. Teaching faculty introduce assignment and objectives to class.

2. Students are assigned to groups of five to six and groups are matched with librarians.

3. Librarians visit class, introduce basic print resources, and make first contact with groups.

4. First library meetings are held between groups and librarians to:
   a. Evaluate Web resources students located prior to meetings
   b. Introduce and explore (hands-on) additional print and electronic resources
5. Librarians make initial report to teaching faculty regarding student progress.
6. Groups divide project tasks among members.
7. Second library meetings are held with groups and librarians to:
   a. Review criteria for assignment
   b. Review and evaluate selected resources for author biography, bibliography, and critical context essays
   c. Discuss citing resources
8. Groups synthesize information, draft biography and critical context essays, and design Web pages.
   a. Groups or individuals consult with teaching faculty.
   b. Groups or individuals consult with librarians.
   c. Librarians consult as needed with teaching faculty.
9. Students present their final Web sites during class at end of semester with teaching faculty and librarians in attendance.

Description of the Instruction Session: What Actually Happened?

Teaching faculty arranged students into groups of five to six according to students' experience and comfort with technology, especially Web design. Each group had at least one member who identified him- or herself as having previous experience with technology. Teaching faculty scheduled one class session to introduce the assignment, to model completed projects from past semesters, and to provide the groups in-class time to select an author or illustrator for their project. The groups also appointed a group Web master to manage the group's contributions for posting to the Web.

Teaching faculty sent a list of the authors and illustrators to the three participating librarians who each chose three to four names from the list so that every option was selected. When the librarians knew the authors they would be researching, the librarian who was the liaison to the English department provided a refresher for the other librarians on standard print and electronic resources that would be applicable to the project. The authors and illustrators spanned the spectrum from established and classic (such as L.M. Montgomery) to new or regional (such as Jon Scieszka or Brad Sneed). This range meant that some authors were more heavily represented in library resources than others. Preliminary research permitted the librarians to communicate any concerns or issues to the teaching faculty and to explore alternative resources.

All three librarians attended a classroom session and were introduced to the students. The English specialist librarian briefly presented print resources the students could expect to use for their research. The class split into project groups and the librarians spent five to ten minutes with each of their assigned groups. This initial meeting was useful because the students spoke about how they chose their subject, what their majors were, and other general topics that permitted librarians and students to become acquainted. The librarians shared why they chose a particular author and offered reassurance that students would be able to find information. Contact information was exchanged, and the initial meeting outside class was scheduled. More pragmatically, students and librarians were now able to recognize each other when they met in the library. One issue that immediately arose during this first meeting was scheduling. Although the librarians were flexible with their schedules and offered evening and weekend times to meet in addition to their normal business hours, it became obvious that finding a time that all students in a group could meet was going to be a stumbling block. Some groups eventually met when the majority of members were available, with the understanding that those present would pass on the needed information to anyone who was absent.

Within one week of the class meeting, the librarians met with individual groups in the Social Sciences/Humanities Reference Collection area in the main library. Public-access computers were readily accessible. Each student was assigned to bring the addresses of two Web sites that provided information about their author. Prior to the meeting, the librarian also explored the Web to locate information and be familiar with those sites the students might find. The students presented the sites they found and the librarian led a discussion on evaluating Web sites. Many of the students were familiar with basic concepts but confessed that they couldn't find a lot of useful information.[3] The librarian walked the group through research sources such as *The Dictionary of Literary Biography, Children's Literature Review*, ProQuest Literature Online, and Gale Literature Resource Center. Students were delighted to find information and immediately began pulling relevant books from the shelves, making copies, and searching the databases and the library catalog. This first meeting lasted about one hour.

Following the first meeting, the librarians sent brief notes to the teaching faculty detailing which students attended, which ones brought two Web sites, and summarized how the session went and if there were any concerns. Group dynamics became apparent by the end of the first meeting. Those groups with strong leadership quickly organized, divided the labor, and planned future group meetings. Groups without a strong leader spent more time figuring out who would do what and less time actually researching.

After the initial group meeting with librarians, teaching faculty provided further instruction in drafting the biography, bibliography, and critical context essays for the selected authors. By the second meeting with the librarians, the students had divided the project so that each member was responsible for a different critical context. Topics for these essays included literary relations, history of literary production, cultural connections, style of illustrations/ art, narrative style and structure, and theme. The second meeting was concerned primarily with helping the students to locate additional resources applicable to the critical context being researched. This meeting lasted between thirty and forty-five minutes. Subsequent meetings between the librarian and individual students occurred as research questions arose. The major obstacle for students at this juncture was that they expected to find resources that contained exactly the information they needed. Information for the biography and bibliography sections was readily found, but placing their author within a cultural, literary, or artistic context required that the students extrapolate information from multiple sources and apply their own evaluation and criticism of the author's or illustrator's work.

At midsemester, teaching faculty presented all students with an in-class, hands-on tutorial about creating a basic Web page in the Web-authoring software Adobe GoLive 6.0. Although students had one additional class session to develop the design of their Web sites and one additional class session to develop its content, they completed subsequent work on the site on their own time. Personalities and scheduling conflicts caused some groups to falter at this stage in the project, but many thrived, amazing themselves at the Web pages and content they had produced. The librarians' direct interaction with the students was mostly complete by this point; students focused on synthesizing the information they gathered and deploying it onto their Web sites.

The semester ended with groups presenting their Web sites to the teaching faculty and librarians. Throughout the semester, the teaching faculty conducted continuous assessment of the assignment and the librarian–student interactions. Librarians offered feedback, but teaching faculty were wholly responsible for grading student work and the final projects.

Reflection on the Instruction Session: Lessons Learned

Due to continuous assessment via surveys, e-mail reporting, and grades, librarians and teaching faculty were able to review the librarian–student interaction, the students' ability to achieve the information literacy competencies and the integration of technology into the lesson plan.

Librarian–Student Interaction

Student Surveys. Teaching faculty administered surveys to the students at the beginning of the semester. Questions asked were:

1. Briefly outline the steps you take when doing research.
2. Describe the last interaction you had in a library with a librarian.

Most students responded to the first question with a logical approach to starting their research (picking a topic, making notes, outlining ideas, and finding information). They did not expand on finding information, but many referred to the Web. Responses to the second question varied from "I don't use librarians" to "my high school librarian she helped me find a book." There was no indication that any of the students had recently worked with librarians for in-depth research purposes.

Follow-up surveys were administered at the end of the semester, and the results indicated the benefits of the collaboration. Students were asked to rank the following statements using a five point scale from "strongly disagree" to "strongly agree":

1. Meeting with a librarian was valuable.
2. After working with a librarian, I believe my research skills have improved.
3. My group's librarian made library technology more accessible.
4. My group found good resources that we likely would not have discovered without our librarian.
5. I would consult with my group's librarian again on a future project.
6. If a friend asked you for advice about doing research, what would be the most important piece of advice you would provide?
7. Any additional comments or suggestions about your group's work with your librarian would be welcome.

Although a quantitative analysis has not been performed on these surveys, it was easy to see the pattern for most respondents. Results ranged from "neutral" to "strongly agree," with just a few "disagree" marked by students who commented they already knew how to use the library. The question about giving advice to friends was added to the second-semester surveys, and a definite majority answered with a recommendation to use the library and ask for help from a librarian.

Librarian surveys. The three librarians were asked the following questions before starting the project.

1. What are the potential benefits to this project?
2. What are the potential pitfalls to this project?
3. If you had to choose just one, what idea would you most like to communicate to the students during your participation in this project?

Potential benefits identified were: increased interaction with students, collaboration with faculty outside the normal liaison relationship, and easing library anxiety of students. These benefits were realized when librarians responded to similar questions at the end of the first semester. Upon completion of the project librarians reported the following benefits: working with students at their "point of need," working in a different-than-usual library atmosphere, and repeatedly interacting with students allowed building on previously developed skills.

In the preproject surveys, potential pitfalls included failure to communicate, unrealized expectations, bad group dynamics, and scheduling conflicts. As the postproject surveys demonstrated, scheduling problems and students' lack of understanding of the overall project were the primary pitfalls. Throughout all semesters, the key ideas that librarians wanted to communicate to the students were that libraries don't have to be intimidating and that students should ask for help when needed. The student surveys, cited above, indicate that the librarians succeeded in this goal.

Student Achievement of Information Literacy Competencies

The final product—the Web sites—best illustrated the extent to which students met the information literacy competencies. Students learned to integrate information in several ways. First, they cowrote the biographical essays. Each student sought out information, returned it to the group, and the group reviewed the gathered pieces and compiled them into one unified piece. Second, each student researched a particular cultural context. Few students found all the information they needed in one source. Instead, they found a snippet in one essay, another aspect in a book, and a new perspective in a review. The students learned to evaluate the fragments, compare the new information to what they knew from the biographies and their own readings of the author's work, and seek out more information to fill gaps or confirm inconsistencies. Finally, the groups had to ensure that the cultural context essays formed a cohesive picture of the author, given that the site would be available to anyone searching the Web. Students' awareness of the need for clear written and visual communication was therefore heightened by the fact that they were designing Web sites about an author or illustrator that others might refer to for information. The majority of students successfully demonstrated achievement of the competencies.

Integration of Technology

The Web project assignment, as currently written, required an ambitious integration of technology by both the teaching faculty and the students. Assessment of its role influenced the ways teaching faculty taught the assignment from one semester to the next.

First, teaching faculty assessed the distribution of students within their groups. To help ease student anxiety about creating a series of Web pages, teaching faculty had initially assigned students to groups according to their stated comfort level or expertise with technology: each group had at least one member who expressed a high comfort level or expertise with technology. However, because groups had such difficulty coordinating their respective schedules, in subsequent semesters the students were organized according to their preferred time to meet outside class. This change did not eradicate the scheduling issues, but it did minimize them without adversely affecting the collective technological skills of each group.

Second, teaching faculty assessed the initial introduction of the assignment to the students. When first meeting with the librarians, students expressed concerns about the technology portion of the assignment. Students' anxiety about creating the Web pages themselves prevented them from focusing on the information literacy skills they needed to complete the whole assignment. In subsequent semesters, when introducing the assignment, teaching faculty addressed this concern by encouraging the students to focus on the analytical aspects of the assignment and on their selection of print and visual resources.

Third, teaching faculty assessed their departmental technology capabilities. Like their students, teaching faculty grappled with the assignment's high-tech components. Teaching faculty had limited tech support beyond their own resources, and the lab classroom's wired connection required an upgrade for speed and efficiency. Consequently, teaching faculty and students experienced technical difficulties that frustrated them and complicated the timely completion of some projects. The classroom's technology resources have since received the necessary upgrades, mitigating some of the initial frustrations. However, in order for the assignment to continue, the teaching faculty have requested additional support (a graduate teaching assistant, for instance) who could be available to assist students with implementing their design ideas and uploading the completed pages. The development of a new studio environment at Kansas State—the Humanities Commons—may provide some of these requested resources.

In all, the students who participated in this project seemed to enjoy and take pride in their final product, when they had overcome their initial anxiety. The librarians enjoyed working with the small groups and with the English faculty. The collaboration allowed librarians to become an integral part of the assignment and has opened doors for further joint projects. With the technology improvements noted above, it is possible this assignment may become a standard part of the Children's Literature class.

Notes

1. Anne Millard-Daugherty and Jan Guise, "Creating a Learning Community: Faculty/Student/Librarian Collaboration at Washburn and Kansas Universities" (paper presented at the annual international meeting for the Society for Information Technology and Teacher Education, Nashville, TN, Mar. 18–23, 2002).

2. Association of College and Research Libraries, *Information Literacy Competency Standards for Higher Education* (Chicago: ACRL, 2000). Available online from http://www.ala.org/ala/acrl/acrlstandards/inform ationliteracycompetency.htm.

3. Note that a quick Google search in late 2005 revealed considerably more free Web resources than did searches in 2002 and 2003 when this assignment was first given.

Teaching Resources

Excerpts: Group Web Project Assignment

Goals
- To learn how to locate, to synthesize, and to document both print and online research materials.
- To learn how to create and upload a Web page.
- To contribute to the ongoing critical conversation about children's literature by building an online Web resource.

Audience
Educated and interested readers of children's literature, including (but not limited to) students of children's literature, prospective teachers, and current teachers.

Components of the Web Page:

(1) Brief biography of the author (500–700 words), in the group's own words, with citations (from at least three sources) and a works-cited list. See sample, though longer, of a biography at http://www.ksu.edu/english/nelp/purple/biography.html or view the "biography" sections of the sites at Children's Literature Online.

(2) A two-part bibliography, in MLA format:
- A bibliography of all works written/illustrated by the author (primary resources), listed by genre and organized by date (oldest first).
- A bibliography of eight to ten selected works about the author and his/her works (secondary resources), annotated with a one- or two-sentence description about each selected work. At least four of these selected works must be available from and listed as library print materials.
- See sample, though longer, of a bibliography at http://www.ksu.edu/english/nelp/purple/bibliography.html or view the "bibliography" sections of the sites at Children's Literature Online.

(3) Five or six of the following Critical Contexts, each 400–500 words in length:
- Literary Relations (comparison with another author writing in similar style or genre) Example: Comparison between Crockett Johnson's presentation of art and the imagination in *Harold and the Purple Crayon* and Leo Lionni's in *Frederick*.
- History of Literary Production (tracing the production history of a particular work) Examples: Discussion of HarperCollins' rejection of Johnson's *Harold and the Purple Crayon* before accepting it for publication,

as described in the letters of Ursula Nordstrom. Discussion of adaptations/ interpretations of *Harold and the Purple Crayon*, such as the animated film and the board game. Discussion of the translations of *Harold and the Purple Crayon*.

- Cultural Connections (using biographical, historical, and/or cultural information to analyze a particular work) Examples: Discussion of Johnson's *Harold's Trip to the Sky* (1957) in connection with the rise in American space exploration in the 1950s. Discussion of how Johnson's fondness for dogs manifests itself in works such as *The Blue Ribbon Puppies* and *Terrible Terrifying Toby*.
- Style of Illustrations/Art (analysis of the visual presentation of a particular work, including comparison/contrast with at least one other author-illustrator) Example: Comparison between Johnson's minimal, representational cartoon-style of drawing in *A Picture for Harold's Room* and the style of Syd Hoff in *Danny and the Dinosaur*.
- Narrative Style and Structure (analysis of the narrative form of a particular work) Examples: Analysis of Johnson's *We Wonder What Will Walter Be? When He Grows Up* as a fable. Analysis of Johnson's *Harold and the Purple Crayon* as a picaresque narrative.
- Theme (analysis of a theme, in one work or several works, by the author) Examples: Analysis of gender in Johnson's Ellen and Harold books and how these characters challenge traditional gender roles by sharing similar qualities (imagination, adventure, concern for others). Analysis of the presence of imaginary companions in Johnson's Ellen and Harold books and how they represent aspects of the child's self (Harold's crayon representing the creative self, Ellen's lion representing the superego).

For more, see the relevant sections of the sites at Children's Literature Online.

Group Web Project: Grading Criteria

Biography
- Clear, concise, and accurate prose narrative that describes key life events of the author, connecting those key events to the history of the time and the author's works whenever possible. Any awards should be included as well.
- 500–700 words length.
- Must draw from at least three different sources.
- Written in the group's own words. Any quotations, ideas, or information not your own should be cited according to MLA format, and you should provide a works-cited list at the end of the biography.

• Names of group members should precede or follow the text of the biography.

Bibliography
• A bibliography of all works written/illustrated by the author (primary resources), listed by genre, correctly cited according to MLA format.
• A bibliography of eight to ten selected works about the author and his/her works (secondary resources), correctly cited according to MLA format.
• Each entry for the secondary resources should be followed by a one- to two-sentence description about the content/claims of the entry.
• At least four of the secondary resources must be available as library print materials (that is, not only available from a Web page).
• Names of group members should precede or follow the text of the bibliography.

Critical Contexts
• Five or six entries (depending on the number of people in your group, one for each).
• Only two of the five to six entries may be from the same category of "Critical Contexts." The categories once again are:
   — Literary Relations (comparison with another author writing in similar style or genre)
   — History of Literary Production (tracing the production history of a particular work)
   — Cultural Connections (using biographical, historical, and/or cultural information to analyze a particular work)
   — Style of Illustrations/Art (analysis of the visual presentation of a particular work, including comparison/contrast with at least one other author-illustrator)
   — Narrative Style and Structure (analysis of the narrative form of a particular work)
   — Theme (analysis of a theme, in one work or several works, by the author)
   — Each entry must be 400 to 500 words in length.
   — The selection of category and the selection of topic for a given category should be relevant and appropriate for the selected author. (For instance, if your selected author writes picture books, your group should have an entry for "Style of Illustrations/Art" in order to provide helpful context for the author.)
• Each entry for the "Critical Contexts" should have a clear thesis

claim and supporting evidence (indirect/direct quotations). It should be clearly written and free of errors in grammar, punctuation, and spelling. The author's name should precede or follow the text of the entry.

• All "Critical Contexts" entries should include works cited in MLA format. And, if other people's ideas or words are included in the entry, they should be cited in MLA format.

Final Group Web Project:

• Effective presentation and selection of all Group Web Project components, including use of hyperlinks and attention to clear graphic and text display

• Attention to audience for Group Web Project, with text written in prose that is free of errors in grammar, spelling, and punctuation

Presenting Your Web Project:

For your presentation to the class, your group should offer your responses to the following questions:

1. What two or three aspects of the Web project (anything from research to content to design) are you most proud of? (If it's an element you can show us on the resulting pages, please do so.)

2. What one or two aspects of the Web project (again, any aspect) was most challenging?

3. If you had more time, what one or two aspects would you like to develop, revise, or complete?

I'd recommend having more than one person offer these responses to the class, so we hear from at least two or three members of the group. Then, after you've made your presentation, we'll offer any comments or questions.

Chapter 7

Inspired Teachers: Providing a Classroom Context for Information Literacy Theory and Practice

Corinne Laverty and Brenda Reed

Introduction

Today's world of learning resources is as engaging as it is complex. Consider the richness of the expanding online universe: blogs, wikis, online newspapers, Really Simple Syndication (RSS) feeds, podcasts, streamed video, e-books and e-journals, software, games, Web sites, and learning objects. Teachers use everything from books (picture books, graphic novels, fiction, nonfiction) to multimedia to virtual sources in the classroom. As librarians at the Queen's University Faculty of Education in Kingston, Ontario, Canada, we wanted to offer a series of information literacy classes that would appeal to preservice teachers on three levels: learning to use resources in our education library to complete their course assignments; learning to identify subject and grade-specific materials to take to their own classrooms during teaching practices; and learning about the concept of information literacy and how to teach research skills when they become teachers in the field.

To inform our choice of classes, we surveyed 522 outgoing teacher candidates in 2005 using twenty questions that examined their understanding of information literacy; their preparedness to teach information literacy skills; their knowledge of how to do research and search the Web; and their knowledge of the role of the school librarian. Key findings from this survey[1] revealed that these teacher candidates:

- Do not understand the concept of information literacy
- Are not prepared to teach information literacy skills when they leave the program
- Prefer to Google for information for their class assignments
- Are unaware of the range of resources they can use in their classrooms and how to find these resources
- Do not have sufficient knowledge of the key education resources through which they will continue their own professional development in the field

On the bright side, these students were asked what topics they would like to learn more about. Almost half of them identified what we would categorize as "information literacy" skills such as how to evaluate resources, use databases, teach the research process, and search the Web. Our INSPIRED Teaching Series (**In**novative **S**tudent **P**articipation **I**n **R**esearch and **ED**ucation) was born from these results. This five-part series offered four sessions on each of these topics over two months: (1) Best Classroom Resources, (2) Assignments Already? (3) Be a Subject Expert, (4) When YOU Teach Research, and (5) Out-Google Your Students. Sixty classes related to this series were given during the fall term to 1,469 students using fifty-two teaching hours.

Analysis of the Learning Situation

Teacher candidates (TCs) from both the concurrent (five-year concurrent undergraduate and BEd degree) and the consecutive (one-year postundergraduate degree) BEd programs at our university spend one academic year at the Faculty of Education, where a separate education library serves their resource and instructional needs. The INSPIRED Teaching Series was designed to provide preservice teachers with the information literacy skills they need as both continuing learners and teachers of K–12 students. The new K–12 curriculum phased in by the Ministry of Education in Ontario from 1998 to 2001 emphasizes inquiry, research, and communications as one of the sets of expectations for grades one to eight, and methods of inquiry as one of the strands of many senior-level courses. In 1999, the Ontario School Library Association published *Information Studies, Kindergarten to Grade 12,* an information literacy curriculum that maps information literacy skills onto the new Ontario curriculum.[2] Teachers in Ontario are expected to work with teacher librarians to prepare lessons that ensure the progressive acquisition of information literacy skills by Ontario K–12 students, and here in the Faculty of Education we want to provide preservice teachers with the information and teaching strategies they will need to do this work.

Our INSPIRED program was designed to ensure that preservice teachers are aware of the *Information Studies* document; that they can teach their students how to find, evaluate, and use information; and that they have the knowledge to continue their professional development independently. These library goals are not currently recognized as part of the Faculty of Education curriculum, so pursuit of these objectives is in noncredit instructional sessions during on-campus instruction weeks of the BEd program. Given the very full schedules of our TCs, the library's best chance of drawing participants to our workshops is during the lunch hour when we can offer forty-minute sessions that still give people time to travel to and from class. With the aim of capturing the interest of as many TCs as possible, we designed a seven-week staged program that moves from the immediate needs of the new preservice teacher (what types of resources are in this library and how do I find them) to a deeper focus on subject-specific resources (and how resources connect to the curriculum) to a sharing of teaching ideas and modeling of strategies for teaching research skills to K–12 students. Throughout the series of workshops, we approached our work with the teacher candidates as professional development with colleagues rather than as instructional classes for students and we aimed to model the passion for learning and the genuine interest in literature and information that can lead to inspired classroom teaching. We publicized our INSPIRED Teaching Series by alerting both faculty and students to the program. We provided faculty with information through librarian participation on faculty curriculum committees and via a faculty listserv. The faculty, in turn, encouraged teacher candidates in their classes to attend the library workshops; and we further publicized our programs to teacher candidates via posters, the teacher candidate listserv, and a large display board located at the entrance to our library.

Information Literacy Standards
(Note: A complete list of ACRL *Information Literacy Competency Standards for Higher Education* [Chicago: ACRL, 2000] appears as appendix A.)

The following chart illustrates which ACRL Information Literacy Competency Standards for Higher Education[3] are met in each of the classes:
Class 1: Best Classroom Resources
Class 2: Assignments Already?
Class 3: Be a Subject Expert
Class 4: When YOU Teach Research
Class 5: Out-Google Your Students.

ACRL Information Literacy Competency Standards[4]	1	2	3	4	5
1.1.a Confers with instructors and participates in class discussions, peer workgroups, and electronic discussions to identify a research topic, or other information need.		x	x	x	x
1.1.b Develops a thesis statement and formulates questions based on the information need.		x		x	
1.1.c Explores general information sources to increase familiarity with the topic.	x		x	x	
1.1.d Defines or modifies the information need to achieve a manageable focus.		x		x	x

1.1.e Identifies key concepts and terms that describe the information need.	X	X	X	X	X
1.2.c Identifies the value and differences of potential resources in a variety of formats (e.g., multimedia, database, website, data set, audio/visual, book.)	X		X	X	
1.2.d Identifies the purpose and audience of potential resources (e.g., popular vs. scholarly, current vs. historical).	X	X	X	X	X
1.2.e Differentiates between primary and secondary sources, recognizing how their use and importance vary with each discipline.	X		X	X	
1.2.f Realizes that information may need to be constructed with raw data from primary sources.	X		X	X	
1.3.b Considers the feasibility of acquiring a new language or skill (e.g., foreign or discipline-based) in order to gather needed information and to understand its context.		X	X	X	X
1.3.c Defines a realistic overall plan and timeline to acquire the needed information.	X	X		X	X
1.4.a Reviews the initial information need to clarify, revise, or refine the question.	X	X			X
1.4.b Describes criteria used to make information decisions and choices.		X	X		X
2.1.a Identifies appropriate investigative methods (e.g., laboratory experiment, simulation, fieldwork).	X	X	X	X	X
2.1.b Investigates benefits and applicability of various investigative methods.	X	X	X	X	X
2.1.c Investigates the scope, content, and organization of information retrieval systems.		X	X		X
2.1.d Selects efficient and effective approaches for accessing the information needed from the investigative method or information retrieval system.	X	X	X		X
2.2.a Develops a research plan appropriate to the investigative method.	X	X	X	X	X
2.2.b Identifies keywords, synonyms, and related terms for the information needed	X	X	X	X	X
2.2.c Selects controlled vocabulary specific to the discipline or information retrieval source.	X	X	X	X	X
2.2.d Constructs a search strategy using appropriate commands for the information retrieval system selected (e.g., Boolean operators, truncation, and proximity for search engines; internal organizers such as indexes for books).	X	X	X	X	X
2.2.e Implements the search strategy in various information retrieval systems using different user interfaces and search engines, with different command languages, protocols, and search parameters.	X	X	X	X	

2.2.f Implements the search using investigative protocols appropriate to the discipline.	X	X	X	X	
2.3.a Uses various search systems to retrieve information in a variety of formats.	X	X	X	X	X
2.3.b Uses various classification schemes and other systems (e.g., call number systems or indexes) to locate information resources within the library or to identify specific sites for physical exploration.	X	X	X	X	X
2.4.a Assesses the quantity, quality, and relevance of the search results to determine whether alternative information retrieval systems or investigative methods should be utilized.	X	X			X
2.4.b Identifies gaps in the information retrieved and determines if the search strategy should be revised.	X	X			X
2.4.c Repeats the search using the revised strategy as necessary.	X	X			X
2.5.a Selects among various technologies the most appropriate one for the task of extracting the needed information (e.g., copy/paste software functions, photocopier, scanner, audio/visual equipment, or exploratory instruments).		X			X
2.5.c Differentiates between the types of sources cited and understands the elements and correct syntax of a citation for a wide range of resources.	X	X	X	X	X
2.5.d Records all pertinent citation information for future reference.		X	X	X	X
3.2.a Examines and compares information from various sources in order to evaluate reliability, validity, accuracy, authority, timeliness, and point of view or bias.			X	X	X
3.2.c Recognizes prejudice, deception, or manipulation.					X
3.4.a Determines whether information satisfies the research or other information need.		X		X	X
3.4.g Selects information that provides evidence for the topic.		X			X
3.6.a Participates in classroom and other discussions.		X	X	X	X
3.7.a Determines if original information need has been satisfied or if additional information is needed.		X			X
3.7.b Reviews search strategy and incorporates additional concepts as necessary.		X			X
3.7.c Reviews information retrieval sources used and expands to include others as needed.	X	X			X
5.3.a Selects an appropriate documentation style and uses it consistently to cite sources.		X		X	X

Lesson Plan

This five-part series was offered sequentially so that library knowledge could be built gradually over time and with opportunities for practice. "Best Classroom Resources" began the series and was a demonstration of how to find a wide range of teaching resources in our library with suggestions for how the resources would be used by teachers. "Assignments Already?" introduced key journals for teachers and the methods for accessing journal indexes. "Be a Subject Expert" introduced students to the best print and online resources for classrooms in a particular discipline. "When YOU Teach Research" introduced students to the stages of the research process and to the Ontario document, *Information Studies.*[5] "Out-Google Your Students" provided advanced Web search strategies and knowledge of the structure of information on the Internet. Classes One, Three, Four, and Five were taught in the library Teaching Corner, which accommodates up to forty students at round tables and has a laptop and portable data projector with an Internet connection. Class Two was taught in an e-classroom equipped with seventeen computers and an instructor's station.

Description of the Instruction Session: What Actually Happened?

The content of each lesson was quite different, but there were common features across the five classes. In Class One and Three we brought physical examples of many resources for display and included computer demonstrations of how to access them. Class Two focused on searching for journal articles with a series of hands-on exercises. Class Four and Five used PowerPoint presentations to illustrate key concepts. Comprehensive handouts were distributed at each class.

Engagement

Each session started with a welcome to the world of resources and an appeal to the audience as educators who would work with us in a librarian–teacher partnership. The INSPIRED Teaching Series and specific learning objectives for the session were introduced. We linked these objectives to students' coursework and to their roles as future teachers. The latter connection was highlighted throughout each session to help participants frame their learning as future teachers rather than as students completing the next assignment.

Connections

We asked several questions, probing prior knowledge and helping direct the level of information we imparted. What types of resources do beginning teachers need to learn about? Responses helped to map out the diversity of formats for exploration (books, videos, pictures, Web sites, etc.). This

INSPIRED Teaching Series	
Best Classroom Resources Display of resources / Computer Demo	You will learn how to find: • Fiction, nonfiction, textbooks, teacher guides, and lesson plans • Multimedia: videos, kits, and posters • Ministry of Ed. elementary "Curriculum Units" and secondary "Course Profiles" • Popular teacher-friendly, classroom idea magazines
Assignments Already? Hands-on in e-classroom	You will learn how to: • Access Queen's online resources from home • Access four education journal indexes • Search effectively to find journal articles online or in print
Be a Subject Expert Display of resources / Computer demo	You will learn how to: • Link specific curriculum units to information literacy objectives within the Information Studies guide for Ontario classrooms • Review journal titles that feature teaching strategies & curriculum ideas • Use subject associations to support your teaching with curriculum ideas and professional development Classes on social studies, language arts, math, science, history, geography, English, social sciences and humanities, health and physical education, and arts
When YOU Teach Research PowerPoint / Computer demo	You will learn how to: • Create research questions that require your students to develop thoughtful answers rather than find text they can copy • Find learning objects that other educators have already prepared that will help make your teaching effective • Identify steps in a research process
Out-Google Your Students PowerPoint / Computer demo	You will learn: • Cool Google search tips that your students probably don't know • Lesson ideas for teaching the critical evaluation of Web sites • Search engine facts that will amaze you!

led to exploration of search techniques. Sample searches revealed how to find some of the materials we had brought to the session, making a connection between the item in hand, the citation on the screen, library locations, and organization of collections. The nine library collections were pointed to (reference, K–12, current periodicals, bound journals, multimedia, textbooks, Ministry guidelines, lesson resources, and the regular book collection). Basic library services were reviewed in the first two classes to encourage TCs to take advantage of their borrowing privileges, allowing students to take out up to fifty items on their practice teaching rounds.

Demonstration and Modeling

An interesting array of resources and their connections to the curriculum was illustrated in Class One (Best Classroom Resources) and Three (Be a Subject Expert) in the hope that learners would be inspired to know more about how to find and use them in their own classrooms. The resources were displayed over five tables around which the students gathered in the library's Teaching Corner. We used a central computer and data display to demonstrate online search tools and techniques, using a thematic approach to resource selection in both these classes. In the generic "Best Resources" class where students were first introduced to the library, we highlighted materials from across subjects in a variety of formats. For example, groups of materials from literature, geography, history, science, and math were reviewed and passed around. In the subject-specific classes (Be a Subject Expert), we shared selected materials related to a discipline or subject area (e.g., social studies in the primary/junior level versus geography or history in the intermediate/senior level).

Modeling of key search principles (e.g., keywords, operators, subject headings) accompanied each online search tool as it was introduced: library catalog (Best Classroom Resources; Be a Subject Expert); education-related journal indexes (Assignments Already); Web searching (Out-Google your Students).

Sample keyword searches in catalog
video? and "flanders fields"   video? and "world war" and 1939 and canad?   kit and history and canad?   (poster or "study print?" or picture?) and war   teaching and "civil war"   curriculum and Ontario and history

The class on journal indexes, held in the e-classroom, introduced the different types of journals in the field of education (academic, peer reviewed, those written by teachers to provide best classroom practices by subject). Instructions on a diagram showed how to access indexes from home. Then, students compared our four "core" databases in terms of size, content, and scope and experimented with searches on two topics across two indexes. Students discussed what worked well and what proved difficult, leading to suggestions for improving searches through changes in search technique and the use of more focused search words or subject headings.

We used hands-on exercises to articulate explicitly the investigative steps that were naturally occurring as students tested their queries: concept identification within the research question; brainstorming for synonyms related to key concepts to serve as keywords; construction of search statements; identification of subject headings or descriptors; revision of search strategies using subject searches, limitation within specific journal titles and by full text; using the "Get-It@Queen's" utility to locate a copy of an article either online or in print; and, finally, downloading or e-mailing online articles or locating paper copy. Handouts included space for recording concepts, search terms, search strings, and relevant subject headings.

In the "When YOU Teach Research," class we modeled the research process as it is described in the OSLA *Information Studies* document (stages are described below).[6] Although there are many models to choose from, this is the approach adopted in Ontario schools. Images of the research process were shown in the PowerPoint so that students could see and better understand the stages and their interconnections.

The OSLA Research Model[7]	
Stages	**The Process of Inquiry**
Stage One: Preparing for Research	Students identify an interest, define and explore a topic, and begin to relate their topic to resources and prior knowledge.
Stage Two: Accessing Resources	Students locate, select, and gather information, and collaborate to share their findings.
Stage Three: Processing Information	Students analyze, evaluate, and sort the information they have gathered; test its usefulness for their topic; and synthesize their findings and draw conclusions.
Stage Four: Transferring Learning	Students continue to make revisions, present their work, and reflect on the research product and process, transferring the skills they used to their understanding of problem solving.

After reviewing the stages of the research process, we selected a topic (life in a medieval castle) from a Grade Four curriculum strand and tracked the topic through the research stages.[8] We also demonstrated how teachers would prepare to introduce a research unit by: (1) identifying specific subjects suited to inquiry, (2) identifying appropriate inquiry objectives for a grade level using the *Information Studies* guide produced by the Ontario

School Library Association,[9] (3) ensuring that adequate and appropriate resources are available for the topics their students are likely to pursue, and (4) referring to resources such as Jamie McKenzie's "Great Question Press" and Benjamin Bloom's *Taxonomy of Educational Objectives* to ensure that research questions are connected to student curiosity and suitable for the grade level.[10] Topics in all classes draw on authentic questions that connect to the real school curriculum.

In "Out-Google Your Students," we solicited search practices and tips from the audience and then explored other ways of thinking about Web search strategy. What types of resources are on the Web and what are the starting points for getting to them? Students were encouraged to brainstorm resources and consider whether a search engine is the best method to find them. This revealed a Web of resources that might have other starting points than Google. A comprehensive Web search strategy also was presented that revealed the "invisible Web." Potential starting points were: virtual reference desk, broad Canadian Web sites, government sources, subject directories, and search engines. Googling tips were demonstrated.

To end the session, we asked students to invent evaluation criteria and identify questions and exploration techniques that would reveal the value, bias, and relevance of Web sites. In one class targeting the primary/junior TCs, we divided students into four groups. Each group took on a different specialist role, reviewing for content, authority, bias, and usability. We asked each group to rank a series of Web sites on dinosaurs.[11]

Feedback
All classes, except "Be a Subject Expert," included a student evaluation constructed on the model provided in the teaching resources section.

Reflection on the Instruction Session: Lessons Learned
One of the problems we encountered was the time constraint involved in offering sessions over the lunch hour, the only "open" slot for all students. Classes were rushed but greatly appreciated as evidenced by these comments from individuals:

> The sessions helped with finding books easily on my own. The best part was having a list of resources; Learning various ways to search on the Web was also beneficial; Going through teacher-related Web sites ... was great; The journals for teachers are good; I am completely useless at searching Google, I didn't realize there was more to searching the Internet. I now have a starting point and am learning as I go; I found them [the sessions] very useful to see how many resources are available to teachers; The wealth

of resources that were shared was amazing; An overwhelming amount of information; Need more time to follow along.

Given the comments made by the teacher candidates, we intend to make each class an hour long next year. Student comments also revealed how little they knew about index and Web searching, their lack of mental models for research, and their realization that teachers spend a lot of time looking for inspirational resources.

The best attendance was in the "Be a Subject Expert" classes, probably because these classes provided the closest subject orientation to a field. Also, some curriculum instructors in the various disciplines specifically confirmed the value of these sessions and encouraged students to attend. Many of the comments on the evaluation forms focused on the participants' surprise that they had not known about the resources in the education library when they were undergraduates, a comment that tells us that we need to pay more attention to the education students who do their BEd concurrently with their undergraduate degree. Moreover, it was clear that students preferred separate primary-junior and intermediate-senior sessions. From the librarian point of view, we see that it will be difficult to achieve our goals of ensuring that all teacher candidates learn about the OSLA's *Information Studies*[12] document, simply because we will not meet all the TCs at every workshop class this year. We are now organizing a workshop for faculty on our progress and methods to ensure that they know about the expectation that teachers need to be prepared to work with teacher librarians in Ontario schools to teach information literacy.

Notes

1. Elizabeth Lee, Brenda Reed, and Corinne Laverty, "Information Literacy, Teacher-Candidates and the School Library: Information Literacy in a BEd Program" (unpublished report, TEACH Grant 2004/05 # 014-518-xx-66, Faculty of Education, Queen's University, Kingston, ON, Canada, 2005).

2. Ontario School Library Association, *Information Studies: Kindergarten to Grade 12* (Toronto, ON: Ontario Library Association, 1999). Available online from http://www.accessola.com/action/positions/info_studies/.

3. Association of College and Research Libraries, *Information Literacy Competency Standards for Higher Education* (Chicago: ACRL, 2000). Available online from http://www.ala.org/ala/acrl/acrlstandards/inform ationliteracycompetency.htm.

4. Ibid.

5. Ontario School Library Association, *Information Studies*.

6. Ibid.

7. Ibid.

8. Ontario Ministry of Education, *The Ontario Curriculum: Social Studies Grades 1 to 6, History and Geography Grades 7 and 8*, Rev. ed. (Toronto, ON: Ministry of Education, 2004), 27–28.

9. Ontario School Library Association, *Information Studies*.

10. Jamie McKenzie, "The Great Question Press: Squeezing Import from Content," *From Now On: The Educational Technology Journal* 13, no.6 (2004). Available online from http://www.fno.org/feb04/questionpress.html; Benjamin Samuel Bloom, *Taxonomy of Educational Objectives: The Classification of Educational Goals, Handbook 1: Cognitive Domain* (New York: D. McKay, 1956).

11. Joyce Valenza, "A WebQuest about Evaluating Web Sites." Available online from http://mciu.org/~spjvweb/evalwebstu.html.

12. Ontario School Library Association, *Information Studies*.

Teaching Resources

Examples of Types of History Resources for Be a Subject Expert, Class 3	
Ontario Ministry of Education documents	Each curriculum document outlines what is to be taught by grade and subject (e.g., Canadian and World Studies 11 and 12)
Textbooks and teacher's guide	Approved Ministry of Education textbooks for use in the classroom (e.g., *World History: Patterns of Interaction* [student text and teacher's guide])
Nonfiction	Books for students to read and books that give teaching ideas for teachers (e.g., *World History Map Workbook: Geographical and Critical Thinking Exercises*)
Fiction describing historical events	For example, *The Middle Passage: White Ships, Black Cargo* illustrates the abysmal journey of slaves from west Africa. How to use A to Zoo, NoveList, or the Children's Literature Comprehensive Database to identify subject content in picture books.
Graphic novels	For example, *Maus, Persepolis, Louis Riel: A Comic Strip Biography, Fax from Sarajevo*
Reference materials	For example, *Greenwood Encyclopedia of Daily Life: A Tour Through History From Ancient Times to the Present*, 6 volumes
Transparencies	For example, Canadian history transparencies
Software	Ontario Software Acquisition Program Advisory Committee (http://www.osapac.org/)
Key history journals	For example, *American History, The Beaver, Canadian Social Studies, Canadian Social Trends, The History Teacher, History Today, The Magazine of History*
Poetry	*In Flanders Fields: The Story of the Poem* by John McCrae
Lesson plans	Books with lesson plans dedicated to specific topics
Posters	Copies of posters made during both world wars
Video kits	For example, *Sacrifice, Achievement, Legacy: Canadians & the Second World War, 1939–1945*. Includes 2 videos, teacher's notes, maps, and study prints. *Powerful and Authentic Social Studies* for teachers.
Videos on World War	For example, *Canvas of War* (account of Canadian war artists in WWII); *Canada's War in Colour; Take No Prisoners.*
Primary source materials & artifacts	For example, *American History in a Box*. Includes copies of newspapers and documents from the 18th century. Replica of the *Rosetta Stone.*

Web sites	Key Canadian Web sites for history educators were highlighted: Library and Archives Canada: http://www.collectionscanada.ca/index-e.html CBC Archives: http://archives.cbc.ca Canada's Digital Collections: http://collections.ic.gc.ca/ Canadian War Museum: http://www.warmuseum.ca/ Department of National Defense: http://www.forces.gc.ca/ Canadian Heritage: http://www.pch.gc.ca/ Archives of Ontario: http://www.archives.gov.on.ca/ Ontario History Quest: http://ohq.tpl.toronto.on.ca/ CBC News in Review: http://www.cbc.ca/newsinreview/
Professional associations for teaching resources	Ontario History and Social Science Teachers' Association: http://www.ohassta.org/ National Council for the Social Studies: http://www.ncss.org/ American Historical Association: http://www.historians.org/index.cfm

Sample hands-on exercise used to focus on concept Identification
What are some strategies for working with groups in primary/elementary classrooms, and is group work even a good idea for these grade levels? What ideas can you find about classroom conditions that facilitate learning by autistic teenagers?

Concept 1	Concept 2	Concept 3

Googling Tips

Operators:	AND is assumed and does not need to be typed. Use * within a phrase for characters or words: Pierre * Trudeau Quotations for phrases: "middle ages"-site:com To remove commercial sites. OR in capitals for synonyms: "middle ages" OR medieval ~in front of a word for synonyms: "middle ages" ~weapons

Google Book Search: Search full text of copyright-free books. Google Scholar: Search what Google classifies as "scholarly" works.
inurl:bbc "middle ages" or intitle: bbc "middle ages" Finds sites with both bbc and middle ages in the URL or the title.
link:www.google.ca for pages pointing to that site
related:www.google.com for similar pages
define:for words in the order in which you type them
Use Advanced Image Search for a specific type or color.
Advanced search options by language, file format, domain, date

Search with word that reflects type of material needed:
    "toxic chemicals" database
    fish "acid rain" research
    life "middle ages" research
    Chaucer "Canterbury tales" analysis
    Mozart mp3 download

Technical/Organizational tips • Use the "cached" feature for missing URLs. • Use Edit >> Find on this page. • Compile Web sites on desktop using drag and drop in IE. • Add your own "Google toolbar" to your browser.

Sample Student Evaluation

Assignments Already

1. Record the keyword searches you would use in a journal index to find articles on:
a) teaching activities on geometry for elementary or high school students

b) teaching strategies for an inclusive classroom

2. I learned how to ...

3. I still don't understand how to ...

Please turn to complete the back of the page

I understand how to:					
	yes	no		yes	no
get connected to library indexes from home			limit a search to full-text journal articles		
select commonly-used education indexes			use subject headings and descriptors to improve searches		
type separate concepts in search boxes			use the Get-It link to find an online or print article		
save, e-mail, and print online articles			locate print articles on the shelf in the education library		

Chapter 8

Weaving the Threads of Early Childhood Curricular Approaches into Preservice Practice: A Course-embedded Information Literacy Instruction Model

Signia Warner and Lolly Templeton

Introduction

What is the most effective way to support early childhood teacher candidates in their efforts to become competent lifelong information seekers and users? As librarians with a background in early childhood education and a faculty member teaching an early childhood curriculum course, we have been collaborating for over a decade in an attempt to answer that question. We use active learning techniques to engage teacher candidates in hands-on information literacy sessions embedded in the course content. Esther Grassian and Joan Kaplowitz define active learning as participatory learning activities that occur in a synchronous face-to-face classroom setting.[1] When working with college students, Patrick Sullivan recognizes that "Active learning incorporated into instruction is more effective than one-way communication such as lecture. Having information reinforced through exercises or activities engages students in the learning process."[2] The collaborative nature of our approach with ongoing consultation between librarian and faculty ensures that information literacy objectives are consistent with education course assignments and national standards.

Our first research assignment in the upper-division early childhood curriculum class at Westfield State College requires teacher candidates to analyze early childhood curriculum models and develop a multimedia presentation encapsulating their research results. The next information literacy instruction (ILI) session uses Intel Teach to the Future (ITTF),[3] a professional development software program designed to help in-service and preservice teachers integrate technology into classrooms to enhance student learning. Our third ILI session introduces Kid Pix Deluxe for Schools[4], a multimedia tool that enables candidates to prepare lesson plans, reports, and slide shows for their interdisciplinary unit of instruction. This course-embedded information literacy approach incorporates concepts developed earlier by Lolly Templeton and Signia Warner in a case study describing how collaboration between teacher and librarian can enrich instruction and make it relevant for learning.[5]

Analysis of the Learning Situation

Westfield State College is a liberal arts college with a student body of approximately 5,200 located in Westfield, Massachusetts. The Education Resources Center (ERC) is on the mezzanine floor of the college library. The ERC maintains a collection of more than 14,000 items including children's literature, curriculum guides, textbooks, tests, children's magazines, kits, games, math manipulatives, photographs, videos, DVDs, and children's educational software. Kid Pix is available on two of the nine computer workstations along the mezzanine wall in the ERC. At one end of the ERC, there is a viewing room for previewing videos and DVDs and listening to audiotapes and compact disks. An electronic classroom at the opposite end of the area is intended for information literacy instruction but is used as a computer lab when there are no scheduled ILI sessions. The ILI classroom is equipped with an instructor's workstation, projection equipment, a whiteboard, and two laser printers. Twenty workstations arranged around the perimeter of the room are loaded with Microsoft Office XP, Intel Teach to the Future, and provide access to more than 150 library databases. In the center of the room are modular tables and chairs that can be rearranged to accommodate diverse learning activities.

Specifically designed to meet the information needs of educators, the ERC is set up according to recommendations discussed in Jo Ann Carr's *A Guide to the Management of Curriculum Materials for the 21st Century: The Promise and the Challenge.*[6] The ERC is staffed throughout the day and evening library hours by one professional librarian and six trained student support staff.

Approximately 889 full-time day students are enrolled in initial teacher licensure programs at Westfield State College. Information instruction librarians introduce first-year students to online catalog and database searching during a formal ILI session as part of a required freshman English composition class. Candidates enrolled in teacher education programs begin using ERC resources for assignments in professional education coursework during their sophomore year. When they enroll in the early childhood curriculum class, many teacher education candidates are already familiar with some of the resources available in the ERC. At this point in their program, teacher candidates are "ideally positioned to take information literacy skills to the next levels," as Warren F. Crouse and Kristine Esch Kasbohm point out:

When they become teachers, these candidates can use their own information literacy knowledge to address, plan, and carry out academic research programs in their classrooms that will enable future students to achieve information literacy. If teacher education candidates are trained and educated to believe in collaboration between teachers and librarians, they will promote the benefits of universal information literacy, thereby enabling information literacy to become a self-sustaining generative process.[7]

We faced several technological challenges in the implementation of our collaborative model. Scheduling ILI sessions is sometimes difficult because there is only one electronic instruction classroom for the entire library. Accessibility to Kid Pix is restricted to two workstations in the ERC causing some frustration on the part of candidates. Technology exposure and information literacy expertise varies, particularly among transfer students. Availability of technology resources and practitioner expertise fluctuates in field experience settings sometimes limiting opportunities for some candidates to implement their lesson plan.

Information Literacy Standards

(Note: A complete list of *ACRL Information Literacy Competency Standards for Higher Education* ([Chicago: ACRL, 2000] appears as appendix A.)

In designing our ILI sessions, we strive to meet the Association of College and Research Library (ACRL) Competency Standards within the context of several other national and local standards, including the National Council for the Accreditation of Teacher Education (NCATE), the National Education Technology Standards (NETS), the National Association of the Education of Young Children (NAEYC) initial licensure program standards, and Massachusetts Recommended PreK–12 Instructional Technology Standards.

The ACRL standards for college libraries specify the need to collaborate frequently with classroom faculty to integrate information literacy into appropriate coursework.[8] As we worked to integrate information literacy into early childhood coursework over the past decade, our ILI model has become increasingly embedded in the structure of the course. As stated in *Preparing Early Childhood Professionals: NAEYC's Standards for Programs:* "The complexity of the process requires candidates, as well as experienced teachers, to go beyond their own basic knowledge to identify and use high-quality resources, including books, standards documents, Internet resources, and individuals who have specialized content expertise, in developing early childhood curriculum."[9] Both sets of standards pose a challenge to continuously identify and use up-to-date high-quality resources.

Although all higher education information literacy competencies are addressed at some point during the three information literacy sessions in the ERC, the main emphasis for our research is on ACRL's Third and Fourth competency standards.[10]

What tomorrow's teachers should *know* and be able to *do*, is the current focus of the national accrediting agencies for teacher education. In the charts below, we outline the knowledge, skills, and understandings that candidates acquire based on ACRL outcomes. We also present the learning activities that serve as lines of evidence for assessing outcomes. The performance outcomes we listed provided focus for our instructional design.

Standard Three. "The information literate student evaluates information and its sources critically and incorporates selected information into his or her knowledge base and value system."[11]

Number	Outcomes	Knowledge, Skills, and Understandings	Candidate Performance
3.2.b.	*Analyzes the structure and logic of supporting arguments or methods*	Candidates understand the logic of teaching and learning models they are researching even when they hold other philosophies of teaching.	Class discussion; multimedia research presentation
3.2.c.	*Recognizes prejudice, deception, or manipulation*	Candidates learn to evaluate information from Web sites and recognize bias and prejudice.	Evaluation of resources
3.3.a.	*Recognizes interrelationships among concepts and combines them into potentially useful primary statements with supporting evidence*	Candidates are able to explain the relationship between the teacher role and the educational philosophy.	Multimedia research presentation
3.3.b.	*Extends initial synthesis, when possible, at a higher level of abstraction to construct new hypotheses that may require additional information*	Candidates are constantly accommodating new ideas into existing schema.	Response journals; class discussion

3.3.c.	*Utilizes computer and other technologies for studying the interaction of ideas and other phenomena*	Candidates demonstrate skill using and combining computer technology with other media.	Multimedia research presentations
3.4.b.	*Uses consciously selected criteria to determine whether the information contradicts or verifies information used from other sources*	Candidates comment when information contradicts or verifies information from other sources.	Oral class discussion; reading response
3.4.d.	*Tests theories with discipline-appropriate techniques*	Although there is no opportunity to test early childhood curriculum models in an experimental setting, candidates report on efficacy of research.	Multimedia research presentations
3.5.a.	*Investigates differing viewpoints encountered in the literature*	Candidates recognize when scholars express different points of view.	Discussion with research partner; Reading response
3.6.a.	*Participates in classroom and other discussions*	Candidates are expected to fully participate in classroom discussion and work with partners.	Response journals; self-reflection form
3.6.b.	*Participates in class-sponsored electronic communication forums designed to encourage discourse on the topic (e.g., e-mail, bulletin boards, chat rooms)*	Candidates continue to discuss topics with research partners both virtually and in person throughout the process.	Response journals; personal comments; self-reflection form
3.6.c.	*Seeks expert opinion through a variety of mechanisms (e.g., interviews, e-mail, listservs)*	Candidates interview professionals and use e-mail to communicate.	Personal interviews; response journals
3.7.a.	*Determines if original information need has been satisfied or if additional information is needed*	Candidates refer to assignment guidelines and decide if more information is needed.	Class discussion; multimedia assignment criteria
3.7.b.	*Reviews search strategy and incorporates additional concepts as necessary*	Candidates experiment with different types of searches and modify their search strategies.	Response journals; observation

3.7.c.	*Reviews information retrieval sources used and expands to include others as needed*	Candidates review the accuracy, authority, and currency of their information. They cite sources using APA citation style.	Evaluation of resources; bibliography

Standard Four. "The information literate student, individually or as a member of a group, uses information effectively to accomplish a specific purpose."[12]

Number	Outcomes	Knowledge, Skills, and Understandings	Candidate Performance
4.1.c.	*Integrates the new and prior information, including quotations and paraphrasings, in a manner that supports the purposes of the product or performance*	Candidates integrate new information with prior knowledge and make comparisons among different early childhood education models.	Response journals; multimedia research presentation
4.1.d.	*Manipulates digital text, images, and data, as needed, transferring them from their original locations and formats to a new context*	Candidates manipulate digital text, images, and data and transfer them to a slide show presentation.	Multimedia research presentation; navigation of electronic sources
4.2.b.	*Reflects on past successes, failures, and alternative strategies*	Candidates write honest self-reflection comments with areas of difficulty and new insights.	Self-reflection form; response journals
4.3.a.	*Chooses a communication medium and format that best supports the purposes of the product or performance and the intended audience*	Candidates select specific communication formats and media to support their research that is appropriate for class presentations.	Multimedia research presentation; bibliography
4.3.b.	*Uses a range of information technology applications in creating the product or performance*	Candidates use primary and secondary source material and different types of media.	Bibliography; response journals; self-reflection form
4.3.c.	*Incorporates principles of design and communication*	Candidates show evidence of awareness of principles of design and communication skills.	Multimedia research presentation

4.3.d.	*Communicates clearly and with a style that supports the purposes of the intended audience*	Candidates are able to communicate findings of their research clearly and maintain audience interest.	Multimedia research presentation; oral presentation rubric

Lesson Plan

Our challenge was to create a standards-based lesson plan with an emphasis on learning outcomes. We selected the Grant Wiggins and Jan McTighe backward design lesson plan model.[13] Wiggins and McTighe define backward design as a process of planning curriculum that begins with desired outcomes as a way to operationalize the standards in terms of assessment evidence. Using this method, the ACRL outcome measures become targeted goals. We base our instructional plan on outcomes for the Third and Fourth higher education information literacy standards. The lesson plan focuses on essential questions, overarching ideas, and concrete evidence of candidate knowledge, skills, and understandings within the context of this early childhood research assignment. We incorporate the higher education competency standards and state and national early childhood licensure standards in the three-stage backward design model that involves: (1) identifying desired results, (2) determining acceptable evidence, and (3) planning learning activities. During collaborative ILI sessions with both librarian and professor present, teacher candidates locate and choose appropriate resources for their multimedia presentations. As a result of this ILI session, candidates begin to differentiate among the models and weave ideas from particular early childhood curricular approaches into their preK–2 pre-practicum field experience.

We use authentic assessment methods that take into account the context of the performance task. We collect evidence of learning based on research outcomes and our observation of candidates' increasingly sophisticated search strategies, multimedia research presentations, class discussion, reading responses, journals, self-reflection comments, and bibliographies of resources. At the conclusion of the project, we both attend candidates' multimedia research presentations in the education department classroom. We assess the content of the early childhood curriculum model presentations and examine data gathered, including a presentation rubric, self-reflection, and journal entries. Further evidence of how candidates incorporate content from the Intel Teach to the Future program and materials from the ERC is apparent in their interdisciplinary units. Candidate lesson plans created with Kid Pix reveal a spectrum of innovative and highly structured ways to use computer technology with young children. Together, we examine and evaluate the candidates' course documents, share field notes, and use assessment data to inform, revise, and improve our collaborative ILI model.

Description of the Instruction Session: What Actually Happened?
ILI Session I

Prior to the first ILI session in the ERC, we discuss course expectations in the education department classroom. We schedule the first class visit to the ERC after the teacher candidates select a curriculum model to investigate with a research partner. Early childhood curriculum models studied included Reggio Emilia, High/Scope, Project Spectrum, Waldorf, Montessori, and Brain-based Learning.

During the initial library visit, teacher candidates are seated around tables in the middle of the ILI classroom. The session begins with introductions. Teacher candidates share background knowledge, experience, and the preconceptions they have about some of the early childhood curriculum models they will research.

We review basic search strategies for locating books and articles available in print and electronically. Descriptors that are apt to yield desired results are suggested along with specific databases and ways to evaluate Internet sites. We discuss the ITTF and demonstrate some of the features of the computer software. The ITTF automatic citation feature for citing sources using different citation formats is explored. Of particular interest to teacher candidates is the automatic citation format designed to be used with young children. Teacher candidates are given opportunities to voice opinions and ask questions about technical and academic aspects of the research assignment.

We recommend two library databases, ERIC and ProQuest's Education Journals, and demonstrate appropriate search techniques. We explore different types of searches using both the online catalog and library databases and explain the difference between subject searches and keyword searches. We demonstrate how to limit searches by time frame and type of publication. A portion of the ILI session is reserved for active hands-on investigation of primary and secondary source material. For homework, the teacher candidates are referred to the Intel Teach to the Future program to review the composition, construction, and organization of multimedia presentations.

During the next two weeks, candidates return to the ERC individually and in pairs to gather multimedia resources and prepare reports on research findings. Teacher candidates present their final research results in an education department classroom equipped with a multimedia podium.

In their curricular model presentations, candidates incorporate visual displays, videotapes, PowerPoint slides, and samples of learning materials from the ERC. They present and critique the educational learning theory and philosophy of the curriculum model they researched and explain how it is implemented in early childhood classrooms. After each presentation, all participants ask questions and raise issues of concern. In their journals, candidates reflect on each presentation and compile a list of common themes.

ILI Session II

During the second ILI session in the electronic classroom, teacher candidates continue working with Intel Teach to the Future. The ITTF program supports student-centered, inquiry-based learning and promotes effective use of technology in the classroom. It contains Internet links for locating resources, framing essential questions, and planning units of instruction. There also are direct Internet links to useful Web sites with curriculum and assessment tools as well as state and national standards, including the National Education Technology Standards (NETS) sponsored by the International Society for Technology in Education (ISTE). Teacher candidates investigate sample units, lesson plans, and learning activities using the ITTF preservice manual and companion CD-ROM for learning about copyright law and fair use policy. They test their knowledge of copyright law with an online copyright quiz.

Prior to the second ILI session, teacher candidates select interdisciplinary unit themes in consultation with their field experience practitioner. Teacher candidates begin researching integrated unit topics for implementation in their pre-practicum sites. We introduce candidates to the unit template available on the ITTF computer software. Approximately half the second session is devoted to active hands-on research of unit topics.

ILI Session III

The third ILI session is designed to involve early childhood teacher candidates in the evaluation of children's computer software. We discuss and demonstrate three different types of computer software: (1) drill and practice software, (2) children's literature software, and (3) simulation and tool software. We note characteristics of each type of software and during the demonstration, candidates complete a software evaluation form for a children's software program of their choice. Although a software evaluation template is on the ITTF compact disk, we use the Software Evaluation Form 2000 developed by Kathleen Schrock[14] because of ease of use and time constraints.

Each teacher candidate creates a lesson plan to include in his or her interdisciplinary unit portfolios using Kid Pix. It is one of the software programs selected for this ILI session because it is an open-ended program that encourages creativity. Most school sites where teacher candidates are placed for their pre-practicum field experience have access to Kid Pix, enabling them to try out their unit lesson plan with young children. Their lesson plans are structured to motivate students to apply content knowledge using creative activities to develop slide shows, label maps, and publish class books and individual stories. Some of their lesson plans incorporate audio into children's pictures and stories using the text-to-speech Kid Pix tool. At the conclusion of the project, candidates share their lesson plans and display samples of student work created with Kid Pix.

Reflecting on Instruction Session: Lessons Learned

Over the past decade, we have learned some important lessons as we devise effective ways to support early childhood teacher candidates in their efforts to become competent lifelong information seekers and users. At the end of the semester, we examine and reflect on student work, discuss the multimedia presentations, complete a rubric, and review teacher candidates' progress in meeting the Third and Fourth ACRL competency standards.

We are impressed with the apparent ease with which teacher candidates are able to integrate different forms of media into their presentations. Although we continue to struggle with the problem of equitable distribution of responsibility within research partnerships, providing in-class time for some of the research alleviates some of the inequity. We also learned to use candidate assessment in a formative manner to improve and restructure information literacy sessions.

Faculty and librarians interested in developing a collaborative, course-embedded ILI program may benefit from our experience over the past ten years. Some key understandings extracted from our reflections include:

- Value the candidate's point of view.
- Provide ways for candidates to construct their own knowledge.
- Connect ACRL standards with other national and state teacher licensure standards.
- Allow time for close collaboration between librarian and faculty member.
- Take time early in the semester to build classroom community.
- Embed ILI into the structure of the course by integrating ILI content and assignments.
- Use the backward design lesson plan to focus on desired outcomes based on ACRL and teacher licensure standards.

• Provide opportunities for candidates to put IL theory into practice during pre-practicum field experiences.
• Create meaningful active learning experiences.
• Use authentic methods to evaluate candidates within the context of performance tasks.
• Schedule time for ongoing consultation between librarian and faculty.
• Provide flexible time lines for course assignments.
• Structure in-class time for candidates to work on group research projects.
• Offer access to and help with a variety of multimedia.
• Provide a full range of services and resources in the ERC.
• Build interconnections between all types of digital and print resources.
• Maintain high standards for in-depth research in early childhood education coursework.

We have found that information literacy instruction must be explicitly embedded into the early childhood course content and not seen as an add-on to the standards-based preservice curriculum. Potential collaborators need to be explicit, deliberate, and public about integrating ILI into a teacher education program. Course-embedded information literacy assignments offer teacher candidates a variety of ways of incorporating information literacy into their own research and practice. The opportunity to assess instruction collaboratively and to use assessment results to modify our own teaching contributes to ongoing improvements in course instruction.

Notes

1. Esther S. Grassian and Joan R. Kaplowitz , *Information Literacy Instruction: Theory and Practice* (New York: Neal-Schuman Publishers, 2001), 116.

2. Patrick Sullivan, "Developing Freshman-level Tutorials to Promote Information Literacy," in *Integrating Information Literacy into the Higher Education Curriculum,* ed. Ilene F. Rockman and Associates (San Francisco: Jossey-Bass, 2004), 74.

3. Debbie Candau, Jennifer Doherty, Robert Hannafin, John Judge, Judi Yost, and Paige Kuni, Intel Teach to the Future (Sunnyvale, CA: The Intel Corporation, 2003). Available online from http://www.intel.com/education/teach/preservice.htm.

4. Kid Pix Deluxe 4 for Schools (Cedar Rapids, IA: Riverdeep Interactive Learning Limited, 2000–2004).

5. Lolly Templeton and Signia Warner, "Incorporating Information Literacy into Teacher Education," *Academic Exchange Quarterly* 6 (winter

2002): 71–76.

6. Jo Ann Carr, *A Guide to the Management of Curriculum Material Centers for the 21st Century: The Promise and the Challenge* (Chicago: ALA, 2000).

7. Warren F. Crouse and Kristine Esch Kasbohm, "Information Literacy in Teacher Education: A Collaborative Model," *Educational Forum* 69 (fall 2004): 45.

8. Association of College and Research Libraries, *Information Literacy Competency Standards for Higher Education* (Chicago: ACRL, 2000). Available online from http://www.ala.org/ala/acrl/acrlstandards/information literacycompetency.htm.

9. Marilou Hyson, ed. *Preparing Early Childhood Professionals for Programs: NAEYC's Standards for Programs.* (Washington DC: National Association for the Education of Young Children, 2003), 44.

10. ACRL, *Information Literacy Competency Standards.*

11. Ibid.

12. Ibid.

13. Grant Wiggins and Jay McTighe, *Understanding by Design, Expanded 2nd Edition* (Alexandria, VA: Association for Supervision and Curriculum Development, 2005).

14. Kathleen Schrock, "Software Evaluation Form." Available online from http://kathyschrock.net/1computer/page4.htm.

Chapter 9

Modeling an Inquiry-based Research Project to Preservice Teachers

Jane A. Smith

Introduction

Teaching Reading through Children's Literature (Reading 302), is a junior-level course required of all preservice teachers with a concentration in early childhood/early elementary education at Texas A&M University. The course is designed to prepare students to teach critical reading and language arts skills through the use of children's literature. One of the methods used to achieve this objective requires the students to validate the cultural authenticity of a picture storybook adaptation of a children's folktale to determine if the author and the illustrator accurately portray the culture depicted in the work.

The project allows the students to direct much of their own learning. The students select the folktale to authenticate, as well as the aspects of the story they want to verify. They design their own research project within the parameters set forth by the instructor and, as a consequence, often discover that research can be an enjoyable activity. In addition to the development of critical thinking skills, the project highlights the need for cultural authenticity in storybook adaptations of folktales. Accurate portrayals of a culture's customs, values, and beliefs can promote understanding and appreciation for diversity;[1] inaccurate depictions can misinform and mislead.[2] The students are reminded that our perceptions are shaped by what we read and see, and are encouraged to carry this awareness into their classrooms when selecting reading material for their own students.

In late fall 2003, one of the instructors for the Reading 302 course, Dr. Patricia Wiese, clinical assistant professor, approached the education reference librarian, Jane Smith, with the following proposal: over several class sessions, the instructor and the librarian would model the authentication process for her students to increase their understanding of the research and documentation required for the complex assignment. To date, Patricia and Jane have modeled the authentication project for five

Reading 302 classes over the course of three semesters. Although the total number of instructional sessions per class was altered each semester to accommodate fluctuating course schedules, the content of the sessions has essentially remained the same.

Analysis of the Learning Situation

The authentication project consists of three major components: selection of the adapted picture storybook folktale, authentication of its text and illustrations, and retelling of the folktale to the class. Students work in groups of three or four and submit the results of their research in writing to the instructor. The groups also share their results and their authentication "journey" with the class after they retell their folktale.

The project is challenging and time-consuming. It requires sustained effort and the willingness to seek scholarly resources, sift through conflicting information, evaluate one's findings, and deliberate the results. In fall 2003, Patricia assigned the authentication project to her Reading 302 students and found that although she gave oral instructions and a detailed rubric outlining the various components, the completed projects were superficial and not well documented. By modeling the assignment, she hoped to illustrate the thought process needed for in-depth research. In addition, she thought it important that the students recognize that we, instructor and librarian, also completed the project—that we did what we were asking them to do.

Patricia selected the children's folktale that would serve as our model example and divided the project between us; she would authenticate the text, I would authenticate the illustrations and together we would retell the folktale. We began our research into the cultural authenticity of our folktale in late fall 2003 in order to be ready for the spring 2004 classes. We met several times over the next two months to discuss our findings, coordinate the class presentations, compose our storytelling script, and practice our storytelling. We decided that we would model the assignment over three class sessions; in late February we would introduce the project, in late March we would share the findings of our own authentication, and in early April we would retell our folktale. The project was due at the end of April.

The first session was the only one held in an instructional classroom in the library. All subsequent sessions were held in the course classroom in the education building. Both rooms contain several long rows of tables with seating for thirty-five to forty students and are equipped with a podium containing a computer connected to a projection device and a screen. The course classroom also contains an overhead projector. Because the setup in both rooms was so similar, it was easier for the librarian to travel to the classroom than for the students to relocate to the library.

Information Literacy Standards

(Note: A complete list of ACRL *Information Literacy Competency Standards for Higher Education* [Chicago: ACRL, 2000] appears as appendix A.)

The following Information Literacy Competency Standards for Higher Education[3] were addressed, with Performance Indicators and Outcomes noted:

Standard One: "The information literate student determines the nature and extent of the information needed"; 1.1.a.

Standard Two: "The information literate student accesses needed information effectively and efficiently"; 2.2.b, 2.2.c, 2.3.b, 2.3.c, and 2.5.b.

Standard Three: "The information literate student evaluates information and its sources critically and incorporates selected information into his or her knowledge base and value system"; 3.1.a, 3.1.b, 3.2.a, 3.4.c, and 3.6.a.

Standard Four: "The information literate student, individually or as a member of a group, uses information effectively to accomplish a specific purpose"; 4.1.a, and 4.3.d.

Standard Five: "The information literate student understands many of the economic, legal, and social issues surrounding the use of information and accesses and uses information ethically and legally"; 5.3.a.

Lesson Plan

Our lesson plan contained the following elements, though the sequence in which we presented these components differed from one semester to the next because of course schedules.

Lesson Goal

The students will gain a thorough understanding of the scope of the authentication project, as well as the steps involved in the authentication process.

Introduction of Project

Instructor: Discuss the need for and importance of culturally authentic children's folktales as the rationale behind the research project. Provide students with an overview of the project, listing its major components. Inform students that we will model the steps involved in the completion of the assignment.

Selection of Folktale
Instructor: Display the adaptation that we selected as our model example and explain the reasons for its selection. Define source notes and emphasize the importance of adequate source notes. Read the source notes in the model example.

Location of Earlier Version of Folktale
Instructor and Librarian: Explain how to use the source notes to locate an earlier version of the folktale. Discuss the use of the library catalog, WorldCat, and interlibrary loan.

Authentication of Text
Instructor: Compare the major events in the earlier version of the folktale to the adaptation. Note differences and similarities. Provide a detailed comparison of the literary elements in both stories. Explain determination of cultural authenticity of the text in the model example.

Authentication of Illustrations
Librarian: Display several illustrations from the model example. Describe the selection of items to authenticate and the process involved. Explain determination of cultural authenticity of the illustrations in the model example.

Demonstrate Library Catalog Search for Folktales
Librarian: Perform several Boolean searches. Discuss location of folktales within the library.

Retell Folktale
Instructor and Librarian

Description of the Instructional Session: What Actually Happened?
The first semester, the class met three times a week for fifty minutes; the second semester, twice a week for an hour and fifteen minutes, and the third semester, once a week for three hours.

Semester One: Spring 2004
Session One. Patricia began the session with an overview and description of the authentication project. After introducing me, she explained that the two of us authenticated the picture book, *The Golden Sandal: A Middle Eastern Cinderella Story*,[4] Rebecca Hickox's version of the Iraqi folktale, *The Little Red Fish and the Clog of Gold*[5]. We would use our experience to model the authentication process for the students. She displayed the

picture book and briefly summarized the tale. She noted our reasons for selecting this picture book: the familiar story, the detailed illustrations, and the comprehensive source notes. She emphasized the importance of adequate source notes in the search for the earlier version of the folktale. She read aloud the source notes in *The Golden Sandal*, noting that the author cites the version on which her adaptation is based. Patricia located a copy of the cited version, *The Little Red Fish and the Clog of Gold*, in *Arab Folktales*[6] in our library. She noted that the students were to find the earliest English version of their chosen tale; if the version on which their tale was based was itself an adaptation of a prior version, they then had to locate that prior version. Satisfied that *The Little Red Fish and the Clog of Gold* was the earliest English version of the tale, she was ready for the next step: authentication of the text.

I told them to begin their search for the earlier version in our library catalog, and if unsuccessful, to search for it in WorldCat. Using the computer/projection device, I showed them how to access WorldCat from our library home page and how to request an item through interlibrary loan. We cautioned them to start the project as soon as possible, as a copy of the earlier version might take some time to obtain.

The instructor explained that authentication of the text in *The Golden Sandal* involved a general comparison of its events to the events in *The Little Red Fish and the Clog of Gold*, as well as a specific comparison of the literary elements (plot, theme, setting, characterization, point of view, style) of each.

I explained that authentication of the illustrations in *The Golden Sandal* began with an examination of each illustration in order to select items or aspects that could be verified as true to the Iraqi or Islamic culture. For example, I recorded detailed descriptions of the clothing worn by each of the characters, as well as descriptions of the furniture, crockery, and buildings. I arranged these notes into broad subject categories and used the subject categories as keywords to search our library's catalog for scholarly resources. I showed the students how subject headings in bibliographic records could provide additional search terms that would lead to further resources. For example, a keyword search using the search terms "Iraq" and "buildings" retrieved records that yielded the terms "architecture," "Middle East," "Islamic," and "Arab" as well as the LC subject heading "Architecture, Islamic," all of which were used to run new searches. A keyword search for "Iraq" and "clothing" produced records containing the LC subject heading "clothing and dress," and when combined with other keywords, subsequently led to records with the LC subject headings "social life and customs," "food habits," and "women." New searches were run using these subject headings. I also showed the students how to use the alphabetical list of LC subject headings to find resources; searching for "Iraq" in the LC list brought up all possible subject headings beginning with the word *Iraq* and provided links to resources not found in a Boolean search.

I explained that I retrieved a total of forty-three resources but, after locating and scanning each one, I selected only nine. I also obtained a copy of the book, *The World of Islam: Faith, People, Culture*[7] which was identified in the source notes of *The Golden Sandal* as the reference work consulted by the illustrator. I examined each resource thoroughly, recording any information about the aspects I had chosen to authenticate. I organized these notes using the same broad subject headings as those used with the illustrations. The instructor encouraged the students to record the citation information for each resource on separate index cards to use when compiling their bibliography.

I also showed the students how to locate folktales in our library using the online catalog. I distributed a handout replicating this search. I also distributed a list of the steps in the authentication of the illustrations and a list of virtual museums with online exhibits.

Session Two. In this session, we shared our research results and our evaluation of the cultural authenticity of the picture storybook. Patricia compared the events and the literary elements in *The Golden Sandal* to those in *The Little Red Fish and the Clog of Gold*, noting the similarities and highlighting the differences. She noted that although some changes seemed inexplicable (for example, the royal family in the original version became a merchant's family in the adaptation), most of the changes made by the author of the adaptation were either consistent with the culture or appropriate for the book's intended audience. She concluded that the text did meet the project's standard of cultural authenticity.

I displayed the two sets of notes from the first session to show the students how to compare them in order to evaluate the authenticity of the illustrations. For example, I displayed the illustration in *The Golden Sandal* depicting the stepsister holding on to an iron bed frame as she dressed for the henna celebration; however, my research found that Iraqi families slept on mattresses spread out on the floor, not on mattresses supported by an iron frame. Another illustration depicted a dining table set for a meal; my research found that Muslim families ate from large trays while seated on the floor. I included several other examples from my research, causing one student to ask if the students would need to go into such detail. We explained that they would choose which aspects they wanted to verify and that much depended on the folktale selected, the quality of its illustrations and the sources consulted. I ended by concluding that the illustrations in the picture storybook adaptation did not meet the project's standard of cultural authenticity.

Session Three. In this session, we retold the folktale to the class. We wrote a script that combined elements from *The Golden Sandal* with elements from *The Little Red Fish and the Clog of Gold*. We memorized our lines, assembled some props and accessories, and practiced several times before we presented it to the class. We managed to deliver it with most lines intact, and it was well received. Some students were dismayed to learn that they would not be allowed to read the story aloud but would need to present it from memory. To reassure them, we admitted to being nervous, but also spoke about the fun we had during our rehearsals, correcting our mistakes and concocting backup plans if we misspoke during our presentation.

Semester Two: Fall 2004
Session One. Patricia decided to model the authentication project over two class sessions, rather than three, as we now had an additional twenty-five minutes per class. The first instructional session mirrored the first session of the previous semester in that we described the project, its components and requirements, and showed the students how to locate folktales within our library. I distributed two of the three handouts, having forgotten to make copies of the handout that listed the online museum resources. The instructor passed it out at a later date.

Session Two. We began the class with the storytelling presentation of our selected folktale and then moved into the modeling of the project. This time, however, we had decided to record our notes and the results of our research in chart form and display them on the overhead projector as we discussed our findings. We anticipated that the addition of visual aids would enhance their understanding of the project.

Semester Three: Spring 2005
This class met once a week for a three-hour period, so the instructor decided to present all the information about the project in one session. We began the class with the storytelling presentation and then described the project, the process, and the results of our own authentication. We made color transparencies of each illustration in the storybook, after obtaining permission from the publisher, and I used these as I talked about the selection of items to authenticate, as well as my findings.

Reflection on the Instruction Session: Lessons Learned
Despite the large collection of children's folktales in our library and the instructional handout provided in the sessions, there were students in each of the classes who opted to purchase their storybooks at the local

bookstore. And though the instructor emphasized the multicultural nature of the assignment, some students selected familiar folktales from their own cultural tradition to authenticate, rather than selecting one from another culture. Because the students were allowed some autonomy in creating this research project to make it more enjoyable, Patricia did not want to restrict their choices. If the students requested our help in evaluating their choices, we confined our critique to the quality of the illustrations and the fullness of the source notes.

The comprehensiveness of the author's source notes was the principal factor in determining the suitability of a particular folktale to authenticate. The folktales with source notes that identified the original version on which the adaptation was based or provided enough information for the student researcher to do so were the best choices for the project. Examples include Steptoe's *Mufaro's Beautiful Daughters: An African Tale*, Jaffe's *The Way Meat Loves Salt: A Cinderella Tale from the Jewish Tradition*, Bruchac's *The First Strawberries: A Cherokee Story*, Zelinsky's *Rapunzel*, Ross's *How Turtle's Back Was Cracked: A Traditional Cherokee Tale*, Martin's *Rough-Faced Girl*, and any of the Native American tales adapted by Paul Goble.[8]

Patricia concluded that the students in the three-hour class submitted "better projects" because, she believed, they "could see the whole project at one time." But I wonder if it also could be attributed to the fact that their instructional session occurred at the time the students were due to start their projects; that is, it was instruction at the point-of-need. In the classes that met for a shorter period of time, we had to begin earlier in the semester to fit in the modeling of the whole project. The students didn't actually begin their research until later in the semester; by that time, they might have forgotten some of our expectations and instructions. But they did have an advantage over the students in the three-hour class in that they had more time to search for the original version of their folktale, if they chose to start their project when it was first presented.

The charts and color transparencies we added in the second and third semesters proved more effective than verbal explanations alone. Rather than reading aloud from the paper that I had written concerning the authentication of the illustrations, as I did that first semester, I used the color transparencies to point out the details I selected to authenticate and the chart to report my findings. My paper (three pages, single-spaced, ever the librarian!) did not have the desired effect; it aroused rather than dispelled the students' anxiety about the project. The charts and transparencies allowed me to impart the same amount of information in a more concise and visual manner without the added stress.

To model the authentication project, I had to complete the assignment in the same manner as the students. In so doing, I gained a clearer understanding of the difficulties they might encounter in their own research and a greater knowledge of our library's holdings. When students asked for my assistance, I was able to provide more extensive research support and direction than with assignments in which I had no prior knowledge or experience.

Notes

1. R.S. Bishop, "Selecting Literature for a Multicultural Curriculum," in *Using Multiethnic Literature in the K–8 Classroom*, ed. V. Harris (Norwood, MA: Christopher-Gordon Publishers, Inc., 1997), 1–19; Donna E. Norton, *Multicultural Children's Literature: Through the Eyes of Many Children* (Upper Saddle River, NJ: Merrill Prentice-Hall, 2001).

2. Elizabeth Noll, "Accuracy and Authenticity in American Indian's Children's Literature: The Social Responsibility of Authors and Illustrators," in *Stories Matter: The Complexity of Cultural Authenticity in Children's Literature*, eds. Dana L. Fox and Kathy G. Short (Urbana, IL: National Council of Teachers of English, 2003), 182–97.

3. Association of College and Research Libraries, *Information Literacy Competency Standards for Higher Education* (Chicago: ACRL, 2000). Available online from http://www.ala.org/ala/acrl/acrlstandards/inform ationliteracycompetency.htm.

4. Rebecca Hickox, *The Golden Sandal: A Middle Eastern Cinderella Story* (New York: Holiday House, 1998).

5. "The Little Red Fish and the Clog of Gold" in *Arab Folktales*, ed. Inea Bushnaq (New York: Pantheon Books, 1986), 181–87.

6. Inea Bushnaq, ed. *Arab Folktales* (New York: Pantheon Books, 1986).

7. B. Lewis, ed. *The World of Islam: Faith, People, Culture* (London: Thames and London, 1976).

8. John Steptoe, *Mufaro's Beautiful Daughters: An African Tale* (New York: Lothrop, Lee & Shepard, 1987); Nina Jaffe, *The Way Meat Loves Salt: A Cinderella Tale from the Jewish Tradition* (New York: Holt, 1998); Joseph Bruchac, *The First Strawberries: A Cherokee Story* (New York: Dial Books for Young Readers, 1993); Paul Zelinsky, *Rapunzel* (New York: Dutton Children's Books, 1997); Gayle Ross, *How Turtle's Back Was Cracked: A Traditional Cherokee Tale* (New York: Dial Books for Young Readers, 1995); Rafe Martin, *Rough-Face Girl* (New York: G.P. Putnam's Sons, 1992).

Teaching Resources

STEPS IN AUTHENTICATION PROCESS FOR ILLUSTRATIONS

1. Examine each illustration in folktale and write down any items that could be authenticated.
2. Arrange items into broad subject headings.
3. Use subject headings to search library catalog.
4. Use subject headings in records found in library catalog to lead to other resources.
5. List possible resources.
6. Use list to locate resources in library.
7. Scan resource to determine usefulness. Discard unsuitable resources.
8. Examine each resource more thoroughly. Note relevant information about any items in list. Make copies of any illustrations from resources that depict items.
9. Organize notes using same broad subject headings as illustrations from folktale.
10. Use side-by-side comparison of notes from folktale and notes from resources to authenticate.
11. Write up findings.

Illustrations Chart		
Detail	Picture Storybook	Findings
Clothing		
Male	Maha's father/Maha's groom Loose-fitting shirt tucked into loose-fitting pants, sleeveless vests Male perfumer Ankle-length jumper dress over long-sleeved shirt	Male Knee-length tunics with long, tight sleeves over formfitting trousers (Lewis, shown on pp. 48, 112, 1976) Long tunic with loose-fitting trousers (Lewis, shown on p. 318, 1976) Hip-length tunic with formfitting trousers (Lewis, shown on p. 221, 1976) Clothing used to identify place in social order (Stillman, 2000), so unlikely poor fisherman and merchant's son dressed alike Fishermen wore short, close-fitting tunic or belted coat, either sleeveless or with elbow-length tight sleeves (Stillman, 2000)
Female	Jumper dress over shirt, dresses with empire waists and wide sleeves, dresses sashed at waist Veils that cover the head, but not the face	Islamic women in Middle Ages wore dresses with belts, sashes and wide sleeves (Guthrie, 2001), (Stillman, 2000) Veils that cover the head, but not the face (Lewis, shown on p. 116, 1976) Women's faces veiled in public from the nose down (Stillman, 2000) Upper-class women wore veils, peasant women did not (Harris, 1958)

Architecture	Buildings have smooth walls as if made of mud or clay	Islamic buildings made primarily of mud brick, either sun-dried or baked, or mud and straw (Ettinghausen, 1976; Jairazbhoy, 2000; Warren, 1982)
	Homes of the poor villagers are nondescript, colorless, rectangular; homes of the wealthy villagers are multicolored and of varying shapes and sizes	Islamic homes have unadorned exteriors (Ettinghausen, 1976; Jairazbhoy, 2000; Warren, 1982) Color rarely applied to outside brick (Warren, 1982)
	Bread oven made of stone, has pitched roof, iron door with bars, and a chimney	Picture of bread oven shows it made of clay, looks more like a large cistern (Warren, p. 107, 1982)
Furniture	Dining table is large plank of wood atop legs of stacked wood or brick; two stools drawn up to table	Muslims had almost no wooden furniture and ate while seated on floor (Ettinghausen, 1976) Meals were served on large trays, not tables (Grabar, 1976; Warren, 1982)
	Maha's stepsister shown holding on to iron bedstead that is on wheels	Islamic people slept on mattresses that were spread out on the floor at night (Ettinghausen, 1976; Warren, 1982) and stored in chests or stacked in corner of room during day (Ettinghausen, 1976)

Chapter 10

Using a Classroom Assessment to Address Diverse Levels of Competence in Education Graduate Students

Susan Ariew

Introduction

How many times have librarians heard graduate students complain just before a library instruction session that they've had a class about library resources before? Ideally, library instruction at all levels would be integrated into the curriculum such that all students would be given the basics and then could build on them as they proceed through their graduate studies. Unfortunately, that is not always feasible and thus many librarians find themselves faced with the problem of the same students having multiple library instruction sessions for several of their core courses. Most students who have had basic assignment-related instruction in education or the social sciences feel they are wasting their time if they think the session they will attend is just a repeat of the same material; and indeed, it will be if the teacher is presenting a preplanned, one-size-fits-all lecture-style presentation. No matter how attractive the PowerPoint slides are, how good the presentation, redundancy can be boring. Moreover, studies have shown that students at all levels generally think their library/information literacy skills are much better than they are, and such overestimation of their abilities can lead to barriers for librarians teaching them.[1]

When faced with a situation where a librarian has both new students and "repeaters," it's time to change things and diversify instruction. To do this, instructors may need to abandon the prepared and structured class and move into a more dynamic, free-flowing, workshop-style environment. Such instruction is not for the faint of heart, but the potential for motivating learners with active learning strategies is well worth the risk. Esther S. Grassian and Joan R. Kaplowitz point out that "students do not learn much just sitting in classes listening to teachers…they must talk about what they are learning, write about it, relate it to past experiences, apply it to their daily lives."[2] Outlined in this chapter is a simple diagnostic tool that allows librarians to enter into meaningful dialogue with students about their prior knowledge, experiences, problems, successes, and queries with regard to their research strategies and tools. Also illustrated are examples of how one can diversify instruction for different levels of students—the beginners versus the more proficient researchers using active, collaborative learning strategies in the same class session.

Analysis of the Learning Situation

Assume for the sake of discussion that the learning situation involves a professional seminar of Instructional Technology graduate students. The librarian has been asked to conduct a three-hour seminar that addresses research techniques and resources in education. The session is taking place in an electronic classroom with approximately twenty-five students, each with a computer workstation. Students wish to learn about researching topics related to instructional technology. Half the class is made up of experienced second- and third-year graduate students in a PhD program, some of whom have had various library sessions before; the other half consists of brand new students in the program, students who know very little about the library. The librarian suspects that the new students will invariably see him or her again with some of the standard core course sessions that will be taught, particularly the basic research methods class in education, so there is no pressure to teach a comprehensive class about research in education. Rather, the librarian wants to engage the entire group in meaningful workshop activities that address learning objectives for both groups of learners.

Information Literacy Standards

(Note: A complete list of ACRL *Information Literacy Competency Standards for Higher Education* [Chicago: ACRL, 2000] appears as appendix A.)

Because the first activity—the diagnostic—assesses the knowledge and experiences students bring to the library session, much of what is going on is a process of discovery for both teacher and students. What do the experienced students think they know? What gaps in their knowledge about the library, educational research, and tools can they identify themselves? What can they share with their lesser experienced student colleagues? This particular activity relates well to ACRL Information Literacy Competency Standard One: "The information literate student determines the nature and extent of the information needed."[3] What can be explored in detail as the discussion ensues is ACRL Standard/Performance Indicator 1.2. Other workshop-style activities related to accessing and evaluating journal articles described in this chapter address ACRL Standards and Performance Indicators 2.1 and 1.3.a. These are all standards that address the early stages of the research process, which would be appropriate for a class introducing education resources, strategies, and techniques to graduate students.

Lesson Plan

The material for the class described here is just an example of what librarians can do to find out more about their students and customize learning for them, as well as how librarians can diversify and tailor learning objectives to various levels of competency within the same session. After initial introductions and orientation to the session, start by using the following questions. If possible, it is helpful to have someone assist the librarian by recording student responses for future reference.

1. How many of you have had library instruction sessions before? For which courses? How many of you have *never* had library instruction?

2. For those of you who have had a library instruction session before, what do you remember about the session or sessions?

3. How many of you have already done research projects before using some of the resources that we may be talking about today?

4. When you employed some of the databases, Web sites, or other resources you learned about in the library sessions or on your own, what problems did you encounter?

5. How did you deal with the problems you encountered?

6. What still perplexes you about the library and its resources?

7. What success stories about your research process, the tools, or the library can you share with the class?

8. For those of you who are more familiar with the library and its resources, what advice would you give to the students in this class who are new to this program?

This part of the workshop should be informal. All questions or comments from students provide the "teachable moment" and create interest and motivation for the group. As the librarian answers students' queries, the students themselves direct the instruction for the group. The instructor may need to slow down and explain the questions and concerns of more experienced library users/researchers to the new students in detail. In the process, the librarian may take the group to electronic information available from the library Web pages to answer specific queries and demonstrate key databases or other resources as he or she answers questions posed by the group. It isn't surprising to get questions and comments about the library and not just about the resources because students associate the library with the research, the tools and the strategies when the physical library presents barriers to them. Addressing all aspects of the research process from a student-centered approach as opposed to a teacher-centered point of view can make the discussion more meaningful for both parties.

Diversifying Instruction: Two Activities for Two Different Levels of Learners

After the opening diagnostic, the teacher then provides more structured teaching and learning activities for the two groups of students, one that addresses the basic needs of the new student and one that poses a challenge for the more sophisticated researchers. For example, the teacher can first present some brief direct instruction about how to locate journal articles both electronically and in print, a basic skill for the new students and a refresher for the more experienced researcher. Next the instructor can ask students to group themselves according to what activity they think they need, the basic one or the one for the more advanced. Students in the novice group would work in pairs on a bibliography of articles in order to determine if they are available online, where to locate them online, if they are only available in print within the library, or if they are not available at all and would have to be requested through interlibrary loan. This exercise reinforces how to use e-journals links, the library catalog, and interlibrary loan services. When working on this exercise, it helps to ask students to click all the way through to get the full text of articles in the bibliography, giving them experience with multiple databases or electronic formats for various journal titles.

The upper-level students, in small groups, examine journal articles in both print issues of scholarly journals and online formats. They are then asked to discuss and analyze what information they gain by seeing an entire print issue of a journal and an article within its issue versus seeing an article online somewhat detached from its context. After about thirty minutes of working in pairs or groups on the two activities, the entire class returns to a group analysis of both sessions. The librarian can lead the discussion with the new students, identifying problems and successes in finding online full-text journal or print-only articles. Students in the upper-level groups can next present their findings about their journal articles to the entire group, discussing what they had learned from the exercise. Allowing upper-level students the opportunity to teach others and share their knowledge as part of any workshop can be a successful way to motivate them.

Description of the Instruction Session: What Actually Happened?

The diagnostic with students in the Instructional Technology professional seminar and other seminars proved to be very successful as students began to realize that this was indeed going to be about them, their ideas, their questions, their experiences, and their concerns and not a repeat of anything they'd had prior to the session. The following are some sample responses from various class participants using the diagnostic assessment tool. Student recollection of prior library sessions included: relief at learning to use new tools and how to access library subscription materials from home; finding the first library instruction class to be an overwhelming experience; instruction occurred too early in the semester—very first class; session was too fast; too much effort had been on keeping up rather than exploring or understanding anything; remembering something about ERIC and InfoTrac databases, but not much of any detail.

Problems with using resources/research process included: accessing full-text articles from various and confusing aggregator services such as InfoTrac, Factiva, Expanded Academic ASAP, Ingenta, and other electronic resources; using hyperlinks from ERIC and PsycINFO databases to get to articles; "refinding" all databases, materials, or resources presented in one session. In other words, students described a lack of connection between the library instruction and the work that needed to be done later on in the semester. Responses about how students dealt with their problems were: consulting the education/social sciences librarian; going to the reference desk for assistance; giving up in disgust; accessing more user-friendly tools and abandoning those sources that presented any barriers. Added perplexities included: a lack of access to physical items in the library because of distance, hours, etc; frustration with the multiprocess steps of going from indexes to articles if articles were not online; overdue notices and fines policies; self-checkout of books and problems with bar codes.

Success stories detailed: Ingenta is great when you get it working for you; Infotrac's Expanded Academic ASAP is useful for this class and all classes; JSTOR materials were very helpful; finding plenty of books in the library made a difference. Advice for new students included: use the reference staff for help if you need it; start early; remember the names of key databases you will need later; learn to master the art of getting to subscription services off campus; use the online Ask a Librarian service; obtain assistance from the education librarian if you need it. Often more experienced students shared their experiences with new students and their voices became the basis for the lessons the librarian chose to develop in more detail for the entire group.

The bibliography assignment kept new students engaged in identifying where to find key journal articles and then in accessing some of them. The upper-level journal comparison activity led to some fascinating discussions about the stability of online resources, the poor quality of diagrams and pictures in online articles compared to print versions of them, and questions about evaluation of journals. Other discussion centered on how much more information students have when viewing an entire print journal in determining the level of scholarship, the reputation of the journal, as well as the browseability of print and how it can lead to serendipity in finding more information (particularly when an entire issue of a journal is devoted to one topic). Discussion followed about how to find the same kind of information about a journal and journal rankings in an online-only environment. Generally, the informal, interactive-workshop-style format meant that everyone participated and had the opportunity to share their expertise and learn from one another.

Reflection on the Instruction Session: Lessons Learned

Querying one's students about what they think they know is very illuminating. One begins to realize that many of the details the instructor previously thought were so important to present in one session (ERIC descriptors versus keyword searching, for example) are not easily retained and are not normally mentioned by students if asked to recall what they learned from prior sessions later on. The initial diagnostic can give the librarian confidence about what can be repeated based on what is revealed about student retention during the interview. Beyond that, one can hear from students about how they learn both during and after library instruction sessions. Using this simple instrument that identifies student questions, problems, and frustrations both motivates and engages them; it encourages students to further their knowledge in meaningful ways. Moreover, it is helpful for the new students to hear the stories of the experienced students simply because they then begin to realize how complex and labor intensive the research process is and that one session on "the library" will not necessarily do it all for them. Following up with some direct instruction and interactive, group activities for both new and experienced students allows them to reinforce earlier skills. Finally, creating the opportunity for the very experienced students to become the teachers and the "stars" of the workshop allows adult learners to lead and guide new students, benefiting both groups. This type of format can make the entire experience more enjoyable and interesting for all parties.

Notes

1. See, for example, Lilith R. Kunkel, Susan M. Weaver, and Kim N. Cook, "What Do They Know?: An Assessment of Undergraduate Library Skills," *Journal of Academic Librarianship* 22 (1996): 430–34; Valerie Perrett, "Graduate Information Literacy Skills: The 2003 ANU Skills Audit," *Australian Library Journal* 53, no. 2 (2004): 161–71; and Heidi E Julien, "Information Literacy Instruction in Canadian Academic Libraries: Longitudinal Trends and International Comparisons," *College & Research Libraries* 61, no. 6 (2000): 510–23.

2. Esther S. Grassian and Joan R. Kaplowitz, *Information Literacy Instruction: Theory and Practice* (New York: Neal-Schuman, 2001), 116–17.

3. Association of College and Research Libraries, *Information Literacy Competency Standards for Higher Education* (Chicago: ACRL, 2000).

Teaching Resources

Sample Activity for Beginning Graduate Students

NAME(S)_____ CLASS_____ DATE _____

Following the Trail—Finding the Articles

For each citation below determine if the article is available online, in print, or unavailable within the USF Library system. *If you find the article is available online, you do NOT need to fill out the print availability.* If the article is not available in print or online, indicate that you need to Interlibrary Loan it by placing an "X" under "Not available except through ILL."

	Available online			Available in print only (fill in only if not available online)		Not available except through ILL
Citation	Yes/No	Name of publisher or service	Years journal is available	Yes/No	Call no. of journal	"X" if this is true
1. Anderson, M.A. (2000). Assessing teacher technology skills. *MultiMedia Schools, 7 (6), Nov–Dec 2000, 25–27.*						
2. Anderson, M.A. (2001) Media specialist and Staff Development. *Educational Media and Technology Yearbook*, 26, 76–82.						
3. Campbell, John Edward, and Carlson, Matt. (2002) Panopticon.com: Online surveillance and the commodification of privacy. *Journal of Broadcasting and Electronic Media.* 46 (4, December), 586–606.						
4. Hayes, K. (2001) School Librarians as Staff Developers. *Book Report*, 19(4) Jan–Feb 2001, 6–8.						

5. Barkley S. & Bianco, T. (2002). Part digital training, part human touch: Rural district mixes its offering of staff development services. *Journal of Staff Development, 23 (1), Win 2002,* 42–45.						

Sample Activity for Upper Level Graduate Students

Summer 2003   Names_____

                 Class_____

The questions below relate to the following article citation:

> Chen, Der-Thanq, Angela F.L.Wong, and Jackie J.F. Hsu. (2002). Dimensions of metaphor consistency in computer-based learning (CBL) design: Lessons learned from project justice Bao. *Journal of Educational Multimedia and Hypermedia* 11 (3): 251–66.

Find this article online listing all services where it is available.

1. Where did you find the electronic versions of this article? List the sources for the journal title and article.

2. Were there differences in the various types of the electronic versions of this article? What kind of impact might the different formats for the electronic version of this article have on researchers?

3. Compare the difference between the paper and the electronic version of this article. What distinctions between the paper and electronic versions did you note?

4. If you were using this article in a research paper, what advantages, if any, are there to accessing the paper version versus the electronic one? What advantages do the online versions offer?

Chapter 11

Vygotsky's Theory and Standards as Frameworks for Library Instruction in a Research Methods Course

Veronica Bielat and Navaz Peshotan Bhavnagri

Introduction

This chapter focuses on collaboration between a librarian (Veronica Bielat) and a faculty member (Navaz Peshotan Bhavnagri) to fully integrate library instruction into an existing master's-level teacher education course. The course content focuses on (1) the use of the library as a resource for empirical research, (2) comprehending and analyzing empirical studies, and (3) learning various empirical research methods.

Librarians understand the importance of linking their library instruction to course content; however, developing and implementing this link is challenging. We therefore recommend that to build this link successfully, it is imperative that faculty and librarians collaborate and, more important, collaborate effectively.[1] In this chapter, we demonstrate how librarians and faculty must not only be fully engaged in the collaborative process, but also how these efforts must be supported with a clear theoretical framework as well as a conceptual framework that is driven by established standards.[2] We also show how our attention to standards not only shaped our teaching, but also clearly had a positive impact on student learning.

Analysis of the Learning Situation

TED7000 is a fifteen-week course titled Introductory Master's Seminar offered to elementary and early childhood graduate students in Wayne State University's (WSU) College of Education. The faculty member has historically included a library instruction session at the beginning of the course. The class had been meeting in a computer lab in the library the second and third weeks of the course, a practice we currently continue. The computer lab has a projector, and each student has a computer with Internet access.

This narrative does not describe a one-shot session but, rather, gives a snapshot of an ongoing integration of library instruction. For the past four years, we have continually refined the library instruction using our three-step process:

1. We frequently discuss strategy and content, which results in revisions to our approaches.

2. These approaches go through further metamorphosis based on student feedback throughout the semester, including a final formal evaluation.

3. We amalgamate our discussions along with student feedback and implement innovations into our teaching, thus transforming the same course the following semester.

This is a cyclical process. It represents a formative and summative assessment process that supports evidence-based teaching practices and effective student learning. Our three steps are integrated into a larger framework, built on Vygotsky's theory[3] and Association of College and Research Libraries (ACRL) Information Literacy Competency Standards for Higher Education (ACRL Standards)[4] complemented by the National Council for Accreditation of Teacher Education (NCATE) Professional Standards for the Accreditation of Schools, Colleges and Department of Education (Professional Standards).[5]

The faculty member encouraged the librarian to learn about Vygotsky's theory because it was highly suitable to our particular teaching and learning situation. As a result, we examined the Vygotskian concepts of "scaffolding" and "Zone of Proximal Development" and how they applied to our teaching. Scaffolding is a process by which individuals gradually learn with support, guidance, and direction from experts (such as adults or peers) until they finally work independently.[6] The Zone of Proximal Development, or ZPD, describes levels of performance. "The lower level of the ZPD is defined by the (learner's) independent performance and its upper level is defined by the most a (learner) can do with assistance."[7] The learning strategies we implemented scaffolded, or lifted, our students to their upper levels of the ZPD. Our strategies helped students improve their understanding of library research concepts and application of library research methods. Students were able to demonstrate this understanding through the use of scaffolding tools incorporated into our instructional activities.

Using the course syllabus, ACRL standards, and NCATE professional standards as our framework, we articulated the learning outcomes we wanted students to achieve with regard to library instruction. From this framework, we connected the faculty member's content and library instruction content for two class sessions. We developed activities for students that required them to demonstrate their understanding of library research concepts. Finally, we developed a survey that reflected students' movement from lower level of ZPD to upper level in relationship to their understanding of the concepts that supported the learning outcomes. The students moved to their upper ZPD based on our "expert" assistance, and at the end of the course, they expressed through our survey that they felt that they had gained expertise in library searching strategies.

Information Literacy Standards

(Note: A complete list of ACRL Information Literacy Competency Standards for Higher Education [Chicago: ACRL, 2000] appears as appendix A.)

ACRL Standards

The ACRL Standards were used as a guide in the development of the library instruction sessions, as they related to the desired outcomes of the course. The faculty member was very pleased to learn that her course outcomes complemented and supported the ACRL standards. The course outcomes were:

• Demonstrate professional knowledge and skills to use various reference aids.

• Demonstrate professional skills in analyzing and synthesizing refereed research as tools of inquiry that are available in the university library.[8]

The following table aligns ACRL standards to our instructional activities. The instructional activities are scaffolding tools that move students to their upper ZPD. These activities are facilitated by both the librarian and the faculty member. Some activities that are introduced collaboratively by the librarian and faculty member are completed over the semester and evaluated by the faculty member.

Table 1 focuses on the Instructional Activities/Vygotskian Scaffolding Tools aligned with ACRL standards. Table 2 aligns students' construction of knowledge with outcomes of particular ACRL standards. The results reported in table 2 are from an anonymous survey administered at the end of the course and responded to by 100 percent of the students. Results reported as before this course (lower ZPD) in the graphs report students' performance at the independent level, without assistance from librarian and faculty member as experts. Results reported as now (upper ZPD) in the graphs refer to students' self-reported understanding of the concept at the end of the course. The results reported as now (upper ZPD) show the students' assessment of their own internal knowledge of the concepts (a result of our expert assistance, or scaffolding), which can be interpreted as the level of their upper ZPD.

The purpose of table 2, which reports the survey results, is to illustrate the shift in students' understanding of research concepts, which we attribute

Table 1. Alignment of ACRL Standards to Instructional Activity/ Vygotskian Scaffolding Tool	
Standard. Performance Indicator. Outcome[9]	**Instructional Activity/ Vygotskian Scaffolding Tool**
1.1.b. Develops a thesis statement and formulates questions based on the information need. 1.1.d. Defines or modifies the information need to achieve a manageable focus1.4.a. Reviews the initial information need to clarify, revise, or refine the questions	Students independently post research question to an online Discussion Board.
1.1.e. Identifies key concepts and terms that describe the information need	Students collaborate to identify dependent and independent variables posted in online Discussion Board.
2.1.c. Investigates the scope, content, and organization of information retrieval systems 2.1.d. Selects efficient and effective approaches for accessing the information needed from the investigative methods or information retrieval system 2.2.a.b.c. The information literate student constructs and implements effectively designed search strategies.	Students record and analyze their searches.
1.2.d. Identifies the purpose and audience of potential resources (e.g., popular vs. scholarly, current vs. historical)	Students respond to questions posted to online Discussion Board previous week.
1.3.c. Defines a realistic overall plan and timeline to acquire the needed information	Students are provided a method to organize their searching.
1.4.b. Describes criteria used to make information decisions and choices 2.4.a.b.c. The information literate student refines the search strategy if necessary.	Students complete a journal detailing their learning about library searching
2.5.b. Creates a system for organizing the information	Students are provided directions on developing a notebook to retain search results, articles, etc.
3.2.a.b.c.d. The information literate student articulates and applies initial criteria for evaluating both the information and its sources. 3.3.a.b.c. The information literate student synthesizes main ideas to construct new concept.	Students complete a Review of Literature as their final project.

to the implementation of the Instructional Activities/Vygotskian Scaffolding Tools aligned to the ACRL standards as outlined in table 1. Students shifted from low levels of skill and understanding (lower ZPD) to higher levels of skill and understanding (upper ZPD) through scaffolding from experts.

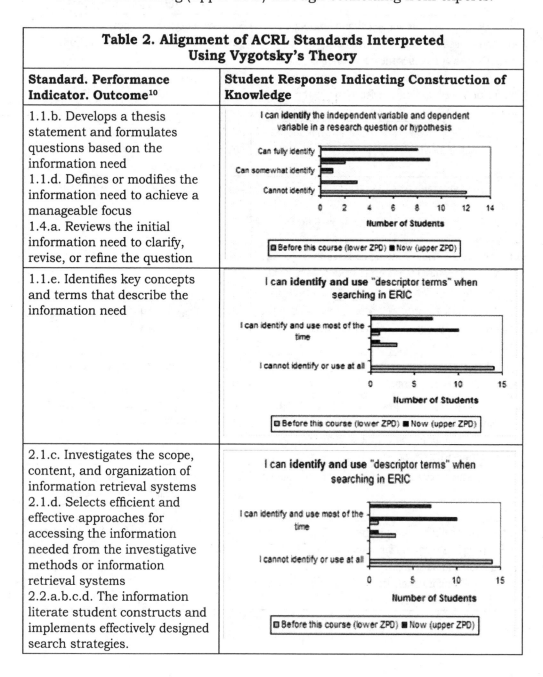

Table 2. Alignment of ACRL Standards Interpreted Using Vygotsky's Theory	
Standard. Performance Indicator. Outcome[10]	**Student Response Indicating Construction of Knowledge**
1.1.b. Develops a thesis statement and formulates questions based on the information need 1.1.d. Defines or modifies the information need to achieve a manageable focus 1.4.a. Reviews the initial information need to clarify, revise, or refine the question	I can **identify** the independent variable and dependent variable in a research question or hypothesis
1.1.e. Identifies key concepts and terms that describe the information need	I can **identify and use** "descriptor terms" when searching in ERIC
2.1.c. Investigates the scope, content, and organization of information retrieval systems 2.1.d. Selects efficient and effective approaches for accessing the information needed from the investigative methods or information retrieval systems 2.2.a.b.c.d. The information literate student constructs and implements effectively designed search strategies.	I can **identify and use** "descriptor terms" when searching in ERIC

Table 2. Alignment of ACRL Standards Interpreted Using Vygotsky's Theory	
1.2.d. Identifies the purpose and audience of potential resources (e.g., popular vs. scholarly, current vs. historical)	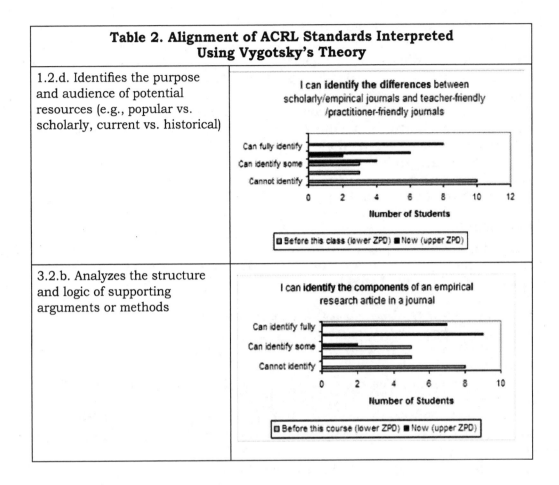
3.2.b. Analyzes the structure and logic of supporting arguments or methods	

NCATE Standards

We also are cognizant that NCATE professional standards complement the development of information literacy skills using technology. The WSU College of Education's Conceptual Framework, guided by the NCATE professional standards, in part states: "[the student]" uses technology as an integral part of one's...learning."[11] Technology was used consistently by the students through the use of PowerPoint, the online course site, and online database searching. This full use of technology was a scaffolding "mental tool" and an organizer promoting higher-level thinking throughout the course, moving students to their upper ZPD. "Mental tools" are learning devices that improve mental functioning.[12] The usefulness of technology was demonstrated in the survey when all students reported that they found the PowerPoint slides "valuable" to "very valuable" in facilitating their learning.

NCATE professional standards additionally emphasize a disposition to learning, particularly in relationship to technology. When asked in our survey regarding their feelings toward technology, only 50 percent of students reported high levels of comfort with technology. At the end of the course, this number had increased to 83 percent. Additionally, students' disposition toward using Blackboard, the online course site, clearly shifted because 27 percent of students reported resistance to learning to use it before the course, whereas none reported that they had any resistance to using Blackboard at the end of the course. The students' overall knowledge and disposition toward using technology increased over the course, supporting the NCATE standards.

Lesson Plan

The following lesson plan, which includes course and library instruction content, method of delivery (such as explanation), and scaffolding tools (such as a rubric) are listed below.

Session I (held the second week in the semester)

Faculty Member

1. Explanation: How to select a research topic (with accompanying PowerPoint)

2. Explanation: Defining variables (with accompanying PowerPoint and rubric)

3. Activity: Students post a research question in Blackboard Discussion Board, followed by student collaborative identification of independent and dependent variables

4. Review of goals and objectives for the next two sessions

Librarian

5. Explanation and Demonstration
   - Review tutorial content and define library terminology
   - Introduce students to ERIC database
   - Demonstrate searching methodology: keyword, descriptor, special fields

6. Application and Demonstration of Knowledge
   - Complete a search using identified variables and record search in matrix
   - Discuss search strategies and add complexity: descriptors and special fields

Session II (held the third week of the semester)

Faculty Member

1. Review of previous week
2. Activity: Research question critique based on rubric provided
3. Activity: Hypothesis based on rubric provided

Faculty Member and Librarian
4. Explanation and Discussion: Textbook, library terms, and concepts handout and library tutorials. Introduction to library vocabulary, including scholarly publishing

Librarian
5. Review: Previous week's searching in ERIC database; discuss problems or issues
   6. Explanation, Demonstration, and Response:
     • Introduce students to additional database resources

Description of the Instruction Session: What Actually Happened?

The faculty member and librarian collaboratively prepared for the library component of the class. The faculty member added the librarian to the online course site (using Blackboard courseware) as a Site-Builder, which allowed her to add content to the site. The librarian posted a Flash tutorial she developed in collaboration with the faculty member about ERIC database searching, along with links to two existing online Wayne State Library tutorial modules,[13] namely Starting Smart and Choosing a Topic. Additionally, the librarian posted library resource pathfinders, instructional handouts, and links to other resources in Blackboard, which provided students with a variety of mental tools that could subsequently be accessed to support their learning.

The librarian sent an e-mail via Blackboard to the students to (1) introduce herself, (2) inform the students that she would be collaboratively teaching them along with their faculty member, and (3) inform students that they needed to come prepared by completing the posted tutorials. (The online tutorials are a scaffolding tool, which provide support and feedback to students to help them develop higher-level thinking on how to develop a search strategy and search the ERIC database.)

During the second class meeting, the faculty member introduced the topic of research question design. Students deliberately revisited the PowerPoint presentation used in this introduction and posted in Blackboard as they revised their research question and hypothesis. For the students, the PowerPoint became what Vygotsky calls a "memory mediator," which facilitated the student's "deliberate memory" or the ability to remember on purpose.[14] Following the introduction, students independently developed their research questions and posted them to a Blackboard Discussion Board. This entire process directly addresses ACRL Standard and Performance Indicator 1.1 that relates to "defining and articulating information need."[15]

The faculty member further refined and scaffolded students' thinking by using another PowerPoint to introduce the concept of independent and dependent variables. She then displayed the Blackboard Discussion Board containing the posted research questions, and all students collaborated in identifying dependent and independent variables in the research questions. This student collaborative work exemplifies Vygotsky's "co-construction of knowledge" resulting in students' better understanding of both variables.[16] By observing this process, the librarian became familiar with the students' research topics. This activity addresses ACRL Outcome 1.1.e. "Identifies key concepts and terms that describe the information need."[17]

At this point, the librarian began an introduction to database searching in ERIC. We queried students to determine if they had completed the online library tutorials. Sixty-four percent of the students reported viewing the tutorials. More important, all the students who had used these tutorials reported in the survey administered at the end of the course that viewing the tutorials improved their understanding of searching ERIC and conducting basic library searches. The tutorials helped move students up in their ZPD, and the librarian provided students with additional scaffolding in class, moving them still further in reaching their upper ZPD with expert assistance.

The librarian then introduced the mechanics of using the matrix, a spreadsheet developed by the faculty member and the librarian as a mental organizing tool for recording new concepts and strategies in database searching. Use of the matrix demonstrates Vygotsky's research method of "double stimulation," which consists of two components: (1) examining learners' processing of new concepts and research strategies, and (2) documenting evidence that the student has a meaningful understanding of the organizing tool.[18] In this application, (1) students used keyword, descriptor, and special field searching as new concepts and strategies to find studies related to their dependent and independent variables; and (2) students showed meaningful understanding of the matrix by using it effectively as a search navigation and organization tool. Students were required to document three searches and submit them to the librarian at the beginning of the next class meeting. The librarian and the faculty member also used the matrix to determine if students were generally meeting ACRL Standard Two: "Accessing needed information effectively and efficiently."[19]

At the end of the class, the librarian posted the three collaboratively developed questions representing articulation of new concepts to a

Blackboard Discussion Board to be answered prior to the next class session. The librarian continually checked the Discussion Board during the week for student responses and posted comments or questions to student postings. The librarian used the Blackboard Discussion Board as an opportunity to engage in Vygotskian "educational dialogue" electronically, to guide students between sessions by responding to their construction of knowledge.[20]

The following week, the completed matrices were collected by the librarian and reviewed according to the double stimulation research method while the faculty member reviewed her content with the students during the first half of the class. At the break, the librarian returned the matrices to the students with written comments and continued the educational dialogue verbally on an individual basis if she were able to identify students with whom a conversation was warranted based on the search strategies documented in the matrix.

The librarian and the faculty member collaboratively facilitated a discussion of scholarly journals and empirical research articles. Together, we reviewed these concepts as presented in the library tutorial and a library terms and concepts handout developed by the faculty member, both of which scaffolded the students. Because we had identified topics that needed additional scaffolding through the Discussion Board postings, we focused on engaging students in educational dialogue to clarify any errors in understanding. In this process, we engaged in intersubjectivity, which means that although we had distinct voices in the dialogue, "each communicant recognize[d] the echo of the original text [the information message] in the other's speech."[21] The content covered in the Blackboard Discussion Board and class discussion addresses ACRL Outcome 1.2.d.: "Identifies the purpose and audience of potential resources (e.g., popular vs. scholarly, current vs. historical)" and Outcome 3.2.b.: "Analyzes the structure and logic of supporting arguments or methods."[22]

The remainder of the class was devoted to applying search strategies learned the previous week to new database interfaces. The librarian actively engaged all students in applying concepts, such as using controlled vocabulary searching, in each interface, so that students participated as a group in the co-construction of knowledge, as they engaged in peer teaching and scaffolding each other. The application of new searching skills repeatedly in different databases and discussion of strategies among the students helped them internalize this new knowledge. Vygotsky explains that this "interpersonal communication" between individuals is necessary because it facilitates internalization, which he calls "intrapersonal communication."[23] As the class ended, both librarian and faculty member encouraged students to contact the librarian any time for personal assistance.

Reflection on the Instruction Session: Lessons Learned

We share our reflections on the lessons we learned in the building of the library instruction sessions based on ACRL standards and Vygotskian theory, and our collaborative focus on using technology in the classroom. We will also share the advocacy position we take based on these reflections, and offer explicit recommendations for librarians and faculty who would like to collaborate.

ACRL Standards

Systematically linking the ACRL standards to course learning outcomes validated our efforts in the teaching and learning process. The faculty member felt reassured that the content of library instruction met national standards. The librarian learned how to connect standards to a theoretical framework and translate them into authentic learning activities. The experience reminded the librarian that it is unrealistic to include all content related to ACRL standards in one or two class sessions. Additionally, faculty may not be aware of the ACRL standards but are already teaching content related to the standards. Therefore, to accommodate time constraints and eliminate redundancies in teaching ACRL standards, we recommend that librarians discuss course outcomes with faculty to discover if this overlap exists.

Vygotskian Framework

The Vygotskian framework provided a base the librarian could return to for ideas and applications and a method of linking the ACRL standards with effective teaching methodology. All instruction librarians need to have a reasonable mastery of educational learning theories and Vygotsky's theory is one such model. The librarian found that it provides a structure and gives specific scaffolding strategies to implement effective teaching of the ACRL standards.

The librarian and faculty member learned that our understanding of Vygotskian theory expanded as we continually assessed and reflected on our teaching effectiveness. Each time we discussed the theory, we both self-reflected on student collaborative opportunities that could be implemented. Additionally, because we had the Vygotskian concept of ZPD as an indicator of learning, we were able to design a survey tool that illustrated students' activities at the independent and assisted level, which allowed us to fully appreciate their growth in learning. (See table 2.) We advocate that librarians and faculty develop methods of continuous self-assessment and student assessment of their teaching.

Technology

We learned that ACRL standards and NCATE professional standards both have components that focus on the learner's effective use of technology. We were both committed to technology as an instructive tool and found methods of using it inside and outside the classroom within the Vygotskian Framework. We recommend that librarians and faculty dedicate effort to using technology vigorously and consistently as a scaffolding tool to promote effective teaching and learning.

Conclusion

Our most satisfying lesson learned was that our collaborative efforts truly benefited students. Students were required, as a course assignment, to complete a reflective journal documenting their experiences, successes, and failures related to completing their library research. We have included below an excerpt from a student's reflective journal that illustrates how our collaborative efforts positively impacted a student.

Notes

1. Richard Raspa and Dane Ward, *The Collaborative Imperative: Librarians and Faculty Working Together in the Information Universe* (Chicago: ACRL, 2000).

2. Navaz Peshotan Bhavnagri and Veronica Bielat, "Faculty–Librarian Collaboration to Teach Research Skills: Electronic Symbiosis," *Reference Librarian* 89/90 (2005): 121–38.

3. Alex Kozulin, *Vygotsky's Psychology: A Biography of Ideas* (New York: Harvester Wheatsheaf, 1990).

4. Association of College and Research Libraries, *Information Literacy Competency Standards for Higher Education* (Chicago: ACRL, 2000). Available online from http://www.ala.org/ala/acrl/acrlstandards/inform ationliteracycompetency.htm.

5. National Council for Accreditation of Teacher Education, *Professional Standards for the Accreditation of Schools, Colleges and Departments of Education* (Washington, DC: NCATE, 2002). Available online from http://www.ncate.org/documents/pdsStandards.pdf.

6. Laura E. Berk and Adam Winsler, *Scaffolding Children's Learning: Vygotsky and Early Childhood Education* (Washington, DC: NAEYC, 1995); and Elena Bodrova and Deborah J. Leong, *Tools of the Mind: The Vygotskian Approach to Early Childhood Education* (Englewood Cliffs, NJ: Prentice-Hall, 1996).

7. Elena Bodrova, "Key Concepts in Vygotsky's Theory of Learning and Development," *Journal of Early Childhood Teacher Education* 18 (1997): 16–21.

8. Navaz Peshotan Bhavnagri, TED 7000 Course Syllabus (Detroit: College of Education, Wayne State University, 2005).

9. ACRL, *Information Literacy Competency Standards.*

10. Ibid.

11. College of Education, Wayne State University, Conceptual Framework. (Detroit: College of Education, Wayne State University, 2006). Available online from http://ncate.coe.wayne.edu/evidence/Conceptual% 20Framework%201-26-06-F.pdf.

12. Commission on Behavioral and Social Sciences and Education, *Eager to Learn: Educating Our Preschoolers* (Washington, DC: National Academies Press, 2000).

13. Wayne State University Libraries, "Searchpath." Available online from http://www.lib.wayne.edu/services/instruction_tutorials/searchpath/.

14. Bodrova and Leong, *Tools of the Mind,* 74–76.

15. ACRL, *Information Literacy Competency Standards.*

16. Joan Wink and LeAnn Putney, *A Vision of Vygotsky* (Boston: Allyn & Bacon, 2002): 61.

17. ACRL, *Information Literacy Competency Standards.*

18. Bodrova and Leong, *Tools of the Mind,* 38.

19. ACRL, *Information Literacy Competency Standards.*

20. Bodrova and Leong, *Tools of the Mind,* 160.

21. Kozulin, *Vygotsky's Psychology,* 186.

22. ACRL, *Information Literacy Competency Standards.*

23. Wink and Putney, *A Vision of Vygotsky,* 151.

Teaching Resources

Teaching Resource 1: Example of a portion of a completed search matrix submitted by a student. Note the addition of more sophisticated search strategies with each iteration.

Researcher: Database: ERIc   Date: 09/18/05   1

Search #	Term 1 IV	Search Strategy	Term 2 DV	Search Strategy	Term 3 OPTIONAL	Search Strategy	Results	Additional Information
1	literature	keyword	multicultural	keyword		keyword	854	Doc. Type: Journal
2	literature	keyword	multicultural	descriptor		keyword	599	Doc. Type: Journal
3	literature	keyword	multicultural	descriptor	research	period type	39	Doc. Type: Journal
4	literature	descriptor	multicultural	descriptor	research	period type	32	Doc. Type: Journal

Teaching Resource 2: Blackboard Discussion Board
This is an example of a Discussion Board used in the classroom. Students articulate their understanding of a concept by responding to questions posted by the librarian and faculty member in the Discussion Board.

Forum: Librarian Discussion Board   Times Read: 49
Date: Mon Sep 19 2005 16:34
Author: Bielat, Veronica <ag6887@wayne.edu>
Subject: Question 1

(Remove)

What is the difference between an ERIC Journal Citation and an ERIC Document citation?

(Reply)

◄◄ Previous Message   **Next Message** ►►

Thread Detail
Question 1	Bielat, Veronica	Mon Sep 19 2005 16:34
Re: Question 1	Student A	Thu Sep 22 2005 19:38
Re: Question 1	Bielat, Veronica	Sun Sep 25 2005 15:54
Re: Question 1	Student A	Mon Sep 26 2005 17:03
Re: Question 1	Student B	Sun Sep 25 2005 22:01
Re: Question 1	Student C	Sun Sep 25 2005 22:18

Teaching Resource 3: Reflective Journal Excerpt

Students are asked to complete a Reflective Journal, assigned by the faculty member, in which students describe their library search strategies, report frustrations, successes, and the new concepts learned. Following is an excerpt from a recent student's library summary, describing how she benefited from our Vygotskian collaboration.

Class Lectures: I think that it is great that Dr.

Bhavnagri has paired up with Veronica to help teach the course. The students benefit a

great deal because we are learning from a research expert and a library expert as well.

Chapter 12

Teacher as Researcher: Librarian and Faculty Collaboration in Teaching the Literature Review in a Distance-delivered Teacher Education Program

Thomas Scott Duke and Jennifer D. Brown

Introduction

A professor of education at the University of Alaska Southeast (Thomas) invited an academic librarian (Jennifer) to co-teach a distance-delivered graduate seminar on qualitative research in school and classroom settings. The seminar, Classroom Research (ED626), was taught via audioconference (i.e., teleconference) and augmented with a course Web site, UAS Online,[1] and an asynchronous online course conferencing system (Discussion Board). This chapter describes a lesson on conducting a *systematic* and *reproducible* literature review, co-taught over the course of several class meetings to the public school teachers who participated in our graduate seminar in fall 2005. These public school teachers, who lived and worked in remote, rural, and Alaska Native communities throughout the state of Alaska, were enrolled in distance-delivered graduate programs in education at our university. Our purpose in co-teaching this graduate seminar was to teach the teachers (i.e., our graduate students) to *systematically* gather and analyze primary and secondary data sources in their own schools, classrooms, and communities in order to empower their instructional practices, (re)discover their status as teacher-researchers and professional educators, and improve the quality of their students' educational experience.[2]

Analysis of the Learning Situation

In partial fulfillment of the requirements of ED626, our graduate students conducted phenomenological self-studies in which they systematically examined their beliefs about education and their school and classroom practices. A phenomenological self-study is a mode of scholarly inquiry in which educators: (1) engage in numerous self-reflection activities to generate primary data sources that represent their beliefs about education and their school and classroom practices, (2) conduct systematic and reproducible database searches to gather secondary data sources that examine and illuminate their research topic(s), and (3) rely on intuition, imagination, and systematic methods of analysis to interpret these data sources.[3]

We required our graduate students to include five sections in their self-studies: (1) an Introduction section with context statement, statement of purpose, and research question(s); (2) a Review of the Literature section; (3) a Methods section; (4) a Results section (with word tables); and (5) a Discussion section where each teacher compared and contrasted the findings of his or her self-study with the findings of the empirical studies or theoretical works he or she reviewed.

We conceptualized the review of the literature conducted by our graduate students as "miniature versions" of the exhaustive literature reviews doctoral candidates conduct when they write their dissertations. We agreed each student should: (1) pose a research question(s); (2) break down the research question(s) into search terms (i.e., keywords, synonyms, and descriptors); (3) use these search terms to conduct searches of ERIC and at least one other database; (4) record the results of each search so that the search could be reproduced by the reader of the literature review; and (5) develop appropriate selection criteria to narrow and refine the findings of his or her search and systematically yield eight to ten empirical studies and/or theoretical works related to his or her research topic(s).

We have co-taught one or more sections of ED626 each semester since fall 2004, and, each semester, we have tried to improve our lectures and instructional materials. It is a challenge to teach students to conduct literature reviews via a distance-delivered format. In previous semesters, we were not satisfied with how students described their database search procedures (i.e., the systematic and reproducible aspect of the literature review); our students also expressed frustration with this process. One student created a note-taking grid and shared it with the class. Jennifer adapted this grid to develop the Search Procedures Notes handout as well as a Translating Your Research Questions into Searchable Terms handout to help students translate their research questions into conceptual categories and use controlled vocabularies (e.g., ERIC descriptors) in the brainstorming process. We codeveloped the Literature Review Template to help the students organize their literature reviews and clearly delineate (and describe) their search procedures and selection criteria.

We developed Macromedia Breeze presentations to augment the course in fall 2005. Macromedia Breeze is software that works as a plug-in with Microsoft PowerPoint. It allows the creator of the slide show to add audio content (e.g., the voice of the narrator). Breeze also allows the creator to publish the presentation online to a Breeze server. A URL is generated and the resulting presentation can be viewed through most Internet browsers with the use of a Flash plug-in. Jennifer narrated two Breeze presentations: *Requirements for the Literature Review* (twelve slides, seventeen minutes long) and *Searching ERIC and Locating Full Text*[4] (twenty-four slides, twenty-one minutes long).

Information Literacy Standards
(Note: A complete list of ACRL *Information Literacy Competency Standards for Higher Education* [Chicago: ACRL, 2000] appears as appendix A.)

Our course syllabus described the Association of College and Research Libraries (ACRL) Information Literacy Competency Standards[5] as an important conceptual framework that guided and informed the course (other frameworks included the Alaska Teacher Performance Standards and the Assembly of Alaska Native Educators Guidelines for *Preparing Culturally Responsive Teachers for Alaska's Schools*).[6] We developed activities and handouts to help our students demonstrate the following ACRL competencies:

Standard/Performance Indicator/Outcome 1.1.a.: Students discussed their respective research topics in class, via audioconference. We set up an electronic Discussion Board to facilitate further peer interaction.

Standard/Performance Indicator/Outcome 1.1.e.: We instructed students to use the Translating Your Research Questions into Searchable Terms handout to independently brainstorm for keywords, synonyms, and controlled vocabularies. We also helped each student brainstorm search terms in class. Jennifer used the ERIC Thesaurus to help students develop search terms and Thomas suggested terms based on his knowledge of the terminology commonly used in the professional education literature.

Standard/Performance Indicator/Outcome 1.2.e.: We required students to conduct primary and secondary research. We defined primary and secondary research, discussed these terms in class, and provided students with examples of primary and secondary data sources.

Standard/Performance Indicator/Outcome 1.4.b.: We required students to develop selection criteria and to use these criteria to decide what literature to include in their reviews. We also required students to explicitly delineate these criteria for the reader in the Review of the Literature section of their self-studies. The Literature Review Template helped students include descriptions of their selection criteria in the bodies of their respective literature reviews.

Standard/Performance Indicator/Outcome 2.5.b.: We instructed students to organize their literature reviews in a thoughtful, thematic manner. We discussed the differences between a literature review and an annotated bibliography in class. We provided the students with examples of previously published literature reviews and of literature reviews written by former students and discussed numerous ways each student might organize his or her own review of the literature. We also discussed the organization of the literature review in the Breeze presentation. Students wrote multiple drafts of their literature reviews and submitted each draft to Jennifer, via e-mail, for editorial feedback. Jennifer used the Microsoft Word Track Changes function to highlight recommended revisions.

Standard/Performance Indicator/Outcome 3.1.b. and 3.1.c.: Students summarized the literature in their own words, paraphrasing and/or using direct quotes, when appropriate. We required students to use American Psychological Association's publication guidelines[7] to cite authors, quote sources, and list references. We discussed APA publication guidelines in class and edited multiple drafts of each literature review to help our students conform to these publication guidelines.

Standard/Performance Indicator/Outcome 4.2.a. and 4.2.b.: We instructed students to use the Search Procedures Notes handout to help them log their database procedures. Through the process of searching databases and coming up with too many results, not enough results, or off-target results, students learned to reflect and improve on their search strategies. Jennifer frequently reminded students that keeping good notes would help them conduct (and describe) searches that were both systematic and reproducible. Students were required to explicitly describe their search procedures for the reader. The Literature Review Template helped students include clear descriptions of their search procedures in the bodies of their respective literature reviews.

Lesson Plan
Week Three (during Class)
- Lecture and class discussion on the importance of conducting a literature review for any research project and an introduction to our expectations and requirements for the literature review.
- A general introduction to and information sharing of the databases available to students at a distance was provided verbally (and reinforced in future weeks with individual students, via e-mail and teleconference, on an as-needed basis).

Week Four (before Class Meets)
Our students were instructed to:
- Watch the two presentations: *Requirements for the Literature Review* and *Searching ERIC and Locating Full Text.*[8]

- Use the handout/grid, Translating Your Research Questions into Searchable Terms to brainstorm for search terms.
- Begin searching. Do preliminary database searches and be prepared to discuss: (1) search terms used, (2) preliminary search results, and (3) any questions about conducting a literature review.
- The instructional handout, Search Procedures Notes, was posted on the course Web site to help students keep track of each and every database search they conducted throughout the semester.

Week Four (during Class)
- Checked in with students and asked them to state their research question(s) and describe their preliminary database searches.
- Consulted with each student about other concepts and terminologies he or she might wish to consider for the database searches.

Weeks Four through Seven
- Students searched databases and wrote drafts of their literature reviews.
- Students were encouraged to contact Jennifer (via telephone or e-mail) with any questions about the literature review. Thomas also was available to answer questions.
- Students were encouraged to use the Discussion Board to ask their classmates questions.

Week Seven
- First draft of the literature review was due. Jennifer provided detailed editorial feedback on each draft.

Week Eleven
- Class lecture and discussion of the Discussion section of the self-study (the Review of the Literature section needed to be fairly complete before students could begin work on the Discussion section).

Week Fifteen
- Final version of entire self-study (including Review of the Literature section) was due.
- Students presented self-studies (including Review of the Literature section) to the entire class, via audioconference.

Description of the Instruction Session: What Actually Happened?
The prep work we asked our students to do (e.g., watching the two

presentations; using the Translating Your Research Questions into Searchable Terms handout to brainstorm search terms; conducting preliminary ERIC searches, etc.) was helpful and made for a dynamic class in which our students asked informed questions. Jennifer was concerned about how the Macromedia Breeze presentations would work so she asked students for feedback. Our students were very enthusiastic about these online presentations because they could revisit them on an as-needed basis and pause the presentations to take notes.

Our students learned to track down research using different search strategies (e.g., ancestral searching, pearl growing, and mining the bibliography). An ancestral search involves reviewing the reference lists of previously published research to identify articles relevant to one's topic of interest. Ancestral searching is sometimes referred to as pearl growing or mining the bibliography.[9] We checked in regularly with each student during our audioconferences to find out how their database searches were progressing. These class discussions allowed our students to learn from their classmates' successes and failures.

The mechanics of locating full-text articles at a distance continued to be a hang-up for many students. Jennifer would like to think that their constant exposure to a working librarian made this task easier. She received many panicky e-mails around week seven, and again toward the end of the semester, from students who were unable to get their hands on enough full text. Jennifer relied heavily on her colleagues at the Egan Library reference desk to help these students while she was busy providing editorial feedback on the drafts students were sending.

By week fifteen, the students had presented their self-studies to the entire class, via audioconference. Our students discussed the professional literature they reviewed with confidence and authority, described how the findings of their self-studies were supported by the professional literature, and described new understandings and conclusions their self-studies might contribute to the professional literature. Many students believed the research process had deepened their knowledge base, transformed their school and classroom practices, and strengthened their identities as competent teacher-researchers.

Reflection on the Instruction Session: Lessons Learned

Thomas: I have broad and deep content knowledge about the discipline of education and have designed and conducted numerous qualitative studies in school and classroom settings. I do not, however, possess a strong information literacy background. I invited Jennifer to co-teach with me because she *does* possess a strong background in information literacy. She also possesses technical skills that I lack. Jennifer and I were effective co-teachers: she taught the students to conduct systematic and reproducible database searches whereas I helped them develop research questions and search terms based on their research topics. Jennifer taught the students (and me) to conduct *secondary* research; I taught the students (and Jennifer) to conduct *primary* research. Learning activities developed by collaborators from diverse disciplines are often more comprehensive, complex, creative, innovative, and sophisticated than learning activities developed by individuals from a single discipline working in isolation. Our students benefited from Jennifer's expertise with information literacy and her experience conducting secondary research; the students benefited from my knowledge of education and my experience conducting primary research. Jennifer and I learned a great deal from each other and are better researchers and more effective instructors because of our collaborative relationship. My work with Jennifer has deepened my appreciation and understanding of libraries, research librarians, secondary research, and interdisciplinary collaboration for the purposes of research and instruction.

Jennifer: I must admit that I feel such ownership of ED626 and our students and their work that at times it becomes blurry regarding what I developed for the course and what Thomas contributed. Although I took the lead on most aspects of the Review of the Literature and Discussion sections of the student self-studies, our work together teaching teachers how to conduct primary and secondary research is an overlap and synthesis of our disciplines, our personalities, and our creative ideas for the improvement of the class. I am very pleased with the quality of the final research studies passed in by our students. Many students commented that the Literature Review section (i.e., their secondary research) was the most rigorous and challenging part of the course. Our students leave ED626 with the ability to: (1) conduct systematic and reproducible database searches, (2) set their own criteria to evaluate the research they find, and (3) write and reflect upon the literature to come to a broader understanding of their topic and its context in educational research and theory. I believe our students mostly appreciated our accessibility as instructors. We gave them a great deal of feedback throughout the searching and writing process. I feel fortunate as a teaching librarian to be a part of our students' entire research process. Collaboration with Thomas has taught me how to improve the educational experience of the teacher-researchers enrolled in the distance-delivered graduate programs at our university.

Notes

1. University of Alaska Southeast, "UAS Online!" Available online from http://www.uas.alaska.edu/online. Includes assignments, announce-

ments, and links to course instructional materials.

2. Joe L. Kincheloe, *Teachers as Researchers: Qualitative Inquiry as a Path to Empowerment,* 2nd ed. (New York: Routledge, 2003).

3. Jennifer Brown and Thomas Duke, "Librarian and Faculty Collaborative Instruction: A Phenomenological Self-study," *Research Strategies,* (forthcoming); John W. Creswell, *Qualitative Inquiry and Research Design: Choosing among Five Traditions,* (Thousand Oaks, CA: Sage Publications, 1998); Jack Whitehead, *The Growth of Educational Knowledge: Creating Your Own Living Educational Theories* (Bournemouth, Dorset: Hyde, 1993).

4. Jennifer Brown, *Requirements for the Literature Review,* 17 minutes, Macromedia Breeze. Available online from http://breeze5.uas.alaska.edu/litreview; *Searching ERIC and Locating Full Text,* 21 minutes, Macromedia Breeze. Available online from http://breeze5.uas.alaska.edu/searcheric.

5. Association of College and Research Libraries, *Information Literacy Competency Standards for Higher Education* (Chicago: ACRL, 2000). Available online from http://www.ala.org/ala/acrl/acrlstandards/inform ationliteracycompetency.htm.

6. Alaska Department of Education and Early Development, "Standards for Alaska's Teachers." Available online from http://www.eed.state. ak.us/standards/pdf/teacher.pdf; Assembly of Alaska Native Educators, *Guidelines for Preparing Culturally Responsive Teachers for Alaska's Schools* (Anchorage: Alaska Native Knowledge Network, 1999).

7. American Psychological Association, "APA Style.org." Available online from http://www.apastyle.org/.

8. Brown, *Requirements for the Literature Review; Searching ERIC and Locating Full Text.*

9. Marshall Welch, Kerrilee Brownell, and Susan M. Sheridan, "What's the Score and Game Plan on Teaming in Schools? A Review of the Literature on Team Teaching and School-based Problem-solving Teams," *Remedial and Special Education* 20 (1999): 36–49.

Teaching Materials

Requirements for the Literature Review
ED626 Classroom Research
Fall 2005

(To view this Breeze presentation online point your Internet browser to: http://breeze5.uas.alaska.edu/litreview.)

❖ This presentation will cover:
  • Guidelines and requirements for conducting and writing the literature review section of the Narrative Report.
  • Search procedures to follow.
  • Evaluating your findings.

❖ Requirements of the literature review
  • Systematic search procedures
  • Reproducible for your reader
  • 8–10 empirical studies or theoretical works
  • Research organized and synthesized in a well-thought-out manner
  • Written in American Psychological Association (APA) publication guidelines

❖ What is an empirical research study?
  • An article that describes research (this can be qualitative or quantitative) conducted by the author(s)
  • Must have a Methods and Results section
  • Author(s) refer to article as a "study" (read abstract)
  • Not an essay or descriptive article

❖ What is a theoretical work?
Theoretical works "provide an explanation, a predication, and a generalization about how the world operates. They may be posed by researchers at the broad philosophical level or at the more concrete substantive level." J.W. Creswell, *Qualitative Inquiry and Research Design: Choosing among Five Traditions* (Thousand Oaks, CA: Sage, 1998), 84.

Phenomenological self-studies produced by students in previous semesters were guided and informed by various (and numerous) theoretical frameworks, including: feminist theories, critical theories, constructivist theories, postmodern and poststructuralist theories, and other theoretical, philosophical, and/or theological perspectives.

❖ What is a descriptive article?
An article that does not include a Method or Results section nor claims a theoretical viewpoint

An article that simply describes a problem or situation. Read closely. For this assignment you are looking for articles with research or theory backing up claims.

Some articles will describe/review the literature and research on a topic. Though it may not have a Methods or Results section, the author may have had a system/method for retrieving the research he or she is reviewing, but not explicitly state his or her method for finding the research. You will need to evaluate the article and decide whether it is worthy of review (e.g., Is it an empirical study? Is it a theoretical work?). At the very least, you can scan it to track down research to include in your own literature review.

❖ Search procedures
  • You must search ERIC and at least one other database (at least 2 databases total).
  • "Full text only" may not be a search limitation.
  • Google (or scholar.google.com) may not be one of your 2 main databases, but you may use these (and other) search engines in addition to your 2 main databases.
  • You also may mine the bibliography of articles to track down research studies (i.e., you can conduct ancestral searches and use pearl-growing strategies). If you do choose to use these strategies, you must inform the reader of your literature review.

You must take thorough and excellent notes on each and every search you conduct so that:
  • Your searches are systematic.
  • Your searches can be reproduced by the reader of your literature review...BE EXPLICIT!

You must define and use criteria to sort out the studies you decide to keep from those you choose not to include in your literature review.

❖ Evaluate your findings...
Read and evaluate each promising article you found. Ask yourself:
  • Is it an empirical research study?
  • Is it a theoretical work?
  • Is it a descriptive article?

Does the article cite empirical research you could track down and use in your own literature review?

❖ Criteria
Does the article fit the criteria you set for the 8 to 10 articles you will choose to review?

Subject matter coverage: Does the article address your research question(s)?
Date range?
Peer-reviewed?
Rigorous research?
Theoretical model?
Other criteria?

❖ Ancestral searching, pearl growing, and mining the bibliography
Does the article you have found cite research studies you would like to track down?

If yes, take the references and refer to the presentation, "Searching ERIC and Locating Full Text," and follow the directions from there! (Look up the references in Journal Search.)

This strategy is called ancestral searching; this technique is also referred to as pearl growing, and mining the bibliography. Ancestral searching is ONE valid strategy to use when you conduct your searches, just be sure to keep copious notes so that you can reproduce how you tracked down your studies for the reader of your literature review.

❖ Draft of literature review
  • Use the Literature Review Template posted to the Resources section of the course Web site.
  • Read student work from previous semesters.
  • You will have multiple chances to pass in your literature review for editing and comments.

ED626 Classroom Research Assignment:
Translating Your Research Questions into Searchable Terms

One of the course objectives in ED626 is that you be able to translate your research questions into searchable terms and use these terms in your database searching. A good first step for you to take when conducting any database search is to brainstorm for **keywords**, **synonyms**, and **controlled vocabularies**. When you have these terms written and organized, you can use them (in varying combinations) as your database search terms.

Below is a grid to help you organize your searchable terms. By being prepared with the words, you formulate your "plan of attack" for locating essential research on your topic. And you start to understand and explore the nuances of your research questions as you conduct your review of the literature.

→ Research Question A (Example)

What are my beliefs about teaching database searching by audioconference?

→ Separate your question into conceptual categories and brainstorm keywords, synonyms, and variations in spelling for each:

belief effectiveness efficacy strategies	instruction teaching instructional practices best practices	computing searching database* information literacy technology literacy	distance education audioconference audio-conference

→ Are there other important concepts or limitations to place on your search strategy? Higher education, teacher education programs, collaborative teaching at a distance, distance teaching in Alaska

→ Is there a controlled vocabulary (also called subject terms, also called descriptors) in the database you will be searching? (e.g., ERIC Descriptors from the ERIC Thesaurus)

ERIC: TEACHER EFFECTIVENESS	ERIC: INSTRUCTIONAL EFFECTIVENESS; TEACHING STYLES; INSTRUCTIONAL IMPROVEMENT	ERIC: INFORMATION LITERACY; COMPUTER LITERACY; LIBRARY SKILLS; TECHNOLOGICAL LITERACY	ERIC: DISTANCE EDUCATION; AUDIOVISUAL INSTRUCTION; COMPUTER MEDIATED COMMUNICATION

→ Research Question #1			
→ Separate your question into conceptual categories and brainstorm keywords, synonyms, and variations in spelling for each:			
→ Are there other important concepts or limitations to place on your search strategy?			
→ Is there a controlled vocabulary (also called subject terms, also called descriptors) in the database you will be searching? (e.g. ERIC Descriptors from the ERIC Thesaurus)			
→ Research Question #2			
→ Separate your question into conceptual categories and brainstorm keywords, synonyms, and variations in spelling for each:			
→ Are there other important concepts or limitations to place on your search strategy?			
→ Is there a controlled vocabulary (also called subject terms, also called descriptors) in the database you will be searching? (e.g. ERIC Descriptors from the ERIC Thesaurus)			

"Search Procedures Notes" – example of note taking. It is very important to your grade and to the integrity of your Narrative Report to take detailed notes on your search process for conducting the literature review. The goal is to provide a systematic and reproducible approach to researching the literature on your topic. The only way to do this is to take the reader through the search procedures that you go through. You will conduct many searches and continue to refine your search terms and refine your selection criteria (see Literature Review Template) before you finally settle on the top 8–10 empirical studies / theoretical or scholarly works you will include in your literature review.

Search #	Database Searched	Keyword #1	Keyword #2	Keyword #3	Keyword #4	Other?	Controlled Vocabulary/ Descriptor?	Controlled Vocabulary/ Descriptor?	Limiters? Date? Full Text? Scholarly?	# Results?
Search #A (Example)	ERIC http:// eric.ed.gov	classroom	inclusion	Special	education				"Reports—Research" Pub. Type	321
Comments on Search #A	I went to the ERIC Web site and clicked on Advanced Search. I typed in Keywords (all fields) CLASSROOM AND INCLUSION AND SPECIAL EDUCATION. I Clicked on Publication Type "Reports—Research", and kept everything else set at the defaults. As 321 were too many results to sort through, I did a second search to narrow my results.									
Search #B (Example)	ERIC http:// eric.ed.gov	classroom	inclusion	Special	education				"Reports—Research" Pub.Type AND Dates 1998-2003	172
Comments on Search #B	The first couple pages of results found on this search were mainly case studies and reports of surveys and not on target to what I was looking for (which is really the effectiveness of inclusion, what does research say about how it works for all kids in the inclusive classroom). I decided to do another search to narrow down my results to a more manageable number, by adding some additional search terms closer to my research question.									
Search #C (Example)	ERIC http:// eric.ed.gov	classroom	effective*				Inclusive Schools		"Reports—Research" Pub. Type AND Dates 1998-2003	68
Comments on Search #C	Bingo! I did a search for the keywords "classroom" and "effective*" (using the * would find me anything using the term effective or effectiveness, etc.) and the descriptor "inclusive schools." When I found that ERIC uses the term "INCLUSIVE SCHOOLS" as the descriptor in this database to describe full integration, I used this term in my search as a Thesaurus Descriptor and this narrowed down the number of my results significantly. I also selected publication type "Reports-Research" and the dates 1998–2003. This brought me 68 results. Though not all of these findings are empirical research, this gave me a good way to start my search process in a manageable way.									

The purpose of this review of the literature was to systematically gather empirical studies and/or theoretical works about (state your topic): _____

_____

_____.

In order to systematically gather this data, I conducted searches in the following databases: *(List the databases you searched. These may include: ERIC, Professional Development Collection, Education Journals Plus Text, Academic Search Premier). "Other" might refer to a method of gathering research studies by reading the references list of an important study (a pearl-growing strategy). Your goal: to write this section about the process of gathering your data so that they are* **reproducible** *and* **systematic** *(i.e., tell the readers your system so they can re-trace your steps).*

Database 1 _____

Database 2 _____

Database 3 _____

Database/Other 4 _____

I used the following keywords to construct this advanced search in:

Database 1 _____

Database 2 _____

Database 3 _____

Database/Other 4 _____

Only articles that met the following criteria were included in this review of the literature:

1. The article examined (state your topic) _____

_____.

2. The article described an empirical study.
3. The article was published in a refereed journal.
4. The article was published before/after _____(date).
5. _____.
6. _____.

This advanced search of the above database(s) yielded (#) _____ articles that met the above-mentioned criteria. This review of the literature summarizes and synthesizes the data presented in these (#) _____ articles.

Chapter 13

Teaching Elementary Education Graduate Students Information Literacy Skills: Collaborating for Success

Collette D. Childers and Christine G. Renne

Introduction

Collaboration between librarians and graduate faculty members is often unique. Dr. Chris Renne, the instructor for a graduate-level education research course for practicing teachers at California State University, Fullerton, teamed with Collette Childers, the education librarian, to teach students the information literacy skills necessary to complete a literature review. All five of the Association of College and Research Libraries' (ACRL) Information Literacy Competency Standards for Higher Education were addressed throughout the semester either in class sessions or as part of the library instruction session.

Analysis of the Learning Situation

As part of Elementary Education 529, a required core master's-level course on learning theory, students must complete a literature review. In the graduate program, the students' abilities range widely. Some have recently completed their degree and credential work and are often familiar with research skills (especially electronic methods) and critical analysis of sources. Others are returning to college after several years away from the university or research environment with little background knowledge. Chris asked Collette to teach a two-and-a-half hour library instruction session for twelve students. This session introduced students to basic library resources, taught them to strategically use databases to find articles, and helped to reinforce the difference between qualitative and quantitative research. The course instructor then followed the library session with several in-class discussions reemphasizing the library presentation.

Writing a good literature review is not easy; however, not having the skills and critical thinking abilities necessary to complete the task makes the process even more difficult. To support the graduate students' learning, their basic skills and abilities were identified using a self-assessment survey drawn from the Information Literacy Competency Standards for Higher Education so instructor and librarian would be able to adapt their instruction to focus on the needs of the students.

During the second week of the course, students identified their research questions, refined their topics in class, and attended the library instruction session on library basics and databases, conducted by Collete.

Following the library session, Chris reviewed areas such as how to further refine a research question, read abstracts critically, formulate a literature review, and use American Psychological Association (APA) style[1] in writing. At the end of the course, students again rated their knowledge, skills, and abilities using the same survey. When the second survey was complete, the students compared their first and second survey responses and then wrote reflective statements about their learning.

Information Literacy Standards

(Note: A complete list of ACRL *Information Literacy Competency Standards for Higher Education* [Chicago: ACRL, 2000] appears as appendix A.)

The following Information Literacy Competency Standards for Higher Education were addressed, with Performance Indicators and Outcomes noted:[2]

Prior to library instruction session:

Standard One: "The information literate student determines the nature and extent of the information needed"; 1.1.a, 1.1.b, 1.1.d, and 1.1.e.

During library instruction session:

Standard One: "The information literate student determines the nature and extent of the information needed"; 1.2.a, 1.2.b, 1.2.c, and 1.3.a.

Standard Two: "The information literate student accesses needed information effectively and efficiently"; 2.1.d, 2.2.b, 2.2.c, 2.2.d, 2.2.e, 2.3.c, and 2.4.a.

Standard Three: "The information literate student evaluates information and its sources critically and incorporates selected information into his or her knowledge base and value system"; 3.2.a. and 3.4.e.

Postlibrary instruction session:

Reinforcement of outcomes taught in prior class sessions and library session, including:

Standard Two: "The information literate student accesses needed information effectively and efficiently"; 2.5.c.

Standard Three: "The information literate student evaluates information and its sources critically and incorporates selected information into his or her knowledge base and value system"; 3.3.a, 3.4.f, 3.5.a, and 3.7.a.

Standard Four: "The information literate student, individually or as a member of a group, uses information effectively to accomplish a specific purpose"; 4.2.b.

Standard Five: "The information literate student understands many of the economic, legal, and social issues surrounding the use of information and accesses and uses information ethically and legally"; 5.2.f. and 5.3.a.

Lesson Plan

During the library instruction session, the following lesson plan was used with the objective that by the end of the session, students could successfully find applicable articles using the ERIC database to complete the literature review assignment. Questions were taken throughout the class session.

1. Welcome and Introduction
2. "Nitty-Gritty" Basics:
   a. Library Home Page
   b. Library Catalog
   c. Interlibrary Loan
   d. Ask a Librarian
   e. Connect from Home
3. Using the ERIC database
   a. ERIC Thesaurus Guessing Game
   b. Using the ERIC Thesaurus
   c. ERIC Features
   d. Interface Features
   e. SFX
   f. ERIC In-class Exercise
4. Short demonstration of Academic Search Elite, Education Abstracts, PsycINFO databases
5. Discussion of qualitative versus quantitative and empirical research design
   a. ERIC Abstracts Guessing Game
6. Short discussion on how to determine key (seminal) authors
7. Self-directed student research time in article databases
8. Questions & Answers/Wrap-up

Description of the Instruction Session: What Actually Happened?
Course Instructor: Christine G. Renne

At the first class session of the semester, students were given a self-assessment to rate their knowledge, skills, and abilities with library and information resources. The survey included items from all five ACRL Information Literacy Competency Standards with a total of twenty-seven questions. The results were shared with the librarian before the session in order to familiarize her with the varying levels of student knowledge.

Designed by one of the authors in the spring of 2001, this survey focuses on key informational skills, library skills, and technological skills. The author shared the results of the first iteration with one of the librarians working with her department as part of the California State University Information Competency Initiative.[3] During the next two years, the survey evolved as library resources evolved and the questions were refined. In the spring of 2003 and in collaboration with the librarian, the ACRL standards became the framework for the survey. The same survey has been used for the past two years.

Prior to the library session, students identified their research topics. The course instructor wrote and provided a question checklist designed to help students develop a more insightful, focused research question. When the students had refined their questions, another tool was provided by way of a Venn diagram. The purpose was to disaggregate the components of the research questions into three subtopics that would familiarize them with the idea of key concepts and to help assist with identifying keywords in order to search the article databases. This was particularly designed to prepare the students to determine which descriptors in the ERIC Thesaurus would yield high-quality results.

Librarian: Collette D. Childers

Although the library instruction session was scheduled for two and a half hours, the actual amount of time I spent in lecture or demonstration was less than ninety minutes. A good portion of the session was self-directed as I wanted to make certain the students had an opportunity to apply the skills I taught them immediately to conduct actual research in ERIC and other databases. I also hoped to reinforce the brief introduction students had in class about how to determine the difference between qualitative and quantitative research and how to locate articles written by key authors.

Twelve students were present for instruction. After a short welcome and discussion of the session's learning goals, I taught some of what I consider to be "nitty-gritty basics" about the library itself (such as where the reference desk is located and how to get more help, how to use the library catalog, how to connect from home, etc.). Immediately following the basics, we began to use the ERIC database to find journal articles. This is where differences in student skill levels and knowledge bases began to appear. We played the ERIC Thesaurus Guessing Game by writing keywords next to official ERIC descriptors on a white board. I asked students to guess which term was the official ERIC descriptor. For example, students were invited to guess whether "classroom techniques" or "classroom methods" was the actual ERIC descriptor (the answer is "classroom techniques"). Thus, students learned that they may have to modify or replace terms with ERIC descriptors for a particular concept or topic in order to most effectively search the database. A student preempted my usual mention of interface features such as e-mailing citations or search history by asking many questions about how to bookmark records and how to save search history for later use. I answered her questions and promised to address any additional questions about database features when I later circulated through the classroom during the self-directed research time.

I gave the students about ten minutes to use the ERIC database and complete the ERIC exercise handout while I circulated through the room. Again, they would have time later in the session to return to ERIC. I then took a few minutes to demonstrate three other databases that are good for research in the field of education and learning theory: Academic Search Elite, Education Abstracts, and PsycINFO. I reminded students that the skills they learned in using ERIC apply to any other database, because although the database interface might look different or a different thesaurus might be available, the search methods remain the same.

Chris wanted the students to find empirical research for their literature reviews. Empirical research was covered in the first chapter of the students' textbooks and briefly discussed in class prior to the session. I used a handout to reinforce the differences between qualitative and quantitative research methods and also what is meant by empirical and primary research. The qualitative/quantitative handout is a generalized list that compares some of the major elements of each type of research to help students easily distinguish between the research designs. I mentioned that research in the field of education tends toward use of qualitative designs, although not exclusively, as some mixed-method research studies use elements of both designs. I also used a handout that described what is meant by empirical or primary research articles, noting that these articles are published in peer-reviewed journals and tend to have common elements such as a stated hypothesis, a methodology section, and a section reporting the results of the study.

Together, we read four ERIC abstracts that were cut-and-pasted into a handout and began the decision-making process about whether an article might be a primary research study or not. I mentioned a few keywords that they might look for in the article title and abstract such as "variables," "analysis," and "results." Most of the students were able to determine if the article was likely empirical by using the keywords method and by simple comprehension of the abstract, as well as using the title of the journal itself as a clue (e.g., *The Journal of Research in Special Education*). The students were cautioned to obtain the actual article itself before making any final determinations.

We then discussed how to find key authors using available library resources, highlighting cues such as the number of journals that the author published in, the quality of the journal the author published in, and how many times the author might have been cited as a reference. Students were told to examine the publication information in the front of the journal or use the Ulrich's Periodical Directory database to help determine whether a publication was scholarly/peer reviewed. I did not teach the students to use an online database to do a cited reference search, as simultaneous user access to this type of database is very limited on our campus due to budgetary restrictions. Instead, Chris encouraged the students to be observant about the number of times an author had been cited by simply noting the reference trail (key authors' work tends to be cited frequently by other researchers in the same field).

Finally, the students had more time to research their topics in ERIC, Academic Search Elite, Education Abstracts, or PsycINFO. Chris and I circulated throughout the room, answering questions and suggesting keywords. I had to guide several students through the use of the ERIC Thesaurus again. The number of steps necessary to actually search, click on a term, read the scope note, and then build a search using the term often confuses the students until they become more familiar with the search interface through repeated use. Chris was present throughout the session, and her presence helped the students to stay on task. I was also able to give more individual time to students than I would have been able to had I been on my own, even though the class size was small.

Course Instructor
For several weeks following the library session, I reiterated several of the items that Collette presented. For example, I presented multiple abstracts for the students to analyze for a variety of items such as the type of article (e.g., empirical research or suggested practices), where the item was published (e.g., journal or ERIC document), and the applicability of the article for a literature review. In addition to the information from the library session, I worked on how to construct an analytical literature review that would inform their individual case studies. Part of the teaching of the actual writing process included instruction on how to properly use APA style. The same self-assessment survey that was given the first night was then repeated at the end of the course to assess student growth.

Reflection on the Instruction Section: Lessons Learned
The collaboration between course instructor and librarian seemed to serve

the students' needs well. Students reported through survey ratings and their reflective statements that their confidence increased pertaining to the five standards. Also, the quality of their literature reviews and final projects as graded by the instructor demonstrated the students' abilities to use their information literacy skills appropriately.

The instruction session appears to have achieved one of its main objectives—to increase students' abilities to successfully complete a literature review as part of a case study based on substantial knowledge of information literacy components. Students were able to apply their knowledge immediately while using article databases to complete research for their literature review during the library session. The follow-up in-class sessions served to clarify and solidify the students' knowledge. As several students noted, the actuality of using information that was later integrated into the final course project helped to increase their information literacy skills.

Reflecting on the effectiveness of this approach, students who initially claim to have extensive library knowledge approach the library session with a bit of skepticism about its value. However, those students who feel well prepared prior to the library session consistently state afterward how beneficial the hands-on collaborative library experience is to their growing professional development as quality-minded educators, due to the additional insights and knowledge gained about accessing previously unknown library resources and targeting highly applicable research articles through effective use of the databases. For those students who were unfamiliar with basic library tools or how to locate pertinent research, the library session was exceedingly appropriate and useful. Because of the success indicated by the students through their survey responses and their coursework, we will not change our basic collaborative style. We do expect that in the future, content will be modified, added, or deleted as continually changing technological advances affect library information resources.

Notes

1. American Psychological Association. APA Style.org. Available online from http://www.apastyle.org/.

2. Association of College and Research Libraries, *Information Literacy Competency Standards for Higher Education* (Chicago: ACRL, 2000). Available online from http://www.ala.org/ala/acrl/acrlstandards/inform ationliteracycompetency.htm.

3. California State University, "Information Competence Initiative." Available online from http://www.calstate.edu/LS/infocomp.shtml.

Teaching Resources

EDEL 529

Identifying Your Research Areas

1. What is your question?

2. What are the key concepts or most important elements inherent in your question? For example, it may involve contexts (first grade, literature circles, etc.), subject areas, or specific content (geometry, decoding, Westward Movement, etc.), processes (using manipulatives, small group discussions, questioning, etc.), or resources (textbooks, dictionaries, maps, etc.). Start with specifics (e.g., first grade); later, if the specifics do not match ERIC descriptors or the search yields very few quality resources, you may need to broaden the concept (e.g., instead of "first grade" try "primary"). Create a Venn diagram using your key concepts.

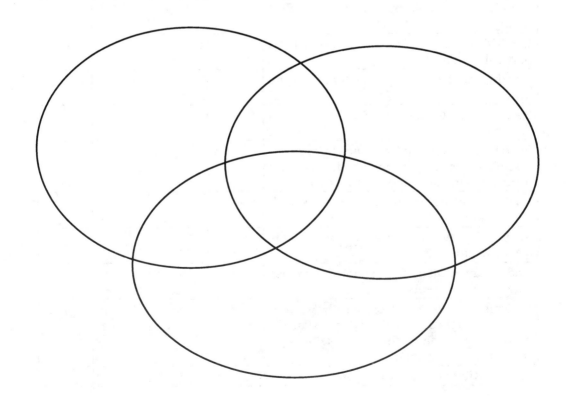

Name _____   **EDEL 529**
Spring 2005

Library Survey

	Don't know	Did it/ worked with it before	Can do on own	Able to teach others
Standard 1: Determines the nature and extent of the information needed				
Identify three key research areas based on a research question				
Know the number of appropriate resources required for the case study				
Standard 2: Accesses needed information effectively and efficiently				
Search for a book by subject in CSUF library				
Use ERIC to search for an article about a particular subject				
Identify and use ERIC descriptors to locate articles				
Locate the full text of some ERIC documents online				
Search for articles in journals from allied disciplines (e.g., psychology, health and medicine, language and linguistics, etc.)				
Able to print out pertinent abstracts with descriptors				
Identify the electronic journal subscriptions available at CSUF				
Understand what an SFX-enabled database is and how to use it				
Understand the layout of the library and locate reference materials, periodicals, curriculum materials, books, and government information				
Locate articles in the CSUF library				

Set up an account in ILLiad and use it to order books or articles from journals not owned by CSUF				
Use Link+ to order books not owned by CSUF				
Set up the proxy server to access CSUF licensed databases from home				
Identify different ways to get assistance with research-related problems (reference desk, e-reference, research consultations)				
Make copies from microfiche				
Understand what a PDF file is, how it differs from other online text formats, and how to read it using Acrobat Reader				
Standard 3: Evaluates information and its sources critically				
Identify empirical studies				
Read and evaluate (tell if it is an empirical study, for example) online abstracts				
Identify the difference between ERIC documents and ERIC journals and why the information is important				
Find articles by major authors for my topic				
Standard 4: Uses information effectively to accomplish a specific purpose				
Write a literature review				
Use a literature review to assist in designing a research project				
Effectively integrate a literature review into a case study final paper				
Standard 5: Uses information ethically and legally				
Recognize the elements of a citation for both paper and electronic sources.				
Use APA format accurately for references				

Chapter 14

Teaching International Students to Access and Use Library Resources

Justina O. Osa

Introduction

The Humphrey Fellowship Program at Penn State is a one-year nondegree program of combined academic and professional development opportunities for midcareer professionals from the designated areas of Africa, Asia, Latin America, the Caribbean, and the Middle East. Often fellows come from information cultures that are different from that of the United States. This usually poses a challenge to their taking full advantage of all the opportunities and resources Penn State, including the University Libraries, has to offer.

Analysis of the Learning Situation

Every year, the faculty who oversee the Humphrey Fellowship Program schedule a library tour and an orientation to library resources for each set of fellows. At the end of the tour and class sessions, I observed that the typical graduate student library orientation did not seem to meet the needs of the fellows. Rather than being a positive learning experience, the session left them confused and frustrated. In a discussion with the fellows affiliated with the College of Education, shortly after they had attended the regular library session, I realized that the library was not succeeding in helping this group to learn to use the library effectively and make the most of the opportunities offered by the University Libraries. They were grappling with one of the major problems international students have—the need to adjust to the information culture of the United States. I knew the library had to do something different to reach these users.

I took this on as a personal challenge. Consequently, I decided to come up with an instruction plan tailored specifically for them. The fellows were excited when we discussed this. I began to ponder how I would design and implement a special library orientation and instruction session that would be customized to the information needs of these Humphrey Fellows. I deduced from our discussion that they had not had time to adapt to the learning and library cultures of the university. The fellows were uncomfortable with the relatively unstructured learning culture in which students take a more active role in framing their own learning and with the library orientation that makes use of pedagogy unfamiliar to them.

Therefore, my task became deciding on a teaching methodology that successfully enables the fellows to acquire needed information knowledge and skills. I believed that the problem was not the level of difficulty of materials presented during the session but, instead, represented other variables, such as presentation of materials and cross-cultural communication differences. Given the fact that most librarians provide excellent library sessions, this chapter does not focus on the usual activities of Penn State library instruction sessions. Rather, it focuses on what was done differently to adequately meet the needs of these international fellows.

The instruction session was held in the instruction laboratory on the Education and Behavioral Sciences Library floor. This laboratory has: (1) one instructor podium equipped with an instructor computer, (2) eight patron workstations, and (3) a data projector.

Information Literacy Standards
(Note: A complete list of ACRL *Information Literacy Competency Standards for Higher Education* [Chicago: ACRL, 2000] appears as appendix A.)

The following Information Literacy Competency Standards for Higher Education were addressed:

Standard One: "The Information literate student determines the nature and extent of the information needed;"

Standard Two: "The information literate student accesses needed information effectively and efficiently;"

Standard Three: "The information literate student evaluates information and its sources critically and incorporates selected information into his or her knowledge base and value system;"

Standard Four: "The information literate student, individually or as a member of a group, uses information effectively to accomplish a specific purpose;" and

Standard Five: "The information literate student understands many of the economic, legal, and issues surrounding the use of information and accesses and uses information ethically and legally."[1]

Given the nature of the instruction session, I was very conscious of the need to present the session using instructional methodology that would meet different learning styles and provide an opportunity for individual practice and feedback. Also, because these students were new to the U.S. information culture, I knew I had to raise their awareness and understanding of copyright laws of the United States.

Lesson Plan
Goal
At the end of the instruction session all Humphrey Fellows will be ushered into previously unfamiliar library and information searching, location, and use experiences.

Objectives
At the end of the instruction session:

1. All Humphrey Fellows will be more familiar with the online library layout.

2. All Humphrey Fellows will be able to identify main concepts in their search.

3. All Humphrey Fellows will be able to select appropriate search terms.

4. All Humphrey Fellows will be able to use the Boolean operators/ connectors.

5. All Humphrey Fellows will be able to locate, evaluate, and retrieve books, articles, and sources for the information they need from the Penn State University Libraries online catalog (the CAT) and other relevant online databases.

6. All Humphrey Fellows will have basic knowledge of the U.S. information culture.

Description of the Instruction Session: What Actually Happened?
Two days before class, I sent an e-mail message to the fellows to remind them of the session, to inform them of the location of the laboratory, and to let them know that I would meet them at the East Entrance. I prepared the instruction laboratory for class, laid out the handouts in order, and turned on the instructor's workstation. I did not turn on the student workstations because I wanted to make sure that each of them knew how to switch on the computer, log in, and go to the library Web page. Then I went downstairs to the East Entrance to escort them to Paterno fifth floor because I did not want them to be stressed out thinking they might not find the right laboratory.

Five fellows attended the instruction session. I told them I was delighted to work with them. I informed them of my awareness of the stress an international student could experience in a foreign country, operating in an unfamiliar environment and educational system. I let them know that almost all students, American students inclusive, are overwhelmed by the size of the Penn State University Libraries. Therefore, they should not be embarrassed if they found the complexity of the University Libraries intimidating. Then I introduced the major goal of the session and reassured them that at the end of the session they would be more comfortable using the library effectively because we would have covered relevant computer literacy, information literacy, information technology, and library skills. That statement caught their attention and I could tell that they would be actively listening to what I shared.

I started off informing them that most libraries in the United States operate with an open-stack system. I gave them this information because I know that there are still libraries in other countries that use the closed-stack system. We then discussed some basic library terms I knew we would find useful during the session and they might need to know as they use the library.

I switched on the projector and requested that everyone start their workstations and log on. I wanted to make sure that they were familiar with our sequence; therefore, I logged onto the instructor's workstation and asked that they replicate what they saw me doing as I started my computer and logged in to the library's Web page. Because the projector was on, they were able to see exactly how I was logging in. I audibly said what I was doing, thereby enhancing the effectiveness of the instruction. I went round to personally make sure that each had successfully logged in. I reminded them that the computers in the libraries were configured to go straight to the library Web page. We then went over the log-on sequence from off-campus. I asked if they knew how to get to the library's Web page from their apartments. They all knew the URL for Penn State, so I brought up Penn State's Web page on the instructor computer and showed them where the libraries' link is and clicked on it. On the libraries' page, I showed them links to pages I believed they would find useful.

Next, I informed them that one of the crucial skills to develop is choosing correct search terms. I spent quite a while on this segment of the instruction session because I knew that the fellows came from countries that are linguistically different from the U.S. One fellow asked that we search for a book on "motivation" in the catalog. This search resulted in 2,338 hits. As none of us desired to browse through the 2,338 hits to locate the ones that would be useful, we discussed limiting our search terms to focus results.

We next discussed the need for conceptualizing search terms. I told them they have to first determine the nature and extent of the information they need to complete their research before they start to perform any search. I explained the need to conceptualize searches by breaking research questions into component parts. One of them suggested we research the topic, How does motivation affect academic achievement in schools? We started breaking the topic into concepts and ended up with three main concepts: motivation, academic achievement, and schools. Then we discussed the need for synonyms.

We continued by discussing Boolean operators. I used the usual three circles to explain the connectors and how each functions in searching. I entered each of the three concepts in three columns and entered the synonyms they generated under each of the concepts. The table below reflects our results.

We then discussed the details of the Search Results page. I showed them vital pieces of information such as the number of books found, item availability, material type, etc. We also discussed important information on the screen such as the information they would need to cite the item. I demonstrated the process of e-mailing a record to myself. I gave them ten minutes to practice the search skills we covered so far. I told them to write down three call numbers for at least three items and to let me know if they needed assistance. I moved around the laboratory offering one-on-one assistance. At the end of the ten-minute period, I observed that they were engrossed in their searches, so I extended the hands-on time by five minutes.

We then proceeded to search for journal articles. I distributed a Types of Periodicals and Journals[2] handout and showed them how to access the information online. I showed them the Libraries' "Try These First" and "Find Articles by Subject" links. When we clicked on Education on the "Find Articles by Subject" page, we found a list of suggested education-related databases. I recommended that they start their search for journal articles from these two links because librarians have carefully created these links and the information found in them. Then we went on to the list of subscription databases that are accessible through Penn State University Libraries.

Motivation	AND	Academic Achievement	AND	Schools
Student motivation **OR**	AND	Success **OR**	AND	High schools **OR**
Learning motivation **OR**	AND	School achievement **OR**	AND	Middle schools **OR**
Academic motivation **OR**	AND	High achievement **OR**	AND	Elementary schools **OR**

Motivation in education	AND	Educational achievement **OR**	AND	Open-air schools **OR**
	AND	Scholastic achievement **OR**	AND	Language schools **OR**
	AND	Scholastic success **OR**	AND	Single-sex schools **OR**
	AND	Student success	AND	Evening schools **OR**
			AND	Private schools **OR**
			AND	Trade schools

I then explained to them that the search strategies and skills we used searching in the libraries' catalog were transferable to searching in the article databases. We discussed the desirability of using the thesaurus attached to a database whenever one is available because of the use of controlled vocabulary; and I explained what controlled vocabulary is. We practiced generating search terms using the Thesaurus in ERIC.

I discussed criteria for evaluating resources. Then we performed some advanced searches as a group.[3] I showed them how to read the result details screen and showed them the full-text availability icon. For non-full-text articles, I showed them how to search for the journal titles in the CAT and how to identify useful information such as article author, article title, volume, number, issue, and pagination that would enable them to access the specific article from either a print or an online journal.

I gave them ten minutes to practice and search for articles they could use for their research. I then suggested that they each choose a different database to perform searches. During all the time they were searching the databases, I moved around the instruction laboratory, volunteered needed assistance, answered questions, and clarified any confusing feature or aspect of the search, database, or article retrieval.

After spending time using the search techniques we discussed, I went over some relevant library policies and procedures, emphasizing policies that may be different in the United States than in their own countries.

I felt it was important to present an overview of the United States' information culture, including laws regarding copyright, licensing, intellectual property, and integrity. I gave them a fairly detailed review of the basics of the copyright system and how it impacts the use of information. I also reviewed plagiarism-related issues, fair use, Penn State Academic Integrity Policy, and Penn State file-sharing policy. Then I showed them the site for "Citing Your Sources."[4]

At the end of our hands-on exercise, we moved to the stacks and periodical areas to retrieve items and journal articles for which they had recorded call numbers and citations. We went as a group to the copying machine area and I showed them how to make copies.

At the end of the session, they all expressed their appreciation for the personalized instruction. I distributed the evaluation form and asked for a volunteer to gather and submit the completed forms to me. Before they left, I distributed my business card, reminding them that they had no reason to suffer in silence because they had my contact information and that I would be delighted to work with them individually or as a group. I was satisfied with the happy and relieved expressions on their faces.

Reflection on the Session: Including Lessons Learned

I learned a lot from working with the Humphrey Fellows. I became more aware of the fact that much of what occurs during instruction involves communication, which is a product of culture. I found that when we were generating search terms, some of the terms they came up with were unique to their experience and culture. When we were using the Thesaurus in the ERIC database, they had a lot of questions as to the meaning of some of the descriptors. The scope notes were very helpful in explaining the meaning of descriptors and showing the context in which each descriptor is used. Using the Thesaurus also helped them become aware of terms that were either unfamiliar to them given their linguistic background or would not have come to their memory during the search exercise.

Another important lesson I was reminded of was how to deal with language barriers that often exist among people who have a different accent or inadequate mastery of a language. I had to pay more conscious attention to the communication process. I reminded myself of some of the information I knew about communicating with people from other cultures, which include speaking clearly, speaking slowly, not using slang, giving specific feedback, establishing a supportive environment, and checking often for understanding.

While I was thinking of the location for the session I planned for the Humphrey Fellows, I was conscious of the need to work in a room with a co-browsing facility. I knew that the session would be more effective and that the fellows would learn better and faster if they could not only hear what I was saying, but also if they could see what I was doing. The projection in the instruction laboratory was very helpful in this regard. Some of the behaviors I practiced while working with the Humphrey Fellows included:

1. Telling them what I was going to do and what I was doing; I audibly worked my way through the searches.

2. Stopping the session at various points and summarizing the session thus far.

3. Providing oral summaries using straightforward grammar and vocabulary.

4. Scanning their faces to know when any of the fellows needed extra directions, help, or support.

5. Giving specific feedback.

6. Encouraging responses and questions.

Often one forgets the crucial role of nonverbal communication in human interaction and communication. I made conscious efforts to remember to control my body language. I reminded myself that my good intentions and efforts to help the Humphrey Fellows could be greatly hampered by any negative nonverbal clues I may send unintentionally. I also reminded myself that nonverbal body language is culture based and does not often have universal interpretation. As an example, raising eyebrows means different things in different cultures. Around the world this simple gesture could mean surprise, skepticism, hello, or no.[5]

When I introduced the e-mail function on the search screen to the Humphrey Fellows, I did not just give them the information. I actually demonstrated how to e-mail records by e-mailing a record to my inbox giving clear verbal directions as we went from step to step. For example, I began by saying "Click on the Mark icon for as many records or titles you need," and so forth. I went into such detail because I knew that at least some of them, if not all of them, had not had previous experience completing such a transaction. The completed evaluation forms the Humphrey Fellows submitted to me confirmed the success of the session. They all indicated that the opportunity to see what I was doing greatly enhanced their learning. The strategy of giving them time (ten to fifteen minutes) to have hands-on practice using search skills covered also was effective. They also stated that the positive, nonthreatening, nonjudgmental, nurturing, warm, and friendly climate I established and maintained throughout the instruction session encouraged them to ask questions. They knew it was safe to risk asking me to repeat or clarify some search skills they did not understand straight away.

The strategy the Humphrey Fellows seemed to understand best was the visual representation of constructing effective search strategies. In my future instruction sessions I will remember to use a chart because it facilitates student learning. Also, I noticed that when I told the fellows that they could search for books and journal articles on their individual research topics, they became engrossed in searching for relevant sources during in-class search session.

One of the fellows indicated that she would have been more comfortable at the initial phase of the instruction session if she were able to work with another fellow. I agreed with her comment because there is often safety in numbers. Therefore, in the future, I will give fellows or other international patrons the option of working in pairs whenever I think such a strategy is appropriate. The session was a huge success and this is what I now do every year to help Humphrey Fellows to take advantage of the opportunities and resources available at Penn State.

Notes

1. Association of College and Research Libraries, *Information Literacy Competency Standards for Higher Education* (Chicago: ACRL, 2000). Available online from http://www.ala.org/ala/acrl/acrlstandards/inform ationliteracycompetency.htm.

2. Pennsylvania State University Libraries, "Types of Periodicals and Journals," Pennsylvania State University, in *Information Literacy & You*. Available online from http://www.libraries.psu.edu/instruction/infolit/ andyou/mod3/types.htm.

3. Pennsylvania State University Libraries, "How to Evaluate Information on the Web," Pennsylvania State University, in *Information Literacy & You*. Available online from http://www.libraries.psu.edu/ instruction/infolit/andyou/mod6/eval.htm.

4. Pennsylvania State University Libraries, "Citing Your Sources," Pennsylvania State University. in *Information Literacy & You*. Available online from http://www.libraries.psu.edu/instruction/infolit/andyou/ mod8/mod8main.htm.

5. Chuck Payne, "I Think I Understand: Tips and Strategies for Successful Cross-cultural Communication," Medicine Hat College. Available online from http://www2.mhc.ab.ca/users/cpayne/portfolio/ cultcomm/understand.htm.

Chapter 15

Digital Resources for Distance Students in a Library Science and Literacy Program

Melissa Cast and Rebecca Pasco

Introduction

For citizens living in Nebraska and the Midwest, there has been limited physical access to colleges and universities offering coursework and degrees in Library and Information Science. As a result, local and regional libraries and information agencies have found it difficult to generate strong pools of credentialed and highly qualified candidates for vacancies and new positions. To address this need, all core library science and some literacy courses offered by the University of Nebraska at Omaha (UNO) were converted into distance-sensitive instructional formats. As a result of this move to distance education, UNO now supports robust undergraduate and graduate programs that generate a steady stream of good candidates for school, public, academic, and special libraries. UNO also hosts a very successful cooperative master of arts in library science degree program with the University of Missouri. The library science education programs attract students from all regions of Nebraska, as well as students from the contiguous states of South Dakota, Wyoming, Colorado, Kansas, Missouri, and Iowa.

Serving library science and literacy students, many of whom live several hours from their home campus, requires information professionals to be creative in the delivery of course content, instruction, and library and information services. The library science and literacy students must quickly develop a wide array of information literacy skills to enable them to identify, locate, and use both digital and print resources to successfully complete course activities and to guarantee success in their professional future. Close collaboration between the faculty librarian and course faculty member is the key to developing meaningful and relevant information literacy instruction.

Analysis of Learning Situation

Ensuring that all coursework within these distance education programs meets high standards of content, rigor, and student engagement requires a great deal of time and energy on the part of both regular and adjunct faculty in terms of instructional pedagogy and course design. In addition to the specific content and skill development identified for each course, meaningful and relevant information literacy instruction is included as a key component. The information literacy instruction in each course has proved to increase the capacity of library science and literature students to successfully complete course activities and assignments. Information literacy instruction is especially important to distance students who are unable to come to the library but need to be able to locate, access, evaluate, and make effective use of online information resources. Faculty working in distance education environments must collaborate closely with faculty librarians to ensure that information literacy instruction directly ties to course objectives and adequately supports students' educational pursuits, regardless of the physical location of the students.

Literature courses are part of the core coursework in the undergraduate and graduate library science and literacy programs at UNO. Students in literature courses are required to use a variety of print and electronic information resources, to find booklists appropriate to age groups or topics, to locate book reviews about specific texts, to gather information about authors and publishers, and to make use of literature resources provided by national organizations (i.e., American Association of School Librarians, Young Adult Library Services Association, and the International Reading Association). Providing information resources and information literacy instruction that support the work of these library science and literacy students (who sometimes live as far as three hundred miles away from their home campus) is crucial to the students' and the program's success. To ensure students are confident in their use of the diverse array of information resources available to them, time is dedicated at the beginning of each literature course for information literacy instruction.

Distance education courses in UNO's library science program and literacy courses are offered in a Web-assisted, hybrid format of monthly, face-to-face sessions combined with online instruction and activities during the weeks between the on-campus meetings. Blackboard, a Web-based course management software, is used by both the faculty member and faculty librarian to provide and enhance access to information resources needed by students for course assignments. Through Blackboard, students are provided with course links by which they can:

• Communicate directly with the faculty member and faculty librarian in an e-mail, a discussion board, or a chat session

• Access and use electronic databases

• Access and use electronic reserves for print resources that have been digitized for Web storage and use

• Make effective use of the campus library's catalog to identify print materials that students may request via interlibrary loan through their local public, academic, or school library

This "distance-sensitive" instructional approach to information literacy instruction requires the program faculty member and faculty librarian to work closely and think creatively to ensure that students:

• Have access to the same information resources, regardless of geographic location, to ensure equity in the instructional process

• Have access to resources that are sensitive to the varying levels of students' technical literacy

• Build professional and supportive relationships with both the faculty member and the faculty librarian

Information Literacy Standards

(Note: A complete list of ACRL *Information Literacy Competency Standards for Higher Education* [Chicago: ACRL, 2000] appears as appendix A.)

The following Information Literacy Competency Standards for Higher Education were addressed, with Performance Indicators and Outcomes noted:

Standard One: "The information literate student determines the nature and extent of the information needed"; 1.1.e, 1.2.a, 1.2.c, 1.2.d, 1.3.a, and 1.4.b.

Standard Two: "The information literate student accesses needed information effectively and efficiently"; 2.1.b, 2.1.c, 2.2.b, 2.2.c, 2.3.a, and 2.3.c.

Standard Three: "The information literate student evaluates information and its sources critically and incorporates selected information into his or her knowledge base and value system"; 3.1.a, 3.2.a, 3.2.d, 3.4.e, and 3.6.a.

Standard Five: "The information literate student understands many of the economic, legal, and social issues surrounding the use of information and accesses and uses information ethically and legally"; 5.1.b. [1]

Lesson Plan
Introduction

1. Introduce the faculty librarian and provide contact information for future assistance.

2. Discuss in-depth the information needs of the immediate assignment and the students' future professional information needs as

school librarians, young adult librarians, and teachers in evaluating and selecting young adult literature. Such information needs include:

- Book reviews
- Author biographical information
- Subject/genres lists
- Book award information

3. Guide students to online Web page, "Young Adult Literature," designed specifically for the class through the Library's Research Wizard.[2]

4. Distribute the Young Adult Literature Information Sources Matrix, which identifies the type of information available in each source. This serves as both a pathfinder and a key to the types of information available in the online resources.

To help students critically analyze information resources, students will:

1. Use university and local public library catalog limiters to narrow search to young adult literature

2. Review book record and use the information available to identify relevant book characteristics for indications of quality and potential interest to young adult readers:

- Examine subject headings and summaries to identify topics potentially of interest to young adult readers and aspects of the book that illustrate how it may be an educational, social, or cultural tool
- Examine subject headings to identify whether the book is an award winner or an honor book
- Explore author tracings to understand the author's publishing history, areas of writing interests (age level, genres, etc.), and possibility of additional awards

To help students identify and evaluate relevant resources, students will:

1. Understand the Nebraska Library Commission's digital resource collection and its availability to state libraries

2. Review book industry vendor resources and issues involved with using them

3. Use search interfaces to narrow results to fit selection criteria

4. Review item records and use the information available to identify relevant book characteristics for indications of quality and potential interest to young adult readers:

- Examine subject headings, summaries, and book reviews to identify topics of potential interest to young adult readers and aspects of the book that illustrate how the book may be an educational, social, or cultural tool

- Examine record to identify whether the book is an award winner or an honor book
- Explore author tracings to understand the author's publishing history, areas of writing interests (age level, genres, etc.) and possibility of additional awards

5. Compare reviews from different professional book review sources for relevant content:
- Which reviews relate it to other young adult titles?
- Which reviews offer thoughts as to a specific audience for the book (e.g., reluctant readers)?
- Which reviews discuss how the work may be an educational, social, or cultural tool?

To introduce students to the value and differences of potential resources, students will:

1. Review annual notable lists such as Young Adult Choices from International Reading Association[3] and Young Adult Library Services Association's Best Books for Young Adults[4]

2. Review online teen discussions of young adult literature on sites such as SmartGirl[5] and reads4teens.org[6]

3. Review online sources for author information including Wilson Biographies, funded by the Nebraska Library Commission for all state citizens, and the Educational Paperback Association's Top 100 Authors[7]

4. Discuss evaluating and verifying author information from sites indexed by search engines

Synthesis
To review the main points of the lesson, the faculty will:
1. Reemphasize contact information for future assistance
2. Reiterate usefulness of the identified digital resources

Description of the Instruction Session: What Actually Happened?

It is important to establish the faculty librarian as an individual resource. The library science and literacy students are a mix of undergraduate and graduate students with different information literacy needs. Information literacy instruction moves from a class focus to an individual focus as the faculty librarian works with students at their particular levels and toward their information needs. The faculty librarian conducts this instruction mostly via e-mail but also may take advantage of telephone and on-campus consultations.

The critical part of the actual on-campus lesson seems to be the initial introduction period and the discussion of information needs. If the students clearly understand what information they need and how it relates to their situation, the rest of the instruction falls into place. Armed with that foundation, students are more attentive, ask better questions, and are more directed in how they use their free time. The individual instruction interactions that occur later also benefit from having a strong introductory foundation. The individual sessions then can be more focused and can build on the initial information literacy concepts.

One challenge to overcome is a disconnect that sometimes occurs between a professional journal review accessed through an intermediary source such as Patron Books in Print and the actual full journal itself. Students often do not realize that these reviews come from professional sources that have a dedication to distribute high-quality and relevant reviews for librarians and educators. As a result, it is important to spend a significant amount of time actually looking at the reviews and asking the questions listed above to get the students to be selective in their choice of an information source.

Class time is always an issue for the face-to-face sessions, which is why a matrix was created to link information types with information sources. If time is short, one information resource can be used as an example with the matrix leading students to additional resources for the information need.

To design directed and meaningful information literacy instruction, close collaboration has to occur between faculty member and faculty librarian. Mutual understanding of the overall program goals and objectives lead to focused information literacy instruction that supports student learning and the students' growth as professionals.

Reflection on the Instruction Session: Lessons Learned
One Digital Tool at a Time
The content faculty member must first ensure that students are skilled at negotiating the online courseware before introducing them to online information resources in an information literacy instruction session. If students struggle to use the online courseware to easily locate the information resources, they will not use the resources provided and will turn to other resources that may or may not supply information that meets the criteria identified for the assignment. At UNO, the faculty member spends time teaching students to effectively use Blackboard (i.e., location and use of External Links and Course Documents to find resources identified by the faculty member) before adding the next layer of information literacy instruction.

Communicate Clearly and Accurately

Faculty and librarians slip into jargon about resources, tools, procedures, and content, often without intending to do so. Jargon is exclusive, intimidating, and reduces the clarity of instruction. Although on-campus students might have a physical context or information professionals close at hand to assist them, distance students are often "text dependent" in garnering information online and are particularly vulnerable to jargon with no one near to explain the use of a term, acronym, or phrase. Using this lesson plan as an example, students will need to know what is meant by "catalog limiters" or "author tracings." They need to be shown what librarians mean when they say a "book has a record." Who is ALA, OCLC, or YALSA? Clarity and context in personal, and especially in online environments, are critical to the development of a depth of understanding that translates into patron confidence and more sophisticated use of the resources.

Think Outside One's Own Box

Make effective use of WorldCat or other resources to show distance students how to identify print and electronic resources in library and information centers in their own geographic region. Students in literature courses at UNO don't need to use only print and electronic resources provided by UNO. Although they can access many digital resources remotely by logging into the library, faculty and librarians should encourage students to make good use of their area libraries and local information professionals to support learning long after the students are done with the course or their program.

Professional Demeanor

Introducing students to the slippery terrain of digital resources requires determination, repetition, and great patience. Faculty and librarians are well advised to remember that tone of voice, enthusiasm, and expertise are as evident online to distance students as they are when working in person with students on campus.

Assessment, Assessment, Assessment

Faculty and faculty librarians need to measure if and how our instruction and tools support student learning. Timely and systematic feedback opportunities enable student voice and student agency. The faculty librarian asks for feedback at the end of each instructional session. The faculty member revisits and reteaches the information during the semester, as needed, to ensure the students are making effective use of resources for course activities. As a result of positive and continual feedback from UNO distance students on the importance of information literacy instruction to their ability to complete course assignments successfully, the faculty member has increased the amount of time given to information literacy instruction in nearly all library science and literacy courses.

Summary

Information literacy initiatives at UNO allow library science and literature students to identify and navigate information resources that enable them to better direct their own work sessions, to customize their pursuits with particular resources that match their own learning styles, and to do so in a timely and efficient manner.

Notes

1. Association of College and Research Libraries, *Information Literacy Competency Standards for Higher Education* (Chicago: ACRL, 2000). Available online from http://www.ala.org/ala/acrl/acrlstandards/inform ationliteracycompetency.htm.

2. The UNO Research Wizard is a customizable portal of digital resources identified and maintained by faculty librarians. University of Nebraska at Omaha Library. "Young Adult Literature." Available online from http://revelation.unomaha.edu:6060/rw2/public/index.php?ctl=re sult&did=39&cid=178&kid=497&dcid=776.

3. International Reading Association, "Choices Booklists: Young Adult Choices." Available online from http://www.reading.org/resources/tools/ choices_young_adults.html.

4. American Library Association, Young Adult Library Services Association, "Best Books for Young Adults." Vilable online from http:// www.ala.org/ala/yalsa/booklistsawards/bestbooksya/bestbooksyoung. htm.

5. "SmartGirl." smartgirl.com.

6. Carmel Clay Public Library, "reads4teens.org: Great Reads for Teens." reads4teens.org.

7. Educational Paperback Association, "EPA's Top 100 Authors." Available online from http://www.edupaperback.org/top100.cfm?page=2.

Teaching Resources

Young Adult Literature
Information Sources Matrix

RESOURCE	BIOS	BOOK REVIEWS	POPULARITY	AWARDS	SUBJECT ACCESS	SEARCH FEATURES
Best Books for Young Teen ReadersLibrary Reference Z1037 .B55 2000		✽			✽	
Books in Print, http://www.nlc.state.ne.us/nebraskaccess/	✽	✽		✽	✽	Use Children's Room search features
Children's Literature Review Library Reference PN1009.A1.C45	✽	✽				Use the cumulative index in the last vol.
Guys Read, http://www.guysread.com/index.html			✽			
Database of Award Winning Children's Literature, http://dawcl.com/				✽	✽	Sophisticated search interface.
Popular Paperbacks for Young Adults, http://www.ala.org/yalsa/booklists/poppaper			✽		✽	Arranged by year and then genre.
Publishers Weekly—Children's Fiction, http://publishersweekly.reviewsnews.com/index.asp?layout=bestsellersMain			✽			Limited searching. Arranged by date.
Reading Rants: Out of the Ordinary Teen Book Lists, http://tln.lib.mi.us/~amutch/jen/		✽			✽	None. Lists are arranged by subject.
reads4teens.org, http://www.reads4teens.org/		✽ by teens	✽		✽	Search by title or broad subject.
SmartGirl Reviews, http://www.smartgirl.org/reviews/index.html		✽ by teens	✽			

						Notes
Something about the Author (130 volumes) Reference PN451.S6	●	●		●		Use the cumulative index in the last vol.
Teen Reads, http://www.teenreads.com/	●	● by teens	●	●		Search using book title. Limited subject searching.
Titlewave, http://www.titlewave.com/login/		●		●	●	Use "Collection Development Search" for subject searching.
White Ravens, http://www.icdlbooks.org:8080/servlet/edu.umd.cs.wira.WhiteRavens			●		●	Keyword
Yahoo! Authors>Young Adult	●					Arranged alphabetically
Young Adults' Choices—Journal of Adolescent & Adult Literacy, http://www.reading.org/resources/tools/choices_young_adults.html		●	●			None. Arranged by year.
Young Adult Library Services Association, http://www.ala.org/yalsa/booklists/index.html				●		Limited

Chapter 16

They Click! Information Literacy and Undergraduates in an Introduction to Management Class

Jennifer S. A. Leigh, Cynthia Gibbon, and Janelle Wertzberger

Introduction

It's a perfect match. Academic librarians often have a "curriculum without a classroom" and management educators often have the "bodies" in need of information literacy instruction. At Gettysburg College, we put these two interests together and developed an evolving partnership between management professor, Jennifer Leigh, and reference and instruction librarians, Cynthia Gibbon and Janelle Wertzberger. Two years ago, Jennifer first met with reference and instruction librarians to address her concern about the quality of student research. What began as an informal conversation has evolved into an in-depth information literacy experience for the students in the introductory management course, Organizations and Society (MGT 111), and a collaborative teaching effort for librarians with Jennifer. In a typical semester at Gettysburg College, four sections of MGT 111 are taught, enrolling about thirty students each. Most students are sophomore- and junior-level management majors. In this ongoing, interdisciplinary effort, we aspire to introduce students to various information literacy skills and continue to meet several times a semester to reflect upon how we can improve students' learning experience.

Analysis of the Learning Situation

Undergraduates in the introductory management course (MGT 111) at Gettysburg College are introduced to a range of discipline-specific information literacy skills and issues. They meet with academic librarians twice per semester in a classroom setting. In the first library session, students learn research techniques that support a specific assignment. In the second session, they are introduced to social and ethical issues that pertain to the scholarly publishing industry.

In the fall 2005 semester, during our most recent iteration of the MGT 111 information literacy partnership, students interacted with information literacy content online, in their class, and in the library instruction classroom. In collaboration, we produced an assignment design that prompts the first library instruction session. Before this first "skills-based" session, students took a twenty-question pretest via Blackboard (a proprietary, Web-based course information system). During the first library session, student comprehension was measured with TurningPoint, a computer-based system that allows students to participate in class by submitting responses to interactive questions using handheld devices, a.k.a. "clickers."[1] After all the responses are collected, TurningPoint software dynamically compiles class statistics, so the instructor can immediately gauge how well the class understands the content, providing an opportunity to review and remediate. In our case, the interactive questions tested student comprehension of newly presented content. After the first session, students took a posttest. The second library session met in the MGT 111 classroom to synthesize the social and ethical issues of information literacy with theory from their coursework.

Information Literacy Standards

(Note: A complete list of ACRL *Information Literacy Competency Standards for Higher Education* [Chicago: ACRL, 2000] appears as appendix A.)

In order to customize our instruction plan by discipline, we used the Information Competency Skills for Business Students, created by the Business Reference and Services Section (BRASS) of the Reference and User Services Association of the American Library Association.[2] The BRASS Standards are comparable to ACRL's Information Literacy Competency Standards,[3] though the language is tweaked to address the business and management discipline. For example, the performance Indicator under Standard One of the BRASS standards is called Identifying Resources, whereas the correlating ACRL Standard's Performance Indicator (1.2) states: "The information literate student identifies a variety of types and formats of potential sources for information."[4] The BRASS standard's performance indicator uses brevity to express the same value. Under the BRASS standards, we specified the outcome: "Understands that business periodical literature can be of a scholarly, popular, or professional nature."[5] The ACRL standards express the same outcome (1.2.d) as: "Identifies the purpose and audience of potential resources (e.g., popular vs. scholarly, current vs. historical)."[6]

Lesson Plan
The Assignment

Reinforcing and utilizing the above information literacy standards are key elements of assignment design. To successfully complete the assignment, students were required to use "information effectively to accomplish a specific purpose"[7] (Standard Four). They practiced effective and efficient information retrieval (Standard Two) while simultaneously refining their topic by determining what type of information was needed (Standard One). In class, groups were asked to reflect upon their search process, determine areas for improvement, and name their next steps for their research. Review

TABLE 1. BRASS Information Literacy Standards	

Standard 1	*The information literate business student determines the nature and extent of the information needed.*
	   Planning and developing a strategy
	      Identifies key concepts and business terms in searching which describe the business problem in a case analysis or other type of assignment
	   Identifying resources
	      Understands that business periodical literature can be of a scholarly, popular, or professional nature.

Standard 2	*The information literate business student accesses needed information effectively and efficiently.*
	   (No Performance Indicator listed)
	      Understands how to effectively develop and utilize keywords and synonyms for business concepts in a search strategy
	      Checks and reexamines the search terms for errors and/or finds better terms when search does not yield desired results.

Standard 3	*The information literate business student evaluates information and its sources critically and incorporates selected information into his or her knowledge base and value system.*
	   (No Performance Indicator listed)
	      Understands the nature of business information published on the Web (timeliness, authority, etc.).

Standard 4	*The information literate business student, individually or as a member of a group, uses information effectively to accomplish a specific purpose.*
	   (No Performance Indicator listed)
	      Can synthesize and evaluate search results congruent with assignment objectives.

Standard 5	*The information literate business student understands many of the economic, legal, and social issues surrounding the use of information and accesses and uses information ethically and legally.*
	   (No Performance Indicator listed)
	      Understands copyright and intellectual property issues as they pertain to the use and distribution of authored material.

and reflection helped students become more effective in using information to accomplish their tasks (Standard Four), in this case, their research papers.

First Library Session

Goals. There are two skill-based goals for this session. First, knowing what tools are available will help students to better discern the type and breadth of information needed (Standard One). Second, this session will demonstrate diverse strategies for accessing information (Standard Two). As a result, students should be able to select information retrieval tools, select search terms, construct an effective search, and evaluate and select sources.

Content/Activities. Students are introduced to article searching and Web site evaluation. Active learning is encouraged in an exercise about distinguishing among popular, professional, and scholarly sources, in searching the Business Source Elite database, and again in evaluating Web sites using the CRAAP test criteria.[8] Keyword and subject searching, Boolean operators, truncation, journal retrieval, and interlibrary loan also are covered.

Assessment. Student understanding of research techniques and tools is assessed throughout the session by using the clickers.

Second Library Session

Goals. Students will demonstrate comprehension of management theory and apply their understanding of management theory to the scholarly publishing industry.

Content/Activities. Students prepare for class by reading assigned pieces; they are given a group reading quiz at the beginning of class, which will be reviewed immediately afterward. Librarians lead a Balanced Spheres model[9] discussion about the legal, economic, and societal dimensions of the scholarly publications industry, including information about copyright, the production and cost of scholarly information, as well as current professional issues (for example, open access movement, Google Book Search lawsuit).

Assessment. We return to the Balanced Spheres model again at the end of the session in order to summarize and synthesize the day's discussion.

Description of the Instruction Session: What Actually Happened?

Pretest

A required pretest was administered electronically to students (via Blackboard) one week before the first library session. The test included twenty questions, which were adapted with permission from the Standardized

Assessment of Information Literacy Skills, also known as Project SAILS.[10] Of the seventy-six students enrolled in MGT 111, sixty-four completed the pretest. The average score was 67 percent (out of 100), with a dramatic range of scores from 15 to 95 percent!

The First Library Session

This session met in the library's electronic classroom and was intended to introduce research tools and techniques to support the assignment. The following goals (based on BRASS standards) were shared with students at the outset of class: select information retrieval tools; select search terms; construct an effective search; evaluate and select sources. The session focused on finding appropriate journal articles and Web sites.

Two interactive exercises were included in the workshop. Because students were required to use academic sources, we facilitated an activity designed to help them differentiate between academic and trade publications. Pairs of students were given a number of publications to determine their classification. Students then convened in a large group to discuss their "magazines." Differentiating among publications helped students to develop Standard One competencies—determining the nature of information and solidifying distinctions within management literature. Small and large group discussion reinforced how to evaluate information and its sources critically (Standard Three).

The second interactive exercise introduced students to a model designed to help in evaluating Internet-based resources using the criteria of credibility, relevance/coverage, authority, accuracy, and purpose/objectivity. These criteria form a memorable acronym: CRAAP.[11] During the session, groups were assigned to assess Web pages that were related to group topics and selected in advance by the instructors. After the students assessed their sites, a large group discussion reviewed their decisions. This second interactive exercise fostered students' critical thinking skills (Standard Three).

Students' short-term learning and comprehension were assessed throughout the session using the TurningPoint clickers. The clicker questions were different from the ones students had already seen on the pretest, but they addressed the same skills. Section A's class average was 62 percent correct, Section B scored 64 percent correct, and Section C scored 57 percent correct. The students' scores on this in-class assessment were not impressive, but frankly, we did not expect them to be. Inclusion of the questions in the midst of class introduced an element of interactivity (always helpful in maintaining student interest); it also provided a vehicle for review of content.

Posttest

During the week after the first library session, we tested students again via Blackboard, using the same twenty questions from the pretest (although the examples used in the content of six questions were changed). Recall that of the seventy-six enrolled students, only sixty-four completed the pretest. Of those sixty-four, forty-seven also took the posttest. Therefore, we only have comparative data for forty-seven individuals. Of those forty-seven, thirty (about 64 percent) improved their scores on the posttest. Eleven students did worse, and six achieved the same score. In total, the class average was 71 percent with a similar, but slightly higher, range than the pretest—a 35 percent for a low score and a 100 percent for a high score.

The Second Library Session

The second session focused on helping management students understand many of the political, economic, and social issues surrounding the use of information (Standard Five). We believe dialogue on information's context and ethical dimensions fosters broader liberal arts goals such as critical and interdisciplinary thinking.

Before class, we assigned the following readings:
- "High Court Won't Review Copyright Lawsuit against Beastie Boys"[12]
- Sticker Shock Web Site[13]
- "Maggie Discovers Copyright," Chapter one of *Complete Copyright: An Everyday Guide for Librarians*[14]
- "Publishers Sue Google to Prevent Scanning of Copyrighted Works"[15]

During class, students began with a reading quiz, which they were allowed to take in their small groups. We reviewed the answers immediately afterward, which generated a fair amount of discussion. Then students were asked to recall and draw the "Balanced Spheres Model" by Sandra Waddock from her book *Leading Corporate Citizens: Vision, Values, Value-Added.*[16] Her model describes the three main arenas of human activity: the political sphere, the economic sphere, and the social sphere.

We discussed the model in terms of the scholarly publishing industry:
- The political sphere is represented by the laws created by our government with regard to copyright and intellectual property. Discussion is supported by a handout entitled, "Copyright: the Big Picture." The handout uses text from the *Complete Copyright: An Everyday Guide for Librarians* to state the rights of copyright owners, the exemptions to copyright law, and the four factors of fair use.[17] Students are told that the handout is biased and are asked to determine how so.
- The economic sphere is represented by the publishing companies and the effect of mergers and acquisitions. Statistics are presented on the

changes in average pricing of business/economics journals. The handout is titled "The Flow of Scholarly Publishing."

- The social sphere is represented by the consumers of scholarly information. Discussion of this sphere focuses on the open-access movement as a social reaction to mergers and acquisitions in the scholarly publishing industry. The lawsuit involving Google Book Search also is used to illuminate the issues at stake.

Student questions raised during the session included:
- "Why do institutions pay more for journals than individuals?"
- "How much do we [Gettysburg College] pay for copyright fees?"
- "Can you sell copyright? Why? When?"
- "Why did they only play the first thirty to forty seconds of songs over the public address system at my high school?"
- "What about corporations that copyright materials?"
- "Does our college radio station pay copyright fees?"

Reflection on the Instruction Session: Lessons Learned
Assignment
The MGT 111 research assignment has been evolving over the previous three semesters, and the professor and librarians are pleased with it. Despite reviewing the distinction between academic and popular sources in the information literacy session and detailed expectations to do so in the assignment, many students turned in annotated bibliographies lacking the required number of academic references. This distinction remains confusing for some students, even though many benefit from tailored instruction. In the future we may address this issue by having students review strong and weak annotated bibliography samples and check in one-on-one with a librarian with a draft of their annotated bibliography before turning it in to the instructor. Reference librarians would be provided a rubric for evaluation to provide standardized feedback to students.

Pretest
We modified Project SAILS questions to construct our pretest, even though we knew that the SAILS team was spending the 2005–2006 year studying the validity of their questions and skill sets.[18] Given the current state of information literacy assessment, we felt that we were using the best questions available at the time. We may change these in the future. Incidentally, we also explored having MGT 111 students take the Educational Testing Services' (ETS) new ICT (Information and Communications Technology) Literacy Test, which was not yet available for purchase in fall 2005.[19] The ETS was willing to let our students take the test twice but would not release

their scores to us. Ultimately, we decided against using the ICT Literacy Test as part of our assessment mechanism this time. This could change in the future.

First Library Session

Some students reported that they found this workshop "boring" because they had experienced it before (for another class). We are considering a more student-driven model, whereby students demonstrate their current level of information literacy skills and then receive instruction for more advanced skills. In addition, we can redesign the session so that students who claim to know these techniques already can help us teach them.

Posttest

To better measure long-term retention of information, we would like to administer the posttest later in the semester. It should still be given before the second library session, but perhaps not right on the heels of the first library session.

Second Library Session

As currently designed, this session is a combination of lecture and discussion. However, the large class size and challenging nature of the topics does not result in a satisfying discussion. We planned moments of interaction for this session, but we need more of them in order to engage student attention for seventy-five minutes. We also need to help students contextualize this session better. We want them to apply theories learned about earlier in the semester to a specific industry sector; application is a higher-level thinking skill than comprehension and requires more active learning to achieve.

Final Thoughts

We recently adapted American University's online IL tutorial and mounted it on our library server.[20] The tutorial was not available for MGT 111 students in the fall 2005 semester, but we would like to assign it in future semesters. It might best be assigned after the first library session and before the posttest so that students could use it as a review and reinforcement mechanism.

Notes

1. "TurningTechnologies Homepage." Available online from http://www.turningtechnologies.com.

2. Nancy A. Cunningham, "Information Competency Skills for Business Students," *Academic BRASS*, 1, no. 1 (2003). Available online from http://www.ala.org/ala/rusa/rusaourassoc/rusasections/brass/brasspubs/academicbrass/acadarchives/volume1number1/academicbrassv1.htm.

3. Association of College and Research Libraries, *Information Literacy Competency Standards for Higher Education* (Chicago: ACRL, 2000). Available online from http://www.ala.org/ala/acrl/acrlstandards/inform ationliteracycompetency.htm.

4. Ibid.

5. Cunningham, "Information Competency Skills for Business Students."

6. ACRL, *Information Literacy Competency Standards.*

7. Ibid.

8. Meriam Library, California State University, Chico, "Evaluating Information: Applying the CRAAP Test." Available online from http://www.csuchico.edu/lins/handouts/eval_websites.pdf.

9. Sandra A. Waddock, *Leading Corporate Citizens: Vision, Values, Value Added* (Boston, Mass: McGraw-Hill/Irwin, 2002), 360.

10. Julia Blixrud, Julie Gedeon, Carolyn Radcliff, Joe Salem, Mary Thompson, and Rick Wiggins, "Project SAILS: Standardized Assessment of Information Literacy Skills." Available online from http://sails.lms.kent.edu/.

11. Meriam Library, "Evaluating Information," 1.

12. Associated Press, *High Court Won't Review Copyright Lawsuit against Beastie Boys*, Lexis-Nexis Academic, Monday, June 13, 2005. Available online from http://web.lexis-nexis.com/universe/document?_m =305d4b74c372660a6a429c02970adc10&_docnum=1&wchp=dGLbVzb-zSkVA&_md5=8137818c67fda3245db167401b4e919f.

13. Gregory Tomso, Jill Powell, and John M. Saylor, "Sticker Shock." Available online from http://www.englib.cornell.edu/exhibits/stickershock/.

14. Carrie Russell, *Complete Copyright: An Everyday Guide for Librarians* (Chicago: ALA, 2004), 1–16.

15. Scott Carlson, "Publishers Sue Google to Prevent Scanning of Copyrighted Works," *Chronicle of Higher Education*, Nov. 14, 2005.

16. Waddock, *Leading Corporate Citizens.*

17. Russell, *Complete Copyright.*

18. "Current News: SAILS 2.0." Available online from https://www.projectsails.org/news/news.php?page=news.

19. Educational Testing Service, "ETS, ICT Literacy Assessment Overview." Available online from http://www.ets.org/portal/site/ets/menuitem.1488512ecfd5b8849a77b13bc3921509/?vgnextoid=fde9af5e44df4010VgnVCM10000022f95190RCRD&vgnextchannel=69d26f1674f4010VgnVCM10000022f95190RCRD.

20. American University Library's Instruction Team, "American University Library's Information Literacy Tutorial." Available online from http://www.library.american.edu/tutorial/.

Teaching Resources
Annotated Bibliography Requirements (5% of final grade)
- Use APA style citation
- 50 percent of sources should be academic references
- For each citation identified in the research you need to track the following information:
  1. How you identified the citation (databases, bibliography, etc.)
  2. Describe how this citation will contribute to your paper
- Keep an activity log of your searches, as demonstrated in the information literacy session at the library. For example, if I were researching wage inequity, I might search with the following terms in the database engines: women and work, gender and work, wage differences and gender, etc. The purpose is to organize your search so that you know what topics you've covered and to provide as a resource to share with reference librarians if you are having difficulty identifying sources.
- Develop a tentative thesis for your paper.

Notes for future reference:
- You will be expected to attach the original annotated bibliography and activity log with a description of how you identified the sources to your final paper.
- Sources of the reference list "match" those cited in the text of final paper
- Cite each source appropriately in bibliography and in the text
- Appropriate use of quotation conventions are required in final paper
- 50 percent of the citations from this annotated bibliography are expected to appear in the final paper

Final Paper and Group Presentation Requirements
You and your teammates are expected to select your final presentation topic based on the list provided in your syllabus. After selection, you will need to divide the subject into distinct subtopics for each group member to research and write a paper. Your group is responsible for this division of labor and I will provide coaching only if needed.

There are two outcomes for the project. The first is a twenty-five-minute group presentation to the class that integrates the major findings from your research. The criteria for evaluation are as follows: creativity, evidence of cohesive team (e.g., not several discrete mini-presentations), class engagement, clarity of material presented, connection to previous class material/theories, and relaying critical concepts about chosen topic area (history, debates, etc.). The second outcome is an individual research paper (five to seven pages) with a minimum of four academic references. See Blackboard for more detailed description.

Prepared by Cinda Gibbon and Janelle Wertzberger, Reference & Instruction Department, Musselman Library, Gettysburg College
4-05

Flow of **Scholarly Publication**

Scholars produce scholarship, using funds from academia, foundations, government, etc.

2+2=4
ADD'S UP!

Scholars give up their copyright to publishers in exchange for publication.

Publishers coordinate peer review function (provided by scholars for free), publish and disseminate information. They generally hold copyright. Publisher types include commercial, society, small presses, university presses.

Publishers must cover their expenses (online publications DO cost money) and may or may not make a profit.

Subscribers/Users Personal subscribers pay for their own subscriptions; institutional subscribers (usually libraries) pay more on behalf of a group of users. Either way, academia usually pays.

Someone must pay for scholar users to access their original work in published form.

Chapter 17

International Legal Research with Undergraduates

David M. Oldenkamp

Introduction

When was the last time you were asked to write a well-researched analysis of a hypothetical international law case involving a revolt of lunar colonists in the year 2387 that incorporates issues relating to de facto and de jure recognition, self-determination, the 1967 "Moon Treaty," and an incident involving a lunar rebel's passport being stamped in France? Not lately?

This is an example of one of the four hypothetical cases assigned to Dr. Christopher W. Herrick's International Law and Organization course at Muhlenberg College in Allentown, Pennsylvania. Hypothetical cases are regularly used in American law schools to test future attorneys' abilities to take established legal principles and apply them to a fictitious set of facts. These hypothetical case assignments were designed to give undergraduate students a preview of law school and to give them some experience with constructing legal arguments; and it was my job as the social sciences reference librarian to design a library instruction session that would provide the international law students with the legal research skills they would need to construct their arguments.

Ultimately, I discovered that imparting these skills to under-graduates takes more time and energy than the average "one-shot" library instruction session. By the end of the semester, I found that I had forged strong relationships with many of the international law students because each assignment found them flooding my office and the reference desk in search of in-depth reference help. Success could only be achieved through a series of librarian–faculty collaborations and by taking library instruction beyond the classroom as I worked with students throughout the semester to develop and apply their research skills to each assignment.

Analysis of the Learning Situation

Muhlenberg College, a small, private, liberal arts college in Allentown, Pennsylvania, prides itself on giving students a high-quality, rigorous undergraduate education. It is typical for the average Muhlenberg student to attend several course-integrated library instruction sessions as he or she progresses through his or her studies. The Political Science Department faculty are particularly heavy users of library instruction.

As the social sciences reference librarian, I was invited to conduct a seventy-five-minute instruction session for International Law and Organization, a 200-level Political Science course. Many of the students who take this course are prelaw political science majors. There are, on average, twenty-five students in each section of the course, which is offered every fall semester. The typical international law student has had a library instruction session in one of his or her previous classes.

The students come to the instruction session with a diagnostic essay assignment that requires them to research and analyze a real international law case. The assigned case for this session was *The Case of the S. S. "Lotus,"* a classic international law case.[1] Later in the semester, students are given four hypothetical case assignments with underlying subjects covering topics from their textbook readings.[2] Complementing the textbook readings are the Muhlenberg library's print and electronic collections. These resources are augmented by the ever-increasing collections of primary and secondary international law resources on the Internet.

The Trexler Library at Muhlenberg College has one computer instruction classroom that is equipped with workstations for thirty-two students. Librarians work from an instructor computer equipped with a document camera and a projector. Librarians typically create a Web-based research guide for each class, and this Web page is usually provided as a handout for the attending students.[3]

Information Literacy Standards

(Note: A complete list of ACRL *Information Literacy Competency Standards for Higher Education* [Chicago: ACRL, 2000] appears as appendix A.)

This library instruction session, combined with the overall aims of the International Law and Organization course, incorporates many of the ACRL Information Literacy Competency Standards for Higher Education, Performance Indicators and Outcomes:

Standard One: "The information literate student determines the nature and extent of the information needed." [4] The students are expected to define and articulate their information needs (1.1), getting assistance when needed (1.1.a.). Through the research process, they will identify the areas to be researched (1.1.b.) using general resources (1.1.c.) and then use these resources to identify the key legal principles, cases, and treaties

(1.1.e) that they will use in their hypothetical case arguments (1.1.f.). Each student will identify and incorporate a wide variety of these primary legal sources (1.2., 1.2.e., 1.2.f.) from a variety of formats (1.2.c) in their final research product. To locate these resources, the students may need to be creative and locate resources from outside the library (1.3.a) and from foreign legal sources (1.3.b).

Standard Two: "The information literate student accesses needed information effectively and efficiently."[5] The students will need to pick the best resources and tools to use in their research (2.1) and use appropriate search terms to access the international legal resources (2.1.d, 2.2, 2.2a-f). When they conduct their online searches, the students will not limit themselves to one particular resource (2.3, 2.3.a). As they search, the students will need to refine their strategy to be able to retrieve the most relevant resources (2.4), assessing the quality of resources as they progress through their research (2.4.a). As they assess their retrieved information, the students will need to be able keep track of where they retrieved their information (2.5.d.) and be aware of the nature of the material, whether it is a case, treaty, law, or convention, that they find (2.5.c).

Standard Three: "The information literate student evaluates information and its sources critically and incorporates selected information into his or her knowledge base and value system."[6] When the students have gathered their resources, they will need to critically examine how the retrieved information fits within the context of international law, within the interaction between national and international law, and how the information supports or refutes their main argument (3.1, 3.1.a, 3.1.b, 3.2.b., 3.2.d., 3.3, 3.3.a., 3.3.b., 3.4, 3.4.a.-c., 3.4.f.-g.). The students can seek the help of their professor to clarify the assignment or to gain insight on profitable avenues of investigation (3.6, 3.7).

Standard Four: "The information literate student, individually or as a member of a group, uses information effectively to accomplish a specific purpose."[7] The students will gather their primary and secondary legal sources and use them in their construction of a well-organized legal argument (4.1, 4.1.a., 4.1.c., 4.3, 4.3.d.).

Standard Five: "The information literate student understands many of the economic, legal, and social issues surrounding the use of information and accesses and uses information ethically and legally."[8] The International Law and Organization students will use proprietary library subscription databases and freely available Internet sources in their research (5.1.b.), and they will need to use all these sources ethically (5.2, 5.2.f.) and properly cite the information used using *The Chicago Manual of Style* and *The Bluebook* (5.3, 5.3.a.).

Lesson Plan
I. Introduction
    A. Begin with a quick overview of the library resource guide created for the class.
    B. Let students know that reference help is available to them throughout the semester.
II. General Principles of International Legal Research
    A. Brainstorming activity on the sources of international law
    B. Modeling the Process: Example of the Pinochet trial[9]
        1. Discuss some of the trial details
        2. Identify the sources of law that were relevant in this case, using a reference source
        3. Generalize these details to the broader process of legal research:
            a. Identify the legal issues
            b. Do some preliminary research to find keywords and primary source citations
            c. Search in appropriate places to find primary sources
III. Learn How to Use the Legal Research Tools
    A. Start with print reference sources
    B. Find articles and cases in Lexis-Nexis Academic's Legal Research section
    C. Find articles in JSTOR
    D. Look at several examples of freely available primary source Web sites
IV. Conclusion
    A. Remind students of the need to cite their sources properly
    B. Review the processes and techniques learned in class
    C. Remind students to seek help when needed

Description of the Instruction Session: What Actually Happened?
As Dr. Herrick's International Law and Organization students enter the library instruction classroom, I recognize many faces from previous library instruction sessions. When all the students are seated at computer workstations, I distribute the library resource guide I have created for the class. The creation of the resource guide was done in consultation with the professor, after viewing the course syllabus and reviewing the diagnostic essay assignment on *The Case of the S. S. "Lotus."*

    Next, I ask the students to turn their computer monitors off for the first part of the instruction session. I do this before I begin teaching because it can be difficult for students to avoid checking e-mail and logging into their instant messenger accounts when there is a glowing computer screen in front of their faces. Even though Dr. Herrick may be in the classroom, turning the computer monitors off helps me to maintain control and signals to students that they need to pay attention to what I am presenting. I also find that, with fewer distractions, they are more likely to actively participate in the first part of the instruction session.

I begin teaching with a quick overview of the handout I have just given them. This handout is much longer than the normal resource guide I create for classes, and I explain that the reason for this is that the upcoming hypothetical case assignments will require that they use a wide variety of research tools. This handout also contains my contact information and my reference desk shift hours. I make it a point to let students know that I am available for individual consultations and that the intensity of the assignments will mean that most, if not all, of the students will seek my assistance at some point during the semester.

I can tell that most of the students do not take this claim too seriously. After all, they have been in a library session before and they have written research papers before, but I assure them that the research they will be doing for this class is different from most of the other kinds of research they have done in other classes. Instead of focusing on secondary sources (books and journal articles), they will eventually need to locate and use a host of primary sources to construct their legal arguments.

I ask the students if they can give me some examples of the major sources of international law, which is a subject covered in first few weeks of the class, so they are expected to be able to come up with some examples. As particular sources are mentioned, such as treaties and judicial decisions, I write them on the blackboard and show them an example of the source. With some prompting, the students are pretty good about coming up with a list of sources. The list includes bilateral and multilateral treaties, national laws, decisions from international organizations (such as United Nations Security Council Resolutions), judicial decisions, customary international law, and the writings of great legal minds.

The sample case I use is the case of the arrest of Chilean General and former President Augusto Pinochet in the United Kingdom in 1998 on an international arrest warrant issued by a Spanish judge for alleged crimes against humanity (specifically torture) committed by General Pinochet during his presidency of Chile (1973–1990). I do not get into the complex and gritty details of the case in the class, but I do mention how we would go about identifying and researching the legal issues involved in such a case. When I asked the students how many of them knew anything about the Pinochet case, I do not receive much feedback. Their lack of knowledge on the subject actually makes a nice segue to the next part of the session.

I begin using the document camera so that we can take a look at one of the key reference sources that will be helpful as they work on their assignments: The *Parry & Grant Encyclopaedic Dictionary of International Law*.[10] Looking at the entry on the "Pinochet Case" gives us a brief overview of the case, the citation to the actual case, the citation for the U.N. Convention against Torture and Other Cruel, Inhumane or Degrading Treatment or Punishment of 1984, and a "*See*" cross-reference to an entry on "head of state immunity." I also look up the term *Universal Jurisdiction*, where we learn that the concept applies to offences such as: piracy, war crimes, crimes against humanity, hijacking, internationally protected persons, and torture.[11] Because the Spanish government made claims of universal jurisdiction in its attempts to extradite General Pinochet, we will need to know about this concept if we are to analyze the case.

The *Parry & Grant* resource shows the students that the Pinochet case involves several major areas of international law: jurisdiction, sovereign immunity, crimes against humanity, the relationship between national and international law, and extradition treaties. And each of these legal topics has related primary sources that would need to be consulted if they were arguing the Pinochet case. For example, they would need to locate the U.N. Torture Convention, learn if and when this convention was adopted in the United Kingdom, and if General Pinochet's alleged crimes against humanity were committed when the U.N. Torture Convention was binding international law.

I make a point of telling the students that this is the same process that they will need to follow as they do their hypothetical case research. First, identify the general legal issues that are present in the case. Second, look these issues up in an appropriate reference source, which will point them to the key cases, treaties, conventions, and other primary legal resources they will need to use in the creation of their arguments. Third, they will need to determine which resource (whether in print, in a library database, or on the Internet) will be the best place to find the primary legal resource in question.

I go on to reemphasize that using a reference source such as the *Parry & Grant Encyclopaedic Dictionary of International Law* can be extremely helpful in pointing them to the most relevant primary sources for their research question. To illustrate this principle again, I locate the entry on "*The Lotus Case*" in *Parry & Grant*.[12] The *Lotus* entry is two paragraphs long and outlines the main details of the case, discusses the case's importance, and provides citations to later international conventions that codify the legal principles raised by *Lotus*. I highly recommend that the students consult *Parry & Grant* for their research on the diagnostic essay assignment and the later hypothetical case assignments, along with *Legal*

Systems of the World: A Political, Social, and Cultural Encyclopedia[13] when they are starting their research on a particular country's legal system.

Transitioning from print sources to electronic sources, I ask the students to turn their computer monitors on, open a Web browser, and find the Trexler Library's home page. On my own computer, I ask students to follow along on their computers as I navigate my browser to the library's databases Web page. I ask the class to select the Lexis-Nexis Academic database because we are going to use this database to find a few law review articles, a U.S. Supreme Court case, and a foreign court case.

When in Lexis-Nexis, we select the "Legal Research" section, and I explain that the structure of Lexis-Nexis is such that researchers must have some preliminary knowledge about what they are looking for before starting their search because Lexis-Nexis does not have one section where they will be able to do all their research. Instead, they will need to know some information as to what nation's laws they are trying to find or what country's court ruled on the matter they are attempting to research.

If they are looking for articles, they can choose the "Law Reviews" section of Lexis-Nexis Academic. If they need a case from the U.S. Supreme Court, they would select "Federal Case Law" or "Get a Case." To find a case from another country, they could choose to search within the "Commonwealth and Foreign Nations" option. As a class, we work together to find a law review article about sovereign immunity in the Pinochet case, we find a U.S. Supreme Court case that is mentioned in their text, and for an international case, we find the Pinochet case we had discussed earlier in the class.

The students do reasonably well when it comes to following my directions on searching, and I mention a few search strategies that work well in Lexis-Nexis, particularly phrase searching and Boolean operators. I warn them about Lexis-Nexis' default "Previous six months" date limitation, which often frustrates Lexis-Nexis novices when they do a search for an older topic and do not retrieve desired results.

Unfortunately, Lexis-Nexis Academic does not have a copy of *The Case of the S. S. "Lotus."* To find the text of the *Lotus* case, they will need to go to WorldCourts.com[14] and search for the case on this Web site. So, we visit this Web site and find that the text of the *Lotus* case is ninety-five pages long and it is in the .pdf format. I ask the students to refrain from printing the case in the class because our one printer would not be able to accommodate their collective printing. Instead, they can make a note of how to find the case and come back to it later.

The process of having to find their diagnostic essay case on a specialized Web site is a great example that illustrates that there is no "one" resource that they will be able to consult that will have all of the information they will need. I point out that they will be able to use Lexis-Nexis for U.S. legislative and case law, as well as the legislative and case law from several foreign countries and multinational bodies (particularly the European Union). However, to locate some major treaties and cases, it will be necessary for them to rely on Web sites, reference books, and government documents. I tell them that it will be up to them to take their list of needed primary documents and determine which resource is most likely to have that information. If they are researching Swiss criminal law or extradition treaties between the United States and the United Kingdom, they will need to go to the source of the law (the Swiss, United States and United Kingdom governments, respectively) to find what they need.

Before launching into an overview of the freely available international law Internet resources, I ask the students to return to the library's databases Web page. When we all are all back to this page, I ask the students to look at JSTOR. I explain that the reason they will need JSTOR is because the database includes the full text of some of the major international law journals, such as *The American Journal of International Law*. Although JSTOR may not have a complete collection of international law journals, the collection of journals is extensive enough for us to find a few excellent articles that analyze the *Lotus* case, in addition to articles about the *Pinochet* case, the Geneva Conventions, and other international law topics.

I ask the students to refer back to the library resource guide handout I distributed at the start of the class. I tell them that we do not have time to go into all the resources listed in the guide, but I do ask them to visit a few of the listed resources. Particularly, I show them the International Committee of the Red Cross's Databases on International Humanitarian Law where we see that they can find entire treaties online (such as the text of the Geneva Conventions) and I show them the U.S. Department of State's Treaties in Force Web site where they will be able to find all the treaties the U.S. is a party to and when they went into effect. While I am showing them these two Web resources, I can tell that some of the students are distracted by researching their diagnostic essay topic, so I am not sure how many students get the message on the Web resources.

Finally, in the last few moments of the class, I remind the students that they need to cite all the materials they are using in these assignments. A brief classroom survey lets me know that most, if not all, of the students have at least heard of the Chicago style of citation. I also hold up a copy of *The Bluebook*, which covers how to cite the legal documents not covered by *The Chicago Manual of Style*.

With the library instruction session ending, I remind the students that I am available for personal reference consultations should they need further help. Research for this class will not be easy, but as long as they are able to identify the issues in a given case, we have the tools available to be able to find the appropriate resources. I reiterate that their research strategy for the hypothetical cases will be to (1) identify the legal issues in the case; (2) do some preliminary research on these topics, which should yield good keywords and specific citations to primary sources; and (3) go to the source to find these primary sources.

Reflection on the Instruction Session: Lessons Learned

The instruction session for International Law and Organization was successful. The students were engaged, participated in the discussions, and were able to walk out of the class with some of their research for the diagnostic essay assignment completed. However, later in the semester, when it came time for the students to start their research on the hypothetical case assignments, I found myself overrun with students in need of in-depth reference assistance. The first time this happened, I patiently walked each student through the assignment, pointing out what resources would best suit the particular question. The students were having a difficult time identifying the general legal issues presented in each hypothetical and seemed to have forgotten many of the resources covered in the instruction session.

As the first cadre of students came and went from my office, I also found that my colleagues were being overwhelmed with international law students at the reference desk. I decided that I needed to make mini-research guides for each hypothetical case to manage the flow of students in need of assistance. The guides were often a brief outline that listed the major resources to consult for each case. The resources listed included reference books, databases, hints about searching strategies, relevant Web sites, and materials that Dr. Herrick had placed on library reserve.

Throughout the semester, I was in regular communication with Dr. Herrick. These interactions were invaluable because the information we shared informed the creation of the mini-research guides, and I was able to provide him with feedback on how his students were doing in their research. The end result is that the students received the best assistance I could reasonably provide as they completed some of the most challenging assignments of their undergraduate careers.

Perhaps the best indicator of success is the feedback that Dr. Herrick received at the end of the course. The students stated the hypothetical cases were challenging, but that they learned a lot from the course. To quote one student: "The hypothetical cases were awesome. I really had to think and apply what I learned in class." Another student commented that they "couldn't have gotten through the course assignments" without the assistance provided by the people at the library.

Ultimately, the instruction session was a good introduction to international legal research, and the students immediately applied these skills to their first assignment. However, legal research is not easy, and the hypothetical case assignments are particularly difficult. A one-shot instruction approach was not sufficient for students to learn and practice all the skills they would need to complete their assignments. My being flexible and responding to student needs meant that the content and goals of the instruction session were informally repeated and reinforced throughout the semester. The faculty member's goals were met when students completed their assignments and in doing so, the students received an introduction to legal research. My goals as a librarian were met as I saw students becoming better independent legal researchers and more information literate.

Notes

1. *The Case of the S. S. "Lotus" (France v. Turkey)*, 1927, P.C.I.J. (ser. A,) No. 10. Available online from http://www.worldcourts.com/pcij/eng/decisions/1927.09.07_lotus/.

2. The assigned textbook is the classic Gerard Von Glahn, *Law Among Nations: An Introduction to Public International Law*, 7th ed. (Boston: Allyn and Bacon, 1996).

3. Muhlenberg College "International Law and Organization." Available online from http://www.muhlenberg.edu/library/guides/libinst/index.html.

4. Association of College and Research Libraries, *Information Literacy Standards for Higher Education* (Chicago: ACRL, 2000). Available online from http://www.ala.org/ala/acrl/acrlstandards/informationliteracycompetency.htm.

5. Ibid.

6. Ibid.

7. Ibid.

8. Ibid.

9. Regina v. Bow Street Metropolitan Stipendiary Magistrate and Others, Ex Parte Pinochet Ugarte (No. 3) (1999) 1 A.C. 147. Available online from http://www.parliament.the-stationery-office.co.uk/pa/ld199899/ldjudgmt/jd990324/pino1.htm.

10. John P. Grant and J. Craig Barker, eds., *Parry & Grant Encyclopaedic Dictionary of International Law*, 2nd ed. (Dobbs Ferry, NY: Oceana Publications, 2004): 387–88.

11. Ibid., 535–36.

12. Ibid., 296.

13. Herbert M. Kritzer, ed., *Legal Systems of the World: A Political, Social, and Cultural Encyclopedia* (Santa Barbara, CA: ABC-CLIO, 2002).

14. WorldCourts.com. Available from http://www.worldcourts.com.

Teaching Resources
This is a truncated version of a research guide distributed to the class. A complete version may be obtained by contacting the author.

Selected Reference Materials
Grant, John P., and J. Craig Barker, ed. *Parry and Grant Encyclopaedic Dictionary of International Law*, 2nd ed. New York: Oceana Publications, Inc., 2004.
    Ref. 341.03 G762p
Kritzer, Herbert M., ed. Legal *Systems of the World: A Political, Social, and Cultural Encyclopedia.* Santa Barbara, CA: ABC-CLIO, 2002.
    Ref. 340.03 K92L v.1–4
Treaties in Force: A List of Treaties and other International Acts of the United States in Force on .... Washington : U.S. G.P.O., 1944–
    Gov. Docs. S 9.14: (Library owns 1956–present)
    Latest Issue Online: http://www.state.gov/s/l/c8455.htm
West's Encyclopedia of American Law. St. Paul, MN: West Group, 1998.
    Ref. 348.7303 W538e v.1–12

Library Databases
LexisNexis Academic: Legal Research
    • Law Reviews
    • US Case Law: Federal & State
    • US Administrative Law: Codes & Regulations
    • International Law: Canadian Law, EU Law, and the
    Commonwealth of Foreign Nations Law.
JSTOR
    Contains several full-text international law journals, such as The *American Journal of International Law.*

Selected Web Sites
Gateway Sites
    Legal Information Institute: Law by Source: Global: http://www. law.cornell.edu/world/
    American Society for International Law: ILM Links List: http:// www.asil.org/ilmlinks.htm
Primary Sources: Treaties and Other Documents
    Avalon Project (Yale University): http://www.yale.edu/lawweb/ avalon/avalon.htm
    International Committee of the Red Cross: Databases on International Humanitarian Law: http://www.icrc.org/web/eng/ siteeng0.nsf/iwpList2/Info_resources:IHL_databases

• Treaty Database: http://www.icrc.org/ihl
• National Implementation Database: http://www.icrc.org/ihl-nat
University of Minnesota Human Rights Library: http://www1.
umn.edu/humanrts/

Specific Courts and Legislative Bodies:

EUR-LEX: European Union Law Portal: http://europa.eu.int/eur-lex/en/index.html
International Court of Justice: http://www.icj-cij.org/
United Nations International Law: http://www.un.org/law/index.html

Citation Guides

The Chicago Manual of Style, 15th ed. Chicago: University of
Chicago Press, 2003.
Ref. 808.027 C632m (kept at Reference Desk)
The Bluebook: A Uniform System of Citation, 17th ed. Cambridge,
MA: Harvard Law Review Association, 2000.
Ref. 347.30847 B658a (kept at Reference Desk)

Chapter 18

Basic Training: Putting Undergraduate Government Students through the Paces

Barbara P. Norelli

Introduction

An information-literate political science major is one who is able to produce a well-written, well-argued, and well-documented research paper that uses the principles and methods of political science and includes a variety of authoritative and primary sources, especially scholarly books and journal articles, and government documents.[1] Determining which fundamental research skills to develop first in the novice-level government student is not obvious. The draft *Political Science Research Competencies Guidelines* developed by the Law & Political Science Section (LPSS) of the Association of College & Research Libraries (ACRL), with input from the American Political Science Association's (APSA) Undergraduate Education and Teaching & Learning sections, begins to address this issue.[2]

Teaching information literacy skills and concepts to undergraduates takes a whole campus, and the faculty–librarian collaborative effort is one of the most important ingredients in this endeavor. A member of the government faculty and I have been discussing and debating discipline-specific undergraduate research competencies for the past several years; he, in fact, read and commented on a draft version of the LPSS Guidelines. These mutually beneficial conversations informed the instructional design of the Introduction to American Government (GO 101) class assignment and the library session described herein.

Analysis of the Learning Situation
Assignment

My teaching assignment was quite specific. I was asked by Robert C. (Bob) Turner, professor of the foundational course in political science, "Introduction to American Government," to instruct students on how to find periodical articles from magazines and newspapers, specifically the *New York Times, Washington Post,* and the *Wall Street Journal*, on a contemporary political issue. The students were assigned to write a seven- to nine-page paper, worth 30 percent of their final grade, in which they analyzed a current issue, drawing on a minimum of three to five magazine articles and five to seven newspaper articles. The professor and I agreed that the three best library resources to ensure the students' successful completion of the assignment were CQ Researcher, CQ Weekly, and LexisNexis Academic. The eighty-minute instruction session focused on the use of these databases and certain database search strategies while also touching on the concepts of topic selection and bibliographic citation.

Students

A check of the registrar's database indicated that there were thirty-three students in the class, with one senior, four juniors, seven sophomores, twenty freshmen, and one nonmatriculated student. Most of the students, 61 percent, were first-semester freshmen; adding in the sophomores, the class was 81 percent underclassmen. At Skidmore, most students are of traditional college age, eighteen to twenty-two years old; indeed, they were all Millennials, members of Generation (Gen) Y. With most of the freshmen just a few short months out of high school, these students also were the first to experience the newly offered freshmen seminars, a piece of the redesigned freshmen-year experience that included a general, though not required, fifty-five minute introduction to the library, its Web page, and online catalog.

Facilities

The instruction session was held in the library's electronic classroom with a full complement of standard instructional technology, Internet access, and the suite of Microsoft Office software. The instructor's station is at the front of the room. The student computer desks are large with a glass plate protecting the completely recessed PC monitor and CPU, freeing the desktop for work-related materials and keeping the line of sight to the front of the room unimpeded. There are five parallel rows of student desks with three computers in each row. Each desk is capable of accommodating two students easily, and three students in a pinch for those stations on the aisle. The classroom was at peak capacity for our instruction session. Also, the classroom is equipped with a wall of white boards, perpendicular to the student desks, and a dedicated laser printer networked to all the computers. All in all, it is a comfortable room in which to teach and, probably more important, the students can easily find the room because it is located immediately inside the front entrance of the library.

Session

The eighty-minute library instruction session was scheduled several weeks in advance of its early November delivery date. Under typical research circumstances, the timing of the session might have seemed a bit late in the semester, but it was really more of the "just-in-time" variety. Students had been exposed to a number of political science concepts, some had already picked a topic, and with one month left in the semester most were ready to tackle the assignment. Also, there was no need to allow time for interlibrary loan because the assignment called for the use of full-text databases.

Information Literacy Standards

(Note: A complete list of ACRL *Information Literacy Competency Standards for Higher Education* [Chicago: ACRL, 2000] appears as appendix A.)

Lesson Goal

The students will become aware of the CQ and LexisNexis periodical databases and knowledgeable about a few database search strategies in order to locate and retrieve relevant and reliable periodical sources on a current political issue for the assigned research paper; and in so doing, the students will begin to develop their information literacy toolbox for political science research.

Applicable ACRL Information Literacy Competency Standards, Performance Indicators, and Outcomes[3]

1. The students will formulate a current political issue research topic.
   • Outcome 1.1.c. "Explores general information sources to increase familiarity with the topic."
2. The students will identify appropriate news sources for a political science paper.
   • Outcome 1.2.d. "Identifies the purpose and audience of potential resources (e.g., popular vs. scholarly, current vs. historical)."
3. The students will understand similarities and differences in the CQ and LexisNexis databases.
   • Outcome 2.1.c. "Investigates the scope, content, and organization of information retrieval systems."
4. The students will be able to compose and implement an effective search query.
   • Outcome 2.2.b. "Identifies keywords, synonyms, and related terms for the information needed."
   • Outcome 2.2.d. "Constructs a search strategy using appropriate commands for the information retrieval system selected (e.g., Boolean operators, truncation, and proximity for search engines; internal organizers such as indexes for books)."
5. The students will be able to cite sources in their research paper according to the *Chicago Manual of Style*.

- Outcome 2.5.d. "Records all pertinent citation information for future reference."

Lesson Plan

The "basic training" lesson plan timetable allows for a five-minute cushion.

1. The warm-up: (3 minutes)
   a. Introduce self, mention contact information on handout, and state learning goals.
   b. Distribute handouts.
      i. CQ Researcher handout
      ii. Library resources for GO 101: Introduction to American Government
2. Jumping Jacks: (15 minutes) CQ Researcher (bring examples of hard-copy issues)
   a. Students search & explore CQ Researcher (5 minutes)—active learning
   b. Discuss results (5 minutes)
   c. Citation information (5 minutes)—demonstrate
      i. CQ Researcher's "Cite it Now"
      ii. How do I...? Cite a Source: Citation Resources Web page
      iii. Style manuals at reference desk—*Chicago Manual of Style*
3. Stretching: (10 minutes) CQ Weekly (bring examples of hard-copy issues)
   a. Students search & explore CQ Weekly (5 minutes)—active learning
   b. Discuss results (5 minutes)
      i. Demonstrate phrase searching in "Search Articles"
      ii. Clarify terminology—periodicals
4. Lifting weights: (30 minutes) LexisNexis Academic News
   a. Students search & explore LexisNexis Academic News (5 minutes)
   b. Discuss results (5 minutes)
   c. LATCH (5 minutes)—coming up with the right words
   d. Demonstrate search strategies (15 minutes)
      i. Limiting to specific publication(s)
      ii. "atleast" command
      iii. Field searching: section(editor!)
5. Running on the treadmill: Student research time (15 minutes)
6. Cool down and weigh in: (2 minutes)
   a. Reinforce availability of reference assistance
   b. Students leave with one or two full-text articles

Description of the Instruction Session: What Actually Happened?

The class began on time with all students in attendance. The professor, however, was attending to a family medical situation. For a variety of reasons, including scheduling availability and familiarity with the professor, the assignment, and the course, I agreed in advance to be the lone "basic training" drill instructor for the session.

The Warm-up

After introducing myself, I distributed the handouts, stated the goals for the library session, and emphasized that the material covered would be directly applicable to the students' research assignment. As is the case in many library instruction sessions, it was difficult to ascertain beforehand exactly what all of the students did or did not know about using the databases or the college library in general. Based on prior experience with the course, I assumed the underclassmen in particular had little knowledge of the CQ and LexisNexis databases and how to retrieve appropriate and relevant periodical articles in general.

Jumping Jacks

To set a baseline of knowledge, I had the students begin with the CQ Researcher database. It is an excellent starting point for current issue research, providing useful and reliable background material, and it is easy to use. Ten minutes before the students arrived, I opened the classroom and turned on all the equipment. The students then only needed to log on to the campus network (something I was fairly confident they all knew how to do) though I was prepared to use a generic log-in if necessary. Without a lot of lecturing, I asked the students to follow along on their computers and then demonstrated how to navigate to and select the CQ Researcher database from the library's government subject page (pointing out along the way that the Find Subjects link is their main entrée to various library resources by subject). The students then were asked to find information on "identity theft" in CQ Researcher.

Given what we know about Gen Y (that these are students who don't read computer manuals, preferring to just jump in and use the computer instead, and who seem to consider technology an extension of their right hands), I decided to get the students engaged with the databases as soon as possible.[4] We shouldn't be surprised by the Nike "just do it" mentality in learning. We only have to recall the whole language movement[5] that had most of these Gen Y students writing sentences, albeit brief ones, in kindergarten, well before they had knowledge of spelling, grammar, or penmanship, certainly a very different learning experience from what baby-boom librarians such as myself experienced with rigid spelling bees, tedious penmanship worksheets, and mind-dulling grammar rule memorization, before attempting to write a sentence or two in the second grade.

Using a large, readable stopwatch/time clock that we keep at the instructor's station, I told the students they had five minutes to find a document on point, browse the document, and be prepared to report back on how they found the document and what kind of information it contained. When time was up, a student volunteered to demonstrate, using the instructor's station (we don't have the ability to switch the display function to student workstations), how the student searched and what he or she found. A simple search for identity theft in the quick search window resulted in an excellent article. We discussed the ease with which one could locate material in the database, pointed out the browse topic feature, and highlighted its usefulness to those who had not already selected their assignment topic. I then circulated a few hard-copy issues of CQ Researcher, appealing to the tactile learning experience, while I used the online version to review the components of a typical weekly issue (i.e., the overview, background, current situation, bibliography, etc.).

At this point I mentioned the need to cite sources and demonstrated the "Cite it now" feature of the database but did not give a lesson in citation mechanics. Instead, I navigated to the library's Web page on citation resources and mentioned that print copies of the various style manuals are available at the reference desk.

Stretching

With students responding positively to using CQ Researcher, we moved on to CQ Weekly. To reinforce what the students had just learned about navigating to the subject databases, I asked one of the upperclassmen to again demonstrate the path from the library home page to the government subject page. The class was again asked to find an article on the topic of "identity theft," but this time using CQ Weekly.

Although CQ Weekly looks similar to CQ Researcher, I wanted the students to discover the differences between the two resources through their own exploration. Based on their discussion comments, they understood pretty quickly that the scope of CQ Weekly was narrower than CQ Researcher, focused as it is on Congress and legislative issues, though the students found it just as easy to search. I took a minute to show the "Search Articles" search screen for a query on the phrase "identity theft" in quotes limited to title, again just scratching the surface of what this database had to offer. I circulated hard-copy issues of CQ Weekly so the students could see what an entire issue of the weekly news publication contained.

Using motion to keep the students' attention, I make a point of walking over to the whiteboards whenever possible. While at the whiteboards, I asked the students to define "periodicals" and to give examples of each kind. After a little bit of prompting, the students answered appropriately, creating a nice segue to LexisNexis Academic News.

Lifting Weights

I knew the real teaching challenge came with LexisNexis Academic. With a student volunteer at the instructor's station keyboard, I directed the students to search the news category, general news, and major papers subdivisions, for the same search as in CQ—"identity theft." It was quite clear that one needed to compose a more sophisticated search query in order to retrieve a reasonable number of relevant results in LexisNexis Academic. The students were now primed to learn how to compose a better query.

I like to teach Richard Saul Wurman's LATCH[6] (Location, Alphabet, Time, Category, and Hierarchy) system as a helpful way to think of words for expressing a topic in a database search. The students seemed to agree. I had the students brainstorm synonyms to identity theft and they came up with "phishing." I reviewed the use of Boolean "AND" "OR" connectors in databases and added "identity theft" OR "phishing" to our search. We then limited the search to the *New York Times* so the students could see this possibility. The results said it all.

One of my favorite search techniques in LexisNexis is the "atleast" command. I had the students try the command using the search atl3(identity theft) in the full-text field for the previous six months. The students readily recognized the value of such a unique command and wanted to know if other databases did the same thing; they were beginning to think about transferring skills from one system to another!

The last search technique I covered was the use of limiting the search by section field. As political science students often are interested in reading editorials and/or letters to the editor, I demonstrated this type of search: identity theft and section(editor!) in full text for the previous year of the *New York Times*. I know I was beginning to push the limit of the number of items to cover in an eighty-minute class, so I stopped there. It was time to let the students do their research and for them to try to use all that they had learned in the lesson.

Running on the Treadmill

There is no better way to learn than by doing, so I try to incorporate student work time in every session. With most students sharing a computer, I asked the students to take turns searching their topics.

Some of the best teachable moments come from this active learning time. In this case, a student found a reference to the *Wall Street Journal* but was distressed to find that it was not in full text on LexisNexis Academic. I quickly demonstrated how to use the library's "Journal & Newspapers" title keyword search to identify which print or electronic library resources contain full text for a particular periodical title, a skill that would transfer to many other databases and obviously would be a big time saver for the students.

Cool Down and Weigh In

With just a few minutes left in the class, I reminded students of the availability of research assistance and invited them to follow up with one-on-one contact either via e-mail or meeting in my office or at the reference desk. Students left the session with at least one article on their topic and the knowledge of which databases to use to complete their assignment. Throughout the session, the students were attentive and engaged, so generally I was pleased with the way things went. I subscribe to the notion of the spiral curriculum, that information literacy takes many passes with a deepening of the level of instruction to produce a lifelong learner. This was just the first pass for government students.

Reflection on the Instruction Session: Lessons Learned

In retrospect, I realize that I could have done more to prepare for the session. Although I had used the registrar's course database to ascertain the demographic composition of the class, I had not retrieved the student contact information that was also readily available. Equipped with this information, I could have e-mailed the upperclassmen in advance of the library session to enlist their help and assign specific tasks without wasting precious class time to do so. Similarly, I could have surveyed the class by e-mail to get a general sense of their research skill level. Additionally, I could have created student name placards to help create a friendlier learning environment in which students are addressed by name.

It would have helped to include the ACRL Information Literacy Competency Standards learning objectives on the handout. As important as it is for the professor and librarian to see the relationship between the outcomes and objectives, students learn best when they are aware of the reason(s) behind the activity.

Adhering to the "less-is-more" principle is often difficult when negotiating the content of the library instruction session. In this case, the professor has offered to help students in future classes to select and focus their topic before coming for the library research session. This will allow more time in the library session to concentrate on search strategies and to address the frequent student lament that they don't know what words to use in the database to achieve effective results. It would be very helpful to be able to provide the students more supervised practice in this area. I do think that the better we are at defining faculty and librarian responsibilities in the information literacy partnership, the better the instruction and subsequent research experience will be for the student.

A true assessment of the instructional session comes from looking at the students' papers, particularly the bibliographies, to see if the students used a sufficient number of articles from appropriate newspapers and magazines and asking the professor to compare the work of this class with previous classes. Generally, the number of sources used by students in their papers was higher than before. Previously, it was more apt to be just two or, at best, three articles cited. Now the number of newspaper and magazine articles was more closely in line with what had been requested in the assignment, with the average papers citing eight to ten sources and the best papers citing ten to fifteen references. Also, the quality of the sources improved. Except for the few really poor papers, every student paper cited CQ Researcher and most made reference to the *Washington Post* or the *Wall Street Journal.* And, of note, a good number of editorials were referenced from those major papers, meaning the students had not only found articles, but used the appropriate type of article for a contemporary political issue research paper.[7] Based on the data, we can rate the instruction session a success, and with the implementation of the suggested improvements above, it should become an even more satisfying teaching and learning experience for all.

Notes

1. Diane E. Schmidt and Kathleen Carlise Fountain, "Locating Research Materials Using Indexes, Databases, and the Internet," in *Writing in Political Science: A Practical Guide,* 3rd ed., ed. Diane E. Schmidt. (New York: Pearson Longman, 2005), 39–73.

2. Association of College and Research Libraries, Law and Political Science Section, "Political Science Research Competencies Guidelines." Availableathttp://www.acrl.org/ala/acrl/aboutacrl/acrlsections/lawpolisci/lpsspublications.htm. Scroll down page to "Miscellaneous Publications and Releases" section for links to draft guidelines (.doc files).

3. Association of College and Research Libraries, Information Literacy Competency Standards for Higher Education (Chicago: ACRL, 2000). Available online from http://www.ala.org/ala/acrl/acrlstandards/inform ationliteracycompetency.htm.

4. Kate Manual, "Teaching Information Literacy to Generation Y," *Journal of Library Administration* 36, no. 1/2 (2002): 195–217.

5. For an explanation of whole language, see Harlow G. Unger, *Encyclopedia of American Education,* 2nd ed., vol. 3 (New York: Facts on File, 2001), 1171.

6. Richard Saul Wurman, *Informationanxiety2* (Indianapolis, Ind.: Que, 2001), 40–45.

7. Robert C. Turner, Assistant Professor of Government, Skidmore College, personal communication, 2006.

Teaching Resources

SKIDMORE COLLEGE
LUCY SCRIBNER LIBRARY

Library Resources for GO 101:
Introduction to American Government

Find Periodical Articles:
- Databases are accessible from Library's Find Subjects / Government/ Resources for Government Web page. http://www2.skidmore.edu/library/subjects/subjects_tabbed.cfm?sub_id=26.00000&format=Articles
- Use the Journals & Newspapers page (mouse over Find Articles) to locate full text of journal articles in Scribner Library or available electronically in the databases. http://www.skidmore.edu/library/journals/index.htm
- For help in locating articles consult How Do I ...Locate Periodicals in Scribner Library http://www.skidmore.edu/library/help/periodicals.htm

- **CQ Researcher** (Ref. H 35 E35) Handout available: http://cqpress.com/docs/CQR_Reference.pdf
CQ Researcher, a weekly publication, covers the most current and controversial issues of the day with complete summaries, insight into different sides of the issues, bibliographies and more. A good starting point for identifying current political issues. Be sure to check out the Bibliography and Pro/Con sections of the publication.

- **CQ Weekly** (Ref. JK 1 C15)
A weekly publication on Congress with in-depth reports on issues looming on the congressional horizon, plus a complete wrap up of the previous week's news, including the status of bills in play, behind-the-scenes maneuvering, committee and floor activity, debates and all roll-call votes.

- **LexisNexis Academic News**
Provides news from a multitude of sources, including newspapers, magazines, transcripts, and wire services.
    News category: General News/Major Newspapers
    Use the **Sources List** link on the Guided Search form to limit

search to specific publications. The limit can be to one title or as many as five titles concurrently.

- *New York Times*
- *Washington Post*

News category: Magazines and Journals

- *Newsweek*
- *U.S. News & World Report*

Search Techniques:

1. **Terms/Topic: LATCH**
   - **Location** – geography of topic – where?
   - **Alphabet** – terms, synonyms, people – who?
   - **Time** – time period for searching - when?
   - **Category** – concepts or type of resource – what?
   - **Hierarchy** – broader or narrower perspective – how?

   Richard Saul Wurman, *Informationanxiety2* (Indianapolis, Ind.: Que, 2001), 40-45.

2. **Connectors**:
   - **and** <mccain-feingold AND campaign finance reform>
   - **or** <voucher OR choice>
   - Proximity:
     - Numerical: **w/n** <school w/5 voucher>
     - Grammatical: **w/s** (sentence) school w/s (voucher or choice)

       w/p (paragraph) <internet voting **w/p** >

3. **Phrases**: " " = use quotation marks <"campaign finance reform">

4. **Truncation**:
   - Root expander = **!** <**govern!**> = government, governor, govern
   - Wild card = ***** <**wom*n**> = woman or women

5. **Limits**:
   - At Least Command = **atl_( )** <atl3(electronic ballot)>
   - Length of article = more than 500 words <**length(>500)**>

6. **Printing/Emailing/Downloading articles**:
   - Print – use the print button in upper right of screen, select display document and then select print icon on browser

- Email – use the email button in upper right of screen, include complete email address, e.g. <bnorelli@skidmore.edu>
- Download – no direct download feature in LN, can select all of the text, copy and then paste in to a word document that you save on DataStor.

Cite Sources:
- **How Do I ...Cite a Source?**
  http://www.skidmore.edu/library/research/citation.htm
  Path: Scribner Library home page/ How Do I?... / Cite a Source?

- **Citing References from LexisNexis™ Academic**
  http://support.lexisnexis.com/academic/record.
  asp?ArticleID=Academic_citing_refs

For assistance:
- **Barbara Norelli,** Social Sciences & Instructional Services Librarian
  - Office: Library Rm. 109; Phone: 580-5513
  - Email: bnorelli@skidmore.edu
  - Reference Desk Schedule: Monday: 6:30–10:00 p.m.
  Wednesday: 12:30–3:00 p.m.

- **Reference Librarian**
  Hours: Monday – Thursday: 10:00 a.m.–5:30 p.m. and 6:30–10:00 p.m.
  Friday: 10:00 a.m.–3:00 p.m.
  Saturday: 2:00 p.m.–5:00 p.m.
  Sunday: 2:00 p.m.–5:00 p.m. and 6:30–10:00 p.m.

Chapter 19

Research in Reverse: Attempting to Retrace a Researcher's Steps

Christopher Cox

Introduction

Too often, instruction sessions run the risk of becoming mechanical "how do you search a particular database" sessions. Searching is usually the least of students' worries. In my experience, students rarely understand the purpose of research and appear to believe that the peer-reviewed journal articles they find (if they understand the concept of peer-reviewed) arrive on the earth with little blood, sweat, and tears on the part of the writer(s). Dr. Elise Weaver, a faculty member in psychology at Worcester Polytechnic Institute, echoed my concern and together we created an assignment that would allow students to explore the research process in reverse, letting them see the finished product, look at its sections, and examine the process by which the article was accepted for publication. Our hope was that students would better understand how peer-reviewed articles are created; and in writing one, they would learn how their work fits into the ongoing conversation of the scientific community.

Analysis of the Learning Situation

I approached Elise Weaver in the winter of 2004. I had taught instruction sessions for her various courses for three years and was interested in expanding the library's presence in one of these courses, Introduction to Cognitive Psychology (SS 1401). One option was to use Blackboard, possibly by posting an assignment prior to the session or offering a communication venue (discussion board, chat) afterward.

Elise shared her frustration over the class's group assignment as well as other concerns she had about her students' research. Students in SS 1401 were asked to conduct a study examining a particular mental process in depth. Typical topics might include the reasons for differences in people's memories of the same event or whether there is any proof that listening to classical music makes infants smarter (the "Mozart effect"). The assignment itself consisted of two parts. The first part was a term paper proposal that asked students to provide their research question, five source citations and abstracts resulting from a literature search, and a brief description of the different experimental approaches the sources illustrated. Had anyone done something similar before? How would the students' research add to the ongoing scholarly conversation? The idea was to monitor students' research and offer them a context for the experiment. The second part was the paper itself, which was structured like a peer-reviewed journal article, requiring literature review, methods, results, discussion, and reference sections.

SS 1401 is a survey course for sophomores exploring psychology as a major. I always thought the assignment described above was difficult for these students because most of them probably never had to conduct research at this level before or might not know what a peer-reviewed article is. In the fifty minutes I was given in previous sessions, I usually demonstrated my search strategy using a sample topic provided by the instructor. I covered the usual subjects. I discussed Google and explained why it wasn't the best tool for the assignment, demonstrated how to search the library catalog and various periodical databases, including PsycINFO, MEDLINE (PubMed), ScienceDirect, and Web of Science. I explained what peer-reviewed journals were, emphasized how to limit a search to them, and along the way discussed how to trace a research topic back to its origin by looking at encyclopedia articles, works cited in article bibliographies, and the number of times cited in the various databases.

Despite the good intentions of my session, students were still encountering problems. They could search and find peer-reviewed articles. However, the students didn't understand the purpose of performing a literature review. They didn't understand how their writing and the articles they found fit in with work others had already done. We needed to find some way of putting their research into context.

Information Literacy Standards

(Note: A complete list of ACRL *Information Literacy Competency Standards for Higher Education* [Chicago: ACRL, 2000] appears as appendix A.)

We primarily emphasized Information Literacy Competency Standard Three: "The information literate student evaluates information and its sources critically and incorporates selected information into his or her knowledge base and value system,"[1] and the following Performance Indicators and Outcomes: 3.2.a, 3.3.a, 3.3.b, 3.4.a, 3.4.b, 3.4.c, 3.4.d, 3.4.f, and 3.4.g.

Lesson Plan

In response to the challenges noted above, we decided to offer students the opportunity to explore the research process in reverse. Elise would assign a reading to be used as an illustration of high-quality scientific writing. She eventually settled on an article from a then current issue of *Science*, "Intersubject Synchronization of Cortical Activity during Natural Vision."[2] The article was pertinent to coursework, as it explores the correlation between different subjects' brain activity in response to viewing parts of the same movie, in this case Grimaldi's *The Good, the Bad and the Ugly*.[3] Elise found the study fascinating and thought students would relate to its hypothesis.

The article was posted on Blackboard and read by students prior to my session. Accompanying the article on Blackboard was a worksheet I had composed consisting of a series of questions about the article. Students were asked about the article's structure, the author's background, and the publication process. These questions encouraged students to think about how the authors addressed the outcomes within Standard Three.

The fifty-minute session consisted of the following:

1. *Review reading and worksheet.* With the instructor, discuss the article and the answers to the questions with the students.

2. *Introduce the library resources Web site.* I created a Web site with links to various resources I covered and showed students how to find it from the library home page.

3. *Brainstorm keywords.* I led the class in brainstorming keywords based on the article's topic. Keywords were written on the board for use in later searching.

4. *Tracing the author's research steps.*

   a. *Google search.* Search a set of keywords in Google. Show the broad scope, non peer-reviewed results. Nothing from the example article's references would show up. The article's authors probably didn't use it.

   b. *Sample searches of keywords in three databases.* The idea was to return results that match items listed in the example article's references.

      i. PsycINFO—Explain that not all journals are indexed in every database and that all cover different time periods.

      ii. MEDLINE (PubMed)—More medical journal coverage. Show adjustment of search strategy. More results from article's references. Probably used by authors of article.

      iii. Social Sciences Abstracts—Show how broad the subject coverage is, but that some multidisciplinary material or duplicates from previous searches may result.

5. *Show movie.* Show movie snippet from *The Good, the Bad and the Ugly* for discussion, reward.

Elise also tightened the description of her assignment, making its goals more apparent.

Description of the Instruction Session: What Actually Happened?

For the session, about thirty-five of the class' fifty students showed up. I conducted the lesson in their normal classroom, beginning by asking students to take out copies of the example journal article and the worksheet. I asked students what they thought about the experiment. Hearing nothing, I asked what the point of the article was. Finally, a lone voice answered. It was unclear if everyone had actually read the article. It also was hard to tell if the silence I was experiencing was the actual class dynamic or if the students just weren't that interested in the assignment.

We discussed the answers to the questions on the worksheet. Much of the time Elise had to call on students to respond. I used the questions to introduce topics such as author authority, the journal's audience, and peer-reviewed article characteristics. We also examined the references list. All this was met with a general malaise.

Next, I showed them the Web site for the course and it was on to brainstorming keywords. We had a number of good responses, though it took a while. The searches of the databases went off without a hitch. Noting a lack of involvement on the students' part, I asked for volunteers to conduct the searches at the computer using keywords from the board. My lesson didn't work as well as I had expected because the keywords they came up with didn't always mesh with my own. We did find some of the same references that the article's authors came up with, however.

Finally, in the last three minutes of the class, we showed a snippet from *The Good, the Bad and the Ugly*. Elise attempted to discuss what they were seeing and how it related to the article they had read, but they either just enjoyed the movie or fidgeted with their backpacks, preparing to leave for their next class.

Reflection on the Instruction Session: Lessons Learned

Elise noted that the students' work did improve as a result of the changes we had made. However, there were a number of things that, if I were to do it all over again, I would do differently.

First of all, Elise and I agree that we could have chosen a different example article in a more predictable format. The *Science* article does include the information required by the assignment, but the sections (literature review, methods, etc.) are not labeled and are difficult to find.

I would have worked with the instructor to get her more involved in the discussion of the article. I also would want to figure out a way to put the movie snippet to a better purpose, rather than just relegating it to the end of the session. Perhaps showing the movie at the beginning of the session would have "set the stage," resulting in more discussion of the article.

The size of the class was also a challenge. At an enrollment of fifty students, the class was unwieldy to begin with. I couldn't bring them to our instruction lab and do any hands-on exercises because our lab only seats thirty. Student involvement in the session was negligible. They just didn't seem as excited about the article as the instructor and I thought they would be. Their lack of preparation and participation seriously hurt the session.

There are a variety of ways this defect could be addressed. Perhaps next time, I will divvy the students up into two groups and hold the class in the lab so that I can conduct hands-on exercises. The students themselves could search in Google, PsycINFO, and the other resources covered and thus explore some of the example article's citations for themselves. In the lab I could also assign groups of two or three students to explore one of the search resources and then ask them to report back to the class with their findings. That would certainly have aided in student participation.

In the larger classroom, there are not quite as many options. In an effort to get students to talk more about the article, I could ask more specific questions, ones that require only a yes or no answer. I could call on particular students in the order in which they are seated. Another idea would be to divide the students into small groups, ask them to discuss their answers first and come to a consensus, and then report back to the class. I have also recently been experimenting with personal response system (PRS) technologies, or "clickers," which have worked successfully in eliciting feedback on questions, particularly in large classes with students who are less apt to actively participate. By offering clicker-friendly yes or no or multiple-choice questions based on the worksheet, I could easily increase class participation.

The reason students were uninterested in the session's content also might have been that many (as indicated on their evaluations) had previously had an instruction session, perhaps taught by me as one of only three librarians teaching sessions. Many of the students may have felt they already knew the material, though few had had a session in another psychology class.[4] The next time I teach this session, I will post a quick five- to ten question survey on Blackboard, asking students if they had had a previous session and get a sense of their strengths and weaknesses with the material so I could adjust the lesson accordingly. To both aid in participation and give students who are more knowledgeable the chance to show what they know, I could involve those students who already had a session or who did particularly well on the survey in the lesson planning, asking them to teach sections of it.

The session also didn't succeed in meeting some of the information literacy outcomes Elise and I had suggested, specifically those relating to the evaluation of information. I could have done a better job of continuing to shy away from merely presenting searching rather than putting the entire research process into context. Perhaps an adjustment to the paper proposal asking students to not only log experimental approaches, but also to evaluate how well they were executed and explain what method(s) they would use now that they have looked at others' approaches.

Despite any setbacks, I still think that the idea behind the SS 1041 assignment and the session supporting it, giving an example article and retracing a researcher's steps, can be used successfully to put students' research experience into context. Class dynamics change and, by implementing the adjustments suggested regarding the lesson plan and its execution, such an exercise will allow students to better understand scholarly publishing as a whole.

Notes

1. Association of College and Research Libraries, *Information Literacy Competency Standards for Higher Education* (Chicago: ACRL, 2000). Available online from http://www.ala.org/ala/acrl/acrlstandards/inform ationliteracycompetency.htm.

2. Uri Hasson, Yuval Nir, Ifat Levy, Galit Fuhrmann and Rafael Malach, "Intersubject Synchronization of Cortical Activity during Natural Vision," *Science* 303 (Mar. 12 2004): 1634–40.

3. *The Good, the Bad and the Ugly*, DVD, directed by Sergio Leone (1967; Santa Monica, CA: MGM, 1998).

4. Worcester Polytechnic Institute, "Student Course-related Evaluation Form." Available online from http://www.wpi.edu/Academics/Library/Help/Instruction/Forms/ studcrsreleval.html.

Teaching Resources

SS 1401: Introduction to Cognitive Psychology

After reading "Intersubject Synchronization of Cortical Activity During Natural Vision," please answer the following questions.

1. In your own words, what is the central question of this article?

   _____

2. In what way does the method used to conduct this study differ from previously published studies?

   _____

3. In what paragraph do the authors discuss the background research or literature review they conducted?

   _____

4. What conclusions did the authors come to, based on their study?

   _____

5. Where does author Uri Hasson work now, and where did he work when he conducted this study?

   _____

6. Has Uri Hasson published anything other than this article? Please explain the process by which you answered this question.

   _____

7. By what process was this article accepted for publication (see General Information for Authors, Manuscript Selection - http://www.sciencemag.org/feature/contribinfo/prep/gen_info.shtml#manuscript)?

   _____

8. Who do you believe the audience is for this article?

   _____

9. Using the style suggested by the article's references, cite the article you have just read.

   _____

Chapter 20

Suntanning as a Risky Behavio(u)r: Information Literacy for Research Methods in Psychology

Allison Faix and Jennifer Hughes

Introduction

The following interactive activities were designed for Research Methods in Psychology (Psychology 226), a course taught at Coastal Carolina University (CCU). According to the CCU course catalog, Psychology 226 is "an examination of the wide variety of procedures available to the behavioral scientist for collecting and analyzing behavioral data." [1] This course is a prerequisite for the senior psychology major capstone course, Applied Research in Psychology (Psychology 497), which is described as "a research experience in which students are required to develop a research project, conduct a literature review, gather and analyze data, prepare a research paper in accord with the standards of the American Psychological Association (APA), and present their research." [2] The session's activities were designed around a hypothetical research project exploring attitudes of college students toward suntanning as a high-risk activity.

Analysis of the Learning Situation

In Psychology 226, students are required to think of a research topic that could, but does not have to, become the experiment they will later conduct in Psychology 497. Students then research this topic, looking for relevant journal articles, and prepare a written research proposal that includes a literature review section. The literature review section of their proposal must contain at least five citations to scholarly journal articles. A majority of these journal articles must not be more than ten years old. Students also may cite books and Internet sources, but they are strongly encouraged to make sure that most of their research is in scholarly journals.

The classroom in CCU's Kimbel Library is furnished with six rectangular tables that can be easily rearranged to accommodate different classroom situations or activities. For this instruction session, we arranged the tables in a horseshoe shape around the outside of the walls, leaving space in between each table so that when we asked students to work in groups, it would be obvious that each table is a group. This configuration made it easy for us to walk around and answer questions. Twenty-four chairs were evenly divided up between the tables. In the space left in the middle, we set up the cart with the library's laptop and projection unit so that examples of online searching could be shown. The library's mobile laptop cart, containing twenty-four wireless computers, is located at the back of the classroom. When it is time for computer activities, students are asked to retrieve laptops from the cart to use in their groups.

By arrangement with the professor, we taught this session during the Psychology 226 weekly lab time slot instead of during their regular, three-times-a-week, fifty-minute class time slots. Because the lab time is scheduled to last three hours, this offers much more time to conduct activities and cover concepts.

Information Literacy Standards

(Note: A complete list of ACRL *Information Literacy Competency Standards for Higher Education* [Chicago: ACRL, 2000] appears as appendix A.)

Our goals for this session are organized around the following ACRL Information Literacy Competency Standards for Higher Education:[3]

Standard One: After the Journals versus Magazines activity, students will be able to distinguish between magazines and journals and will be exposed to many different publications related to their discipline.

Standard Two: After the Brainstorming Keywords activity, students will be able to identify a wide variety of appropriate search terms on their topics.

Standard Two: After the Using and Comparing Databases activity, students will be able to use several different online databases and compare and analyze search results.

Lesson Plan
Brief Introduction
The librarian introduces herself to the class and explains the purpose of the instruction session.

First Activity: Journals versus Magazines
This is an active learning session where students are asked to walk over to the current periodicals section of the library and bring back one journal that might be a good source for a psychology research project. They then share the reason they thought that their periodical was a journal and not a magazine. We then discuss the differences between magazines and journals and why it is important to use journals for this assignment.

Second Activity: Brainstorming Keywords
The librarian proposes a sample research topic and breaks students into groups. Each group is asked to think of as many different search terms as possible for three different keywords in the sample topic. As each group reports, the librarian offers suggestions about each term, including truncation, synonyms, or possible databases.

Third Activity: Using and Comparing Databases
Each group is asked to perform the same keyword search in four different databases and compare the results. As each group reports, the librarian asks questions about the results and uses students' examples to underline the importance of searching more than one database and trying different variations of keywords to narrow or broaden searches.

Lesson Conclusion
The librarian points out specific hints, such as article location, remote database access, interlibrary loan, Ask a Librarian, and Research Appointments. The librarian concludes by addressing any remaining questions from students.

Description of the Instruction Session: What Actually Happened?

Although this session was initially designed to be taught by one librarian, we decided to experiment with team teaching. Before the session, it was decided that one librarian would be the primary instructor and the second librarian would provide additional assistance to students during group activities.

During the first activity when students were asked to retrieve a psychology-related journal, we led the students to the current periodical shelves because most students did not know where they were located. In the periodical section, most students flocked to the "J" section to find "Journal of." Because many psychology journal titles do not include the word *journal,* the students quickly ran out of choices in the "J" section. Students quickly realized that psychology-related journals can be found throughout the current periodical collection.

When students showed their selections to their classmates in the instruction room, many were hesitant to reveal their title because they were unsure that they had chosen a relevant periodical. We encouraged the students by pointing out the appropriateness of each choice, being careful to highlight titles outside the discipline that were still excellent selections. We were surprised that no one brought a magazine, so we showed students a copy of *Psychology Today.* Students were asked why they had not chosen a periodical such as this. This led to a discussion about the difference between magazines and journals. The professor's enthusiastic participation in this discussion was greatly appreciated because it seemed to increase the students' interest and reinforce the importance of the activity.

We pointed out that when looking for an article on a specific topic, browsing the current periodicals collection is not an efficient method. Students will need to search online databases. This led to the next activity, which helps the students become better database searchers.

The second activity focused on keyword brainstorming. We introduced our preselected topic of research "Attitudes of college students toward suntanning as a risky behavior: a preliminary investigation." Because the university is located ten miles from Myrtle Beach, we felt this topic was one that students could easily relate to and actively contribute to brainstorming. We used this preselected topic because most students had not chosen their own topic at this point in the semester. We chose a topic that would be appropriate, contain a significant number of variables, but would be unlikely to be chosen by a student.

We wrote the topic on the white board and divided the topic into three categories: attitudes, suntanning, and related concepts. Each group was given a sheet of paper and told to write as many keywords as the group could think of in five minutes. As we circulated around the room, students were actively engaged in group discussion of keywords. We encouraged the groups and offered suggestions to those that did not have many terms.

After five minutes, we asked each group to tell us the terms they had written. We wrote these on the white board in the appropriate category. Although we were pleased with the number and variety of terms the groups had thought of, we added several more that we thought were important from our previously compiled list. As terms were displayed, we discussed the challenges of searching, including alternative spellings, international spellings, scientific terms, and truncation. Students seemed to display enthusiasm for this activity, and even competitiveness among groups in the class.

We ended this activity by reminding students that they would want to brainstorm keywords to use in their database searching after they develop their own topics for research.

Before the library session, we had prepared a guide to resources specifically for the class. This guide was available from the library's Web page throughout the semester and provided quick links to online databases and other resources appropriate for the class.

The next activity allowed students to get hands-on experience by searching in four specific databases from the online guide. Each group was asked to get two laptop computers from the back of the room. We used the projection unit to demonstrate the online guide. Each group was given a list of four databases: PsycINFO, EBSCO Academic Search Premier, MEDLINE, and ScienceDirect. In addition, each group was given a sheet of paper with a different set of keywords related to the original suntanning topic. We chose the keywords in advance because we knew they would provide good examples.

Each group was asked to perform the same, exact search in all four databases and compare the results. We asked the groups to write down the number of articles found in each database and the number of articles from magazines as opposed to journals. Students also were asked to note any interesting differences they found between the databases and to remember any questions about searching techniques they might have.

In the beginning, the exercise seemed to confuse students because they focused more on how the students should fill in the worksheet instead of analyzing the databases. By the second or third database, the students began to catch on. We went around to each group to answer questions and ensure that groups were successfully searching.

After all the groups had finished searching, we asked each group to tell the class what their search terms were and how many articles they found in each of the databases. This was effective because students were able to see that some terms resulted in many more articles in a database than others. The value of this activity is to show that it is important to use a variety of keywords as well as to search in a variety of databases. Students noticed that they found different articles in each database, although we had to prompt them to come to this conclusion by asking questions.

At the end of the group activity, we asked for questions about searching. When students did not offer any questions, we took the opportunity to clarify some issues, including how to use our open URL link resolver hosted by UNC Greensboro, JournalFinder, to tell which journals the library owns and how to request an article through interlibrary loan. We also mentioned that students could sign up for research appointments for additional assistance.

Reflection on the Instruction Session: Lessons Learned

One of the important things that we learned from this session is that team teaching was successful in this type of interactive session. In the future, even if two librarians are not available to teach at the same time, it would be useful to bring along an experienced student assistant (especially a psychology major) to help in directing students to the periodical section, writing on the board, and answering basic library questions.

Using a sample topic seemed to help students alleviate the anxiety they felt about choosing a topic for themselves. We think it was important for the students to realize that their topic could be something from everyday life, not necessarily from textbooks or the science lab. The topic we chose seemed to engage the students in brainstorming.

Another lesson we learned was that during the third activity, students were reluctant to note interesting features of each database or questions that they had. Our instructions for this part of the exercise were too vague, and there was no specific place for the students to write these things on the handout. The handout we provided was meant for them to note observations; however, the students assumed that it was a "fill-in-the-blank" exercise. We will consider revising either our instructions or the handout itself in the future to make expectations more clear.

Collaboration with the psychology professors who have taught this course over many years has greatly contributed to the development of these instruction activities. Over the past six years, more than five professors have taught the course. Each year, the librarians consult with the professor to determine the current content and focus of the course. After each instructional session, the librarians again talk with the professor to evaluate the effectiveness of the session for the students. The content of the instructional session is then revised.

At the end of the most recent session, the professor mentioned that she would like to make sure the students have their topics ready before the library session, next semester, so that they can brainstorm their own topics in between the second and third activities. Making this change will allow us to model brainstorming and allow students to gain experience on their own. We are currently planning an activity that will allow students to do this in the allotted time.

We taught this session twice in the same week, and we noticed that each activity took a different amount of time in each class, although, fortunately, we did not run out of time. If we had not had a three-hour timeslot, we would have had to be much more careful about timing activities. It is beneficial to have the extra time so that each class can work through the activities at their own pace.

Notes

1. Coastal Carolina University, *Coastal Carolina University Catalog* (Conway, SC: Coastal Carolina University, 2005). Available online from http://www.coastal.edu/catalog/2005_2006/index.html.

2. Ibid., 370.

3. Association of College and Research Libraries, *Information Literacy Competency Standards for Higher Education* (Chicago: ACRL, 2000). Available online from http://www.ala.org/ala/acrl/acrlstandards/inform ationliteracycompetency.htm.

Teaching Resources

Sample Brainstorming Keywords Handout

Attitudes:

Attitudes	*Perspectives*	*Beliefs*	*Knowledge*
Awareness	*Risk Taking*	*Views*	*Risky Behavio(u)r*
Carelessness	*Perceptions*	*Objections*	*Thoughts*

Suntanning:

Sun Tan	*Suntanning*	*Sun Tanning*	*Sunbathing*
UV Rays	*Ultraviolet*	*Sun Exposure*	*Wrinkles*
Tanning Parlors, booths, beds			

Related Concepts:

Melanoma	*Skin Cancer*	*Skin Neoplasm*	*Sunburn*
Sunscreen	*Self-Tan*	*Prevention*	*Education*
Gender Differences		*SAD seasonal affective disorder*	

Sample Using and Comparing Databases Handout

Combine the keywords your group was given to create searches that retrieve relevant articles in the following databases. Record notes about each of your searches and indicate the number of results for each search.

Keywords: *sun* and attitude* and neoplasms*

PsycINFO: *57 results, many full text, 50 peer reviewed*

Academic Search Premier: *1 result, full text article*

MEDLINE: *390 results, many not full text*

ScienceDirect: *No Results*

Chapter 21

Into the Breach: Teaching Graduate Students to Avoid Plagiarism

Patti Schifter Caravello

Introduction

Graduate students in the social sciences are eager to engage in the scholarship of their subject disciplines, with their successful record of undergraduate research papers behind them and the prospect of an advanced degree before them. Faculty and others assume that these students possess the knowledge and skills to properly document their sources and ethically use the ideas and words of others. But some literature counters this assumption,[1] and a great deal of literature indicates that students plagiarize when they are undergraduates.[2] The Office of the Dean of Students at the University of California, Los Angeles (UCLA), is probably not the only university administrative body to observe that graduate students are not always fully prepared in this area. Although undergraduates who are referred to the dean because of academic integrity breaches have a workshop to attend at UCLA, no preventive or instructive program existed for graduate students. This provided a perfect opportunity to collaborate with the Office of the Dean of Students to tackle a problem of mutual interest that lies at the intersection of information literacy and academic integrity. The central challenge in designing a workshop for graduate students on avoiding plagiarism was to create an engaging session, adaptable to multiple settings and topics that would offer something valuable about a sensitive subject to advanced, experienced students in various disciplines.

The library had collaborated with the Dean's Office to develop an online tutorial[3] and to give citation classes to undergraduates well before they contacted me to discuss ideas for graduate students. The workshop we created was given four times in summer–fall 2005, in three distinct programmatic settings.

• Graduate Summer Research Mentorship Program: Directed by the UCLA Graduate Division, this program enables about thirty doctoral students in the social sciences and humanities to work closely with faculty mentors to accelerate the progress of their research over the course of one summer. The ninety-minute "Avoiding Plagiarism" workshop was held in a classroom outside the library.

• New Graduate Student Orientation: Created by the UCLA Graduate Student Resource Center, this one-day, fall event is open to all new graduate students and includes a plenary session, a resource fair, and over twenty workshops to choose from, on topics such as funding opportunities and keys to success in grad school. The fifty-minute "Avoiding Plagiarism" workshop was held in a nonlibrary classroom.

• Young Research Library (YRL) Workshops: Offered by the YRL (the main library for social sciences and humanities graduate students and faculty), this program presents online catalogs, article databases, bibliographic management systems, and other topics of interest to YRL's primary clientele. The sixty-minute "Avoiding Plagiarism" workshop was given twice in a YRL electronic classroom.

Analysis of the Learning Situation
The programs in which the workshop has been taught so far provided learning situations with the following in common:
• Attendees were all graduate students.
• Attendees came from various disciplines/departments, mainly social sciences.
• The workshop was optional.
• The sessions were not associated with a particular course or writing program.
• The workshop was one offering among several within a larger program.
• The workshop was held in a classroom equipped with a computer and projection screen.

The fact that the workshops were neither compulsory nor associated with a course meant that attendance at some sessions was low, publicity was limited, and, in one case, the workshop competed for attendees with sessions held simultaneously. It also meant that many students who might have needed the session did not attend.

Each discipline presents some unique documentation problems and conventions. To neutralize this potential difficulty, I have taken the following approaches: (a) the PowerPoint presentation I created and the UCLA Avoiding Plagiarism Web site[4] provide essential information and background needed by all at an advanced level, (b) during the workshop students explore specific examples carefully selected from real situations that arise in social science disciplines, and (c) I invite students to submit in writing their unique questions, which I answer later by e-mail. The presentation makes clear that principles surrounding the ethical use of information apply generally to writing at American universities and all the social sciences. However, it is also critical for graduate students to know that the instructor recognizes the citation/documentation problems that arise in their disciplines and can answer specific questions students ask at the workshop or later. For graduate students, this topic is not hypothetical, but directly applicable to their work: they are all, or soon will be, engaged, in research and writing. They are using and building upon the works of others, and they need to impress faculty with their scholarship. Yet, some come to this workshop topic with old habits and preconceived ideas, and some come from other countries where rules and conventions about plagiarism can be very different. With their awareness that the stakes are high, graduate students who choose to attend this workshop geared to their level are quite receptive to the subject of avoiding plagiarism.

Information Literacy Standards

The workshop is designed to address Association of College and Research Libraries (ACRL) Information Literacy Competency Standard Five, specifically Performance Indicator and Outcome: 5.2.f. ("Demonstrates an understanding of what constitutes plagiarism and does not represent work attributable to others as his/her own").[5] The workshop addresses a few other ACRL performance indicators/outcomes in support of this main outcome. The subjects of intellectual property and copyright inevitably arise in discussions about plagiarism; therefore, the presentation provides information related to 5.1.d. ("Demonstrates an understanding of intellectual property, copyright, and fair use of copyrighted material"). The workshop also addresses 5.3.a. ("Selects an appropriate documentation style and uses it consistently to cite sources") by emphasizing the need to learn and use the correct style for the discipline and highlighting some lesser-known details about citation techniques, although no particular citation style is taught. The session introduces sophisticated strategies for note taking and proper paraphrasing because these are essential methods for avoiding plagiarism; this is in Standard 3.1.b. ("Restates textual concepts in his/her own words and selects data accurately"). Although graduate students are not specifically mentioned in the ACRL Standards, they need to achieve these outcomes as much as or, arguably, to a higher degree than do undergraduates. Their literature reviews have to be far more extensive. Appropriately acknowledging intellectual debt is an essential part of becoming a scholar, and graduate student research has the potential to be used later by others who will need to count on scrupulous documentation.

Lesson Plan
Learning Objectives
Students will:

- Consider afresh the problem of plagiarism, understand its meaning, and be introduced to university policies
- Review research practices and strategies to avoid plagiarism
- Demonstrate that they can identify situations in which citation is necessary and can properly paraphrase
- Know where they can obtain more information and help

Basic Lesson Plan

- Introductions (Dean of Graduate Division)
- Informal Talk (Dean of Students):
    — The meaning and significance of academic integrity
    — The rules, policies, and consequences at UCLA regarding academic integrity, especially plagiarism
- PowerPoint Presentation and Active Learning Exercises:
    — Definitions, societal context, recent instances (academia and journalism)
    — Cyberplagiarism: special challenges
    — Strategies: what and how to cite
    — Active learning exercise on what does/doesn't require citation and why
    — Strategies: criteria for proper paraphrasing, novel approaches to note taking
    — Active learning exercise to read and select the best paraphrase for a short text
    — Detection: low-tech and high-tech methods available to faculty
    — Active learning exercise to write a paraphrase of a piece of academic writing, exchange it with another student and offer critique
- Additional question-and-answer opportunity
- Students write a quick assessment and submit questions in writing (optional)

Description of the Instruction Session: What Actually Happened?
The first time the workshop was given (for the Graduate Summer Research Mentorship Program), we had ninety minutes and included all the components described above: the deans spoke on university policies and the seriousness of academic integrity at the graduate level and I used PowerPoint to present the context for plagiarism in our society, problems inherent in a copy-and-paste environment, and how graduate students in the social sciences can develop or alter their research habits to avoid

it. Students participated in all three active learning exercises and asked questions during the session. However, timing was a major challenge; the deans' part went longer than expected, and I hurried through some of the slides in order to get to the third active exercise, which still had to be abbreviated.

Based on the first experience and the pertinent questions students asked, the workshop was tightened up the second time it was given (for the New Graduate Student Orientation) and the following changes were made: the PowerPoint presentation went first, punctuated by just two of the active learning exercises, and the dean's part, condensed, came afterward. The PowerPoint was edited to reduce redundancies and the exercises were altered to include topics students had raised in the first workshop. Timing was still problematic and the dean had less time than expected. This fifty-minute session was the best attended of the four workshops (thirty students) and generated the most dialogue. Both sixty-minute sessions given through the YRL Workshop program followed the pattern of the second workshop, except no one from the Dean's Office attended one of them. With each session, less time was spent on the topic of detection (which was less germane to workshop goals) so that more time could be devoted to prevention principles and strategies. The optimal length of the session is sixty to ninety minutes in order to address the critical issues and actively engage in learning.

Based on the written and verbal feedback, students were most enthusiastic about the active learning exercises. When students apply and discuss what they hear in the presentation, it engenders a deeper understanding. I would not attempt a session on this topic without the active components. Descriptions of the exercises follow:

To Cite or Not to Cite—and Why

This exercise generates much discussion because the answers are not all straightforward. For some of the situations, the answer to (a) is yes *and* no (e.g., where a parenthetical reference is required, but an entry in the Works Cited list is not [#7], or where an acknowledgment [not a bibliographical reference] is needed, but the quoted person's identity is disguised because of confidentiality [#3]). Other situations can be substituted to best suit the target audience, focus on a single discipline, or emphasize certain rules.

This exercise can be done aloud with the whole group, or the students can work alone or in pairs followed by group discussion. The latter method takes more time, so I prefer the full-group approach. Students are encouraged to write answers and notes on their handouts for later reference. The instructor must be prepared to highlight all nuances in each situation if the students themselves do not identify them in the discussion.

Paraphrasing Activity 1: Identifying Plagiarism

The instructions for this activity are to read an original source paragraph and three paraphrases of it, and to answer the questions, Which is plagiarized? Which is paraphrased correctly? Why? I used an example from a book for sociology students;[6] many examples like it are available on the Web.[7]

After the students read the text, the discussion can begin by either asking which is the good paraphrase and why, or taking the paraphrases in order and asking what is good and bad about each one. A few students challenge the solution to this exercise. At one session, a student claimed that the plagiarized sentence could be construed as common knowledge and therefore did not require citation or rewriting; the dean and I pointed out that what is common knowledge in one field is not in another, and because the source was cited at the end of the paragraph, it was not possible that the nearly identical wording was coincidental. The student understood but seemed unhappy that he would have to change his understanding and habits. To the question on the evaluation form, What did you find most interesting or helpful from this workshop? he wrote "That I am a plagiarist, unfortunately." (He showed me this ironically at the end of the session.)

Paraphrasing Activity 2: Writing and Critiquing a Paraphrase

Students read a piece of text,[8] write a paraphrase of it, exchange it with another student, and discuss and critique the other student's paraphrase. An alternative to the last step (if time is short) is to discuss as a group what was difficult about paraphrasing the text. As this activity takes about fifteen minutes, it can be included in the workshop only if there is time, or if it will be used in place of one of the other exercises.

The best choice of text for a graduate student audience is one that is appropriate to the students' subject discipline, includes more than one concept to rewrite, uses some distinctive phrases that either need to be quoted or rewritten completely, and has some detail to capture for accuracy. For graduate students, a relatively complex piece of text offers challenges, provides ample opportunity to apply the criteria, and generates discussion.

The workshop's active learning discussions and written feedback provide assessment of student learning. Students are asked to fill out two cards at the end of the session, one to note a strategy they heard that they would try to use and the other to ask their remaining question about plagiarism (answered later via e-mail). The organizers of the New Graduate Student Orientation workshops also distributed a generic evaluation form, which yielded very positive responses. The questions students asked during the workshop and in writing reflect the sophisticated nature of graduate work. Students reading foreign-language material asked about citing their own translations. Those who were also teaching assistants asked about handling instances of plagiarism with undergraduates they teach. And those involved in field research asked about citing interviews. Questions received in writing included how to quote a professor's lecture, the meaning of self-plagiarism, citing an unpublished article when unsure if the author is ready to circulate the ideas in it, and whether/why to cite an author after discovering your "original" idea is not original. I answered all written questions by e-mail, in some cases checking with the dean first. I also received a few follow-up questions from the students.

Reflection on the Instruction Session: Lessons Learned

A student who attended one of the sessions told me weeks later at the reference desk that she thought all new graduate students needed the workshop because many are not aware that some of their practices can lead to plagiarism. The workshop brings this topic out in the open for discussion and learning. It remains to be seen how or if we can reach all new social sciences graduate students if the workshop remains optional, or even whether taking one workshop is enough to make the difference. Because the workshops are given as one-shot sessions, the assessment of student learning has to be immediate. Subsequent assessment or follow-up assignments would be required in order to evaluate if any success (e.g., increased understanding, more ethical practice) was lasting. Teaching this topic in the context of course-related instruction could provide access to the students later in the term for this purpose. If faculty are receptive to librarians incorporating techniques for avoiding plagiarism into library instruction, more students could be reached, given that contextual instruction is normally a mandatory part of a course. All or part of the workshop content can be used (e.g., one of the active learning exercises can easily be adapted for a specific group and incorporated into a class session). A colleague asked me for the exercises so he could adapt them for graduate students to do *prior* to an instruction session, and another has asked me to present the whole workshop as one part of a three-hour instruction session for a graduate course. Developing and presenting the "Avoiding Plagiarism" workshop can thus inform teaching in various instructional settings. It can even prepare a librarian to discuss documentation or plagiarism issues during individual consultations with graduate students.

The collaboration with the Dean's Office to develop the workshop, explain university policies, and answer student questions enriches the workshop content and lends it a valuable perspective. The session can be given without a dean present as long as the deans' informative brochures are introduced and handed out. The disadvantage to this is that the dean is not immediately available to answer questions on policy; the advantage of the dean's absence is that students may feel freer to reveal their past lapses or misperceptions when no authority figure is there, especially in cases when they have been referred by the Dean's Office to take the workshop. Like all the other research strategies we impart, the ethical use of information and other people's intellectual property is something that many graduate students need us to teach; they are not receiving systematic instruction in this anywhere else. Collaboration—with the dean, graduate division, and graduate orientation programs—is an effective approach. By stepping into the breach, librarians become an integral part of the budding scholar's training.

Notes

1. For example, Patrick G. Love and Janice M. Simmons, "Factors Influencing Cheating and Plagiarism among Graduate Students in a College of Education," *College Student Journal* 32, no. 4 (Dec.. 1998): 539–50; Barbara J. Fly et al., "Ethical Transgressions of Psychology Graduate Students: Critical Incidents with Implications for Training," *Professional Psychology: Research and Practice* 28, no. 5 (Oct. 1997): 492–95.

2. Zorana Ercegovac and John V. Richardson, "Academic Dishonesty, Plagiarism Included, in the Digital Age: A Literature Review," *College & Research Libraries* 65, no. 4 (July 2004): 301–18.

3. "Bruin Success with Less Stress," UCLA Library. Available online from http://www.library.ucla.edu/bruinsuccess/.

4. Patti Schifter Caravello, *Avoiding Plagiarism: Strategies & Resources*, PowerPoint. Available from the author; UCLA Library, "Avoiding Plagiarism," http://www.library.ucla.edu/yrl/reference/avdplagiarism.htm.

5. Association of College and Research Libraries, *Information Literacy Competency Standards for Higher Education* (Chicago: ACRL, 2000). Available online from http://www.ala.org/ala/acrl/acrlstandards/inform ationliteracycompetency.htm.

6. Judith Richlin-Klonsky and Ellen Strenski, eds., A *Guide to Writing Sociology Papers*, 5th ed. (New York: Worth Publishers, 2001), 39–40.

7. Two examples: Indiana University Writing Tutorial Services, "Plagiarism: What It Is and How to Recognize and Avoid It," Indiana University, available online from http://www.indiana.edu/~wts/ pamphlets/plagiarism.shtml; University of Alberta Libraries, "Proper Paraphrasing," University of Alberta, available online from http://www. library.ualberta.ca/guides/plagiarism/handouts/paraphrasing.pdf.

8. The paragraph used for this exercise is the one that begins, "Bias is an uncontrolled form of interest..." in Jacques Barzun and Henry F. Graff, *The Modern Researcher*, 5th ed. (Boston: Houghton Mifflin, 1992): 186–87.

Teaching Resources

UCLA LIBRARY

To Cite or Not to Cite—and Why

Many circumstances pose subtle problems for writers who want to be certain not to plagiarize. For each situation below, (a) note whether a citation is needed and (b) identify hard or tricky issues in the situation, or note why you don't need a citation.

1. You are writing about your experiences and impressions of people you encountered on an archaeological trip to Peru.
(a)

(b)

2. You use data you found on the Web from the U.S. Government in your writing. (Note: U.S. government publications and information are not copyrighted.)
(a)

(b)

3. You are quoting a person you interviewed in the course of your field research.
(a)

(b)

4. You translate a sentence from a French-language article and use it in your paper.
(a)

(b)

5. In your thesis proposal, you mention that there were mass protests against the Vietnam War in the late 1960s.
(a)

(b)

6. You want to incorporate another scholar's idea, without actually quoting him, in the handout you are creating to distribute at a conference where you are making a presentation.

(a)

(b)

7. In a paper you are writing, you relate your friend's story of her experience conducting research in China.

(a)

(b)

8. You want to put into your paper a diagram you found on a Web site (personal author unknown) that illustrates a complex political process.

(a)

(b)

9. In your thesis, you want to use some background information you found in a handwritten letter from a World War II soldier to his parents.

(a)

(b)

The idea for this exercise came from "Exercises for Practice" at the Purdue University Online Writing Lab "Avoiding Plagiarism" Web site, although the format and all the "situations" are different.

9/05

Chapter 22

Undergraduate Social Work Students and Government Documents: An Integrated Approach to Contextual Learning

Chantana Charoenpanitkul and Ryan L. Sittler

Introduction

As undergraduate social work students advance through their coursework at Shippensburg University of Pennsylvania, their information requirements grow and change. This change exposes a true need for these students, not just to receive more library instruction, but also to receive instruction that is more comprehensive. Our interest in achieving this goal led to the creation of instruction sessions that are course specific and integrated across the curriculum for the Social Work Department. Skills are leveled and built on as the students progress from their first year to completion of their degrees. This approach to information literacy is supported by the description of the social work curriculum in the undergraduate catalog:

> The social work program is organized by learning objectives and competencies that are integrated throughout the curriculum.... The social work curriculum builds upon this foundation in a sequence of courses designed to prepare the entry-level social worker for practice. These courses prepare students to know about and to be able to work with individuals, families, groups, organizations, and communities.[1]

Essentially, students need to develop an understanding of contemporary social work practice by examining its history, professions, knowledge base, and values. Specific library instruction sessions have been developed for three required courses in the undergraduate social work curriculum; this ensures that all students will be exposed to the same information, at a time when it is needed in their studies, without repeating "everything they already know." Each new instructional meeting allows for skill development by building on what was taught in the previous session, as well as integrating with the sequence of required courses in the program.

Analysis of the Learning Situation

Three classes were selected, with collaboration from Professor Elizabeth Fisher, Department of Social Work and Gerontology, Shippensburg University, for this cross-curricular approach. These classes are: Social Work in Social Welfare (SWK102); Assessing Individuals in the Social Environment (SWK250); and Assessing Organizations and Communities (SWK340). In brief, skills expected to be learned in each session include: searching for biographical information about social workers and basic research skills (SWK102); advanced information searching using online databases, including an introduction to government documents (SWK250); and finally, advanced searching using government documents (SWK340). Librarians Chantana Charoenpanitkul and Ryan Sittler shared responsibility in teaching the first two courses in this sequence. Chantana Charoenpanitkul taught the third course.

Students learn and retain information better, in many instances, in a contextual learning environment. Considering this factor, a hands-on laboratory approach was implemented for all classes. Additionally, undergraduate social work students need information provided in government documents as their research skills become more advanced. Given the unique nature of government documents, their uses and applications are reserved for the second and third library instruction session, with U.S. Census data being a highlight of the third session. This chapter focuses on the third session, which was taught by Charoenpanitkul.

The students taking Professor Fisher's Assessing Organizations and Communities class are expected to be able to demonstrate advocacy for empowerment; develop and manage professional relationships; and manage the change process in their organizations and communities. Therefore, the objectives of the course are for students to:

• Understand the behavior of organizations, communities, and neighborhoods from a systems/ecological perspective, including life span and aging issues.

• Understand the importance of advocating for systems development and change on behalf of clients needs.

• Identify issues of discrimination and oppression that have a community or organizational context.

Each student is required to do an assessment of his or her home community, as a requirement of this course. Utilization of U.S. Census data is part and parcel of this assignment. One library instruction session, therefore, highlights the effective use of Census data as a means for community assessment.

Information Literacy Standards
(Note: A complete list of ACRL *Information Literacy Competency Standards for Higher Education* [Chicago: ACRL, 2000] appears as appendix A.)

The following Information Literacy Competency Standards for Higher Education were addressed:

Standard One: "The information literate student determines the nature and extent of the information needed."

Standard Two: "The information literate student accesses needed information effectively and efficiently."

Standard Four: "The information literate student, individually or as a member of a group, uses information effectively to accomplish a specific purpose."[2]

Specific Information Literacy Competency Standards, Performance Indicators, and Outcomes are correlated with the librarians' learning objectives for this session, as follows:

• To locate background information using the U.S. Census Web site. (Performance Indicators 1.1 and 1.2)

• To access and retrieve needed data effectively (Performance Indicators 1.1)

• To organize and analyze data into a logical framework (Performance Indicators 2.2 and 2.5)

• To integrate the research technique into one's own set of research skills (Performance Indicators 4.1 and 4.2)

Lesson Plan
Introduction
Present an overview of government documents. Review the use of the Web and how to evaluate information available through the Internet. Highlight official and reliable resources available from federal and local government agencies' Web sites, such as the Bureau of U.S. Census Web site.[3]

Discussion of the Census:
• Community characteristics
• Geographic areas
• Time frame
• Data sets, reports or files

Description of the Instruction Session: What Actually Happened?
This seventy-five-minute session took place in the library computer lab so that each student could have access to a computer. I (Chantana Charoenpanitkul) started by introducing myself. I provided my contact

information in case the students needed further assistance. Professor Fisher and I shared the introduction of the assignment. I then reminded the students that whether they are using the library catalog, databases, or the Internet to search for information, they need to first determine the type of information for which they are searching.

I reminded the students of our overall objective for the class and its related assignment on community assessment, in which the students need to understand their neighborhood from a systems/ecological perspective.

The U.S. Census of Population provides a vast amount of information about general, social, and economic characteristics of the population. In order for students to effectively locate and use Census data for Population and Housing Characteristics, and Social and Economic data, they need to understand the types of data available and the ways in which the data are organized. The students also need to know how to use American FactFinder (AFF),[4] the site's search tool.

To begin using the Census Web site, students needed to identify four things:
1. Community characteristics
2. Geographic areas
3. Time frame
4. Specific data sets, reports or files.

Community characteristics: We then discussed what variables the students needed to locate. For example: Shippensburg is a small college town (home of Shippensburg University)—but who lives here? Population can be examined in regard to both size and diversity in terms of race and age group. Additionally, thought is given to whether this is considered to be a rich or poor community (socioeconomic status and education levels, income and poverty rate). Finally, quality of life in and around Shippensburg is considered (housing situations, rental or ownership, price range, etc).

Geographic areas: Most of the students clearly knew the geographic areas for which they were looking. However, there were some students whose communities or hometowns were difficult to clarify and they needed special assistance in finding data for a very specific region. At this point, the students began using the Census Bureau site. I asked them to enter their home town into the Population search area. I demonstrated how to search by address as well. The students had an opportunity to look at information from the results, the Fact Sheet, which includes basic demographic information for a location. Many of them were able to get the data they required from this basic search.

Time frame: The students also were required to see the growth or changes in their neighborhood and make a comparison across time. The students were reminded that they might need to compare data from the most current census to the previous one, as well as look into data from population projection and annual population surveys and estimates.

Data sets: The data provided by the U.S. Census Bureau are in various "sets," for example: Decennial Census, American Community Survey, Annual Population Estimates, and Economic Census and Annual Economic Surveys. Depending on the type of information or data needed, the students will learn to search using these data sets. Most of the time, data from the Decennial Census will provide adequate information for analysis of a community's characteristics. The next step was to introduce the more sophisticated search tool, American FactFinder. The students were able to use AFF to create a customized table allowing them to compare their chosen community to other neighboring towns, as well as to the entire state of Pennsylvania. I also mentioned that if they need more in-depth information they should use the AFF with Decennial Census Data Sets, which are tables of data including far more detailed demographic characteristics than are otherwise available.

At this time, students were asked to follow my demonstration by creating a Custom Table for poverty data of Shippensburg, Cumberland County, PA, and by comparing it with Carlisle, Cumberland County, PA, and with Chambersburg, Franklin County, PA. Carlisle and Chambersburg are neighboring communities of Shippensburg and similar in many demographic aspects. Finally, students were given the opportunity to individually locate and retrieve the data for their own hometown. They were given fifteen minutes to search. I circulated and consulted individually with students as they explored the Census Web site. By the end of the session, students were able to locate and retrieve the baseline information for assessing their home communities. During the last five minutes of the session I distributed handouts, which introduced the students to other federal and local government Web sites that provide demographic data.

Reflection on the Instruction Session: Lessons Learned

Having taught this session numerous times, we found that a seventy-five-minute session gave us more time to effectively cover this complex topic than did the fifty-minute-session we had previously tried. Although the Census Web site and American FactFinder provide the user with high-quality data about our nation's people and economy, inexperienced users find the applications somewhat cumbersome to use. The types of data provided by the U.S. Bureau of Census are difficult for students to grasp, as well. Some data sets represent the "complete" population of the United States, and other data sets are representative rather than complete. This makes it very necessary for us to provide more instructional detail, with more emphasis on demonstration, than we would normally provide with a less complex topic.

Another problem we encountered is that although maps, which can be created from Census data at this multifaceted Web site, are very useful as visual representations of the data, during the instruction session students retrieving these maps can became so interested in them that they do not follow the demonstration. We have found that we need to mention this and ask the students not to download the maps until they have finished their initial search.

Overall, this session successfully helps students to find the statistical and demographic data that they require for assignments in SWK340 by teaching them in a contextual, hands-on environment. However, the whole of this program is greater than the sum of its parts. Teaching different sets of information literacy skills at different points in the curriculum, as a means of skill building, has proved to be very successful—and a good approach for this type of instruction.

Notes

1. Shippensburg University, *Shippensburg University 2005-2007 Undergraduate Catalog.* Available online from http://www.ship.edu/catalog/ug05-07/Courses.pdf.

2. Association of College and Research Libraries, *Information Literacy Competency Standards for Higher Education* (Chicago: ACRL, 2000). Available online from http://www.ala.org/ala/acrl/acrlstandards/informationliteracycompetency.htm.

3. U.S. Census Bureau. http://www.census.gov/.

4. U.S. Census Bureau, "American FactFinder." Available online from http://factfinder.census.gov/home/saff/main.html.

Teaching Materials

Library Resources for Social Workers

Reference Materials:
- Encyclopedia of Social Works (Reserve Desk)
- Reference sources in Social Work: An Annotated Bibliography (Ref Collection)
- Guide to information sources for social work and human services (Gen Collection)

Finding Scholarly Resources:
- SocINDEX with Full Text
- Social Services Abstracts
- Haworth Journals Online

List of Journals on Social Services and Welfare:
- From Journal List browse by subject
- SU Library subscribes to about sixty-two related journals

Consider Related Fields:
- Sociological Abstracts
- CINAHL
- Medline
- Criminal Justice Abstracts
- ERIC
- Professional Development Collection
- AgeLine

Biographies Search:
- Wilson Biographies (ON CAMPUS ONLY)

APA Style Manual:
- http://webster.commnet.edu/mla/index.shtml

Internet Resources:
Organizations:
- National Association for Social Workers—*http://www.naswdc.org.* Founded in 1955, the NASW is the largest association of professional social workers in the world. Site includes catalog of publications, Code of Ethics, accreditation information, and links to job resources.

- International Federation of Social Workers—*http://www.ifsw. org.* Founded in 1950; affiliated with 59 national organizations. Site includes IFSW publications (some full text), current activities & conferences, and contact information.
- Clinical Social Work Federation—*http://www.cswf.org.* The CSWF is a confederation of 31 state societies for clinical social work. Site includes links to clinical social work resources on the net, news items, and legislative alerts.

Chapter 23

Library and Information Literacy Built into a Social Work Credit Course

Grace Xu

Introduction

The School of Social Work at the University of Southern California (USC) traditionally offers information literacy instructional programs to its master's degree students. During orientation, students are required to take a library tour, a computing workshop, and a library research workshop. In 2005, the school revised its curriculum. The library workshop and an online information literacy tutorial were built into a newly created foundation course. In this chapter, I highlight the library research workshop, online information literacy tutorial, and the creation of library assignments related to the social work course syllabus.

Analysis of the Learning Situation

The two-year master of social work degree program admits about 280 students each year on three campuses: the main campus in Los Angeles, and two satellite campuses in Orange County and Skirball. All library collections are located on the main campus.

A social work library previously existed in the school's building. In 1998, the university closed the departmental library, replacing it with an information center: two group study rooms, and a lab with instructional equipment and twenty computers to access the Internet and other electronic research tools. A social work librarian responsible for library instruction and research help, as well as collection development and outreach is housed at the information center. The former library's print collections were integrated into the university's main social science book stacks and the other libraries.

Most social work students have limited time to visit the campus libraries in person due to internships and tight class schedules. The program requires all students to complete internships in local social work agencies two days per week during a semester. When the students are on campus, they usually have classes from 8:00 a.m. to 4:00 p.m. As a typical urban university, USC has limited dorm space on campus and almost all social work students live off campus.

As a result, the students make use of electronic resources. In 2004 and 2005 new student library surveys, all social work students said they had computer and Internet access at home. The 2005 library survey of students on the satellite campus showed that 55.3 percent of the students had never checked out a book in the previous semester and that 50 percent of the students said that library books were less important than journal articles.

The new digital research environment has brought excitement for students as well as a challenge: how to find resources online. I often found that students didn't know the distinctions between the OPAC and the article databases, they depended on Google to search for articles, and they did not know how to search the library online catalog and locate resources in different libraries. The teaching faculty and the school's administrators also realized the need to improve the students' research skills.

As a consequence, since the social work library was closed in 1998, the school has required all new students to take a library orientation tour and library research workshop. The social work librarian has been invited to meet with the school's orientation committee each summer to plan the library tours and to schedule library workshops with the leading instructor of the policy course.

USC encourages its faculty to apply innovative approaches to teaching. In spring 2005, the university offered a series of "Learner Centered Instruction" workshops for the teaching faculty from different schools and programs. I attended the workshops. I not only learned how to design a lesson plan based on students' learning needs and how to use class activities based on learning outcomes, but also found the opportunity to collaborate with a social work professor who was also attending the workshops.

In the 2005 fall semester, the social work professor, Esther Gillies, was to be the lead instructor for Policy and Practice in Social Service Organizations (SOWK534), a new foundation course to replace the former policy course. She was preparing the syllabus and hoped to use a "learner-centered" approach for the new class. I told her about my ideas for creating an online information literacy tutorial for the social work students. She was very impressed and suggested the tutorial be an addendum to SOWK534. We also agreed to create weekly information literacy assignments related to the social work course.

In the 2005 spring semester, we researched other university's information literacy tutorials through the Web, selected one open source model suitable for us, and drafted each class session's research activities based on the content of the tutorial. During the summer, I was responsible for modifying the tutorial and importing our assignments into the course management courseware, while she wrote social work vignettes. Our project won the support of the school's vice dean of academic affairs. In the 2005 fall semester, we had permission to launch a trial in two SOWK534 classes.

Information Literacy Standards

(Note: A complete list of ACRL *Information Literacy Competency Standards for Higher Education* [Chicago: ACRL, 2000] appears as appendix A.)

The social work professor and I used the following standards:

a. Information Competencies for Social Work Students, EBSS/ACRL 2003[1]

b. Information Literacy Competency Standards for Higher Education, ACRL 2000[2]

In the hands-on workshop, we focused on the Information Competencies for Social Work Students because of their relevancy to our students. As a result of completing the library workshop, we expected the following learning outcomes. Students should:

• Know how to access materials on the home library online system

• Be knowledgeable about the ability to obtain items not physically available at the home library (interlibrary loan and document delivery)

• Recognize that the mastery of the research process goes beyond the assignment at hand

• Recognize the necessity for scholarliness and discipline in research

• Know their local resources

The following Information Literacy Competency Standards for Higher Education, with Performance Indicators and Outcomes noted,[3] were addressed in the online tutorial:

Standard One: "The information literate student determines the nature and extent of the information needed"; 1.1.b, 1.1.e, 1.2.a, and 1.2.d.

Standard Two: "The information literate student accesses needed information effectively and efficiently"; 2.1.a, 2.1.c, and 2.3.c.

Standard Three: "The information literate student evaluates information and its sources critically and incorporates selected information into his or her knowledge base and value system"; 3.2.a.

Standard Four: "The information literate student, individually or as a member of a group, uses information effectively to accomplish a specific purpose"; 4.2.a.

Standard Five: "The information literate student understands many of the economic, legal, and social issues surrounding the use of information and accesses and uses information ethically and legally"; 5.3.a.

Lesson Plan
Library Workshop
The library workshop is offered during the first month of each fall semester as part of SOWK534, which is required for all first-year students. Each session is about forty-five minutes and includes twenty students per session.

Learning Activities:
1. Completion of library survey (five minutes)
2. Introduction to online resources and library services using the Randall Information Center Research Gateway Web page (five minutes)
3. Discussion of the library research process (fifteen minutes)
4. Creation of library and interlibrary loan system accounts (five minutes)
5. Practice (ten minutes)
6. Review of library research steps, and introduction of the online information literacy tutorial (five minutes)

Online Information Literacy Tutorial
In the six weeks following the library workshop, the students are required to work through the online information literacy tutorial, one session per week. The tutorial includes six sessions, each taking about thirty minutes.

Learning Objectives:
The students will be able to identify research topics, access information via the Internet, evaluate the found materials, and apply the preferred citation style.

Learning Activities:
• Work through online tutorial text and Flash animated exercises, and take an optional self-graded information literacy quiz
• Finish a weekly task on Blackboard, using the information literacy skills learned from the online tutorial to solve the problems described in the vignettes

Description of the Instruction Session: What Actually Happened?
Library Workshop
At the beginning of each library workshop, I required all students to take an online survey. The survey questions examine the students' basic knowledge about library research and the Internet. One objective of the library workshop was to introduce new students to the library's electronic resources. To make a clear presentation and to give students an easily accessible reference "handout," I created a research gateway Web page before the workshop.

The Information Center Gateway Web page[4] highlighted the library catalogs, social work–related databases, the social work print collections scattered in different libraries on campus, and some helpful Internet search engines and Web links to other social work libraries. During the workshop, the Web page was set up as the default home page for all students' computers. I gave an introduction to the library services and resources using this Web page, allowing time for hands-on exploration of the page.

Another goal of the library workshop was to teach formulating research strategies. Starting with class discussion, I asked the students where to start their research when there were so many tools and resources. Most of time, their initial response focused on whether to start with general interest databases or subject-specific databases. Then I would ask questions, such as: "How many sources do you need?" "How recent should your sources be?" or "Can you use news articles?" The students normally concluded "it really depends." Before the workshop, I prepared an online flowchart highlighting key library research steps: Think, Find, Evaluate, and Cite. Critical thinking was the main theme of each step in the chart. After the discussion, I referred students to this handout.[5]

The rest of the workshop was hands-on. The students created library and interlibrary loan accounts. I gave them several social work topics and citations and time to practice. They asked me questions or compared search results among themselves. I usually gave a brief review at the end of the workshop[6] and recommended that students take the online information literacy tutorial.

Online Information Literacy Tutorial

There are many well-designed open-source information literacy tutorials available. We selected Research 101[7] and modified it for the social work students. The tutorial includes text, Flash animated exercises, and self-graded quizzes. The six sessions of the tutorial introduce key concepts of information literacy. In our modified tutorial, many original examples were replaced by social work related topics, as well as USC library and the southern California regional information.

In the 2005 fall semester, the online tutorial was added into the syllabus for a foundation credit course for first-year social work students. As a trial, the students were required to read one section of the tutorial per week in the six weeks following the library workshop. In addition, a weekly information literacy task counting 10 percent of the course credit was posted on Blackboard. The students were asked to read the social work vignettes first and then use the information literacy skills learned in the tutorial to answer the questions. All vignettes were written by the social work faculty based on real cases.

Reflection on the Instruction Session: Lessons Learned

As a solo librarian serving a school with almost six hundred students and faculty on three campuses, I have a heavy workload in reference and instruction. I have found that instruction immediately eliminates a large number of frequently asked reference questions. And according to the teaching faculty, the quantity and quality of the resources used in students' research papers and field reports have improved dramatically following library workshops. However, I have found that forty-five-minute workshops were far too short to introduce the various library collections and research tools, let alone the information literacy competency standards. I believed that we should provide an instructional service that could be accessible by the students at any time and from any location.

The instructional research gateway Web page was one of my solutions. On the Web page, I listed not only the social work journals, books, videos, and archival materials, but also the steps to find these collections. If students needed further help, they could click the buttons marked "Teach Me More," linking them to Flash animated search demonstrations. I created these interactive demonstrations with a software program called Viewlet Builder. I found that my research gateway Web page has been an effective tool in classroom instruction and a helpful guide for the students afterward.

The online tutorial is a supplement for the workshop. It covers information literacy and library research skills that I don't have time to cover in the workshop. The students can learn at times convenient to them and focus on information needed at that time. Many students told me they found the online tutorial fun and helpful. They enjoyed the self-paced learning. Instead of producing an online tutorial from scratch, modifying the open-source Research101 saved me time and energy.

Most of my students had work experience before their graduate study. They commonly demonstrated two attitudes toward library instruction, either assuming they knew everything about library research or considering library research as not relevant to practitioners. I found that a few challenging survey questions at the beginning of the workshop could increase their awareness of their own information needs. And the weekly task related to the social work field practice, especially the vignettes, helped the students to understand that library instruction and information literacy instruction could benefit their future social work careers.

I also realized that the success of our library and information literacy program could not occur without collaboration with the teaching faculty and the administrators. The credit-bearing weekly task pushed the students to take part in the online tutorial. Information literacy instruction should not be an independent library program but, rather, should be emphasized in every course, taught by every educator.

Notes

1. Association of College and Research Libraries/ Education and Behavioral Science Section, Social Work/ Social Welfare Committee, "Information Competencies for Social Work Students." Available online from http://www.lib.msu.edu/corby/ebss/socialwork/competencies/basics.html.

2. Association of College and Research Libraries, *Information Literacy Competency Standards for Higher Education* (Chicago: ACRL, 2000). Available online from http://www.ala.org/ala/acrl/acrlstandards/informationliteracycompetency.htm.

3. Ibid.

4. Grace Xu, "Randall Information Center Research Gateway," University of Southern California. Available online from http://sowkweb.usc.edu/library/.

5. "Library Research Strategy," University of Southern California,. Available online from http://sowkweb.usc.edu/library/handout/process.pdf.

6. Grace Xu, "Information Literacy Tutorial—An Addendum to SW 534." Available online from http://sowkweb.usc.edu/library/research101/index.html.

7. University of Washington Libraries, "Research 101." Available online from http://www.lib.washington.edu/uwill/research101/.

Teaching Resources
A sample weekly Information Literacy Task:

Directions:
Read the short vignette below and select those answers that apply

Your field placement is in a private non-profit agency providing child abuse treatment services in South Central Los Angeles. Your assignment is to identify and discuss state policy related to the population for which the agency provides services.

Question 1. Which question might be the most effective to initiate your search?

[ ] How many other agencies in my community provide child abuse treatment services?
[ ] What are the laws in California relating to child abuse?
[ ] Are there any government funded programs to provide treatment of child abuse victims?
[ ] Is a child more likely to be abused in a lower income family?

Question 2. Which key words would be the most effective in your search?

[ ] Child abuse policy and California
[ ] Non-profit agency and California
[ ] Child abuse treatment and California
[ ] Child abuse treatment and South Central Los Angeles

Targeted Instruction Programs for Students in Graduate Professional Programs at a Large Research Institution: Lessons from Business, Journalism, and Social Work

Kathleen M. Dreyer, Alysse D. Jordan, and Deborah Y. Wassertzug

Introduction

Within Columbia University Libraries' structure, the Business, Journalism, and Social Work Libraries are all part of the Social Science Division. The Business Library offers "on-demand" instruction sessions, as well as reference desk and on-call hours and individual consultations. The Journalism Library does not offer traditional desk hours, relying exclusively on consultations (mostly unscheduled). At the Social Work Library, research consultations have proved to be a valuable enough service to justify eliminating traditional desk reference in favor of a consultation model, which blurs the line between reference and instruction. Our experience supporting students in these programs has shown that not only do the needs of graduate students in the social sciences differ from those in the humanities and sciences, but a further distinction can be made between students in graduate academic programs and those in graduate professional programs.

Master's students in business, journalism, and social work are enrolled in one- to two-year programs that include practical components such as internships, beat reporting assignments, and field placements, which limit the amount of time they spend on campus. Adding to their limited time on campus, students' work is often accomplished under tight deadlines, meaning that they are most focused on results rather than on the research process. In order to best reach students in business, journalism, and social work, we have designed innovative, highly specialized services that offer students more in-depth and individualized assistance than could be provided within the confines of a traditional reference desk or general instruction session.

Business School students have responded enthusiastically to the Business and Economics Library's on-demand sessions, which are most often requested by students working in groups. The Business and Economics Library supports MBA and PhD students and faculty in the Graduate School of Business and the Department of Economics. During orientation sessions at the beginning of each semester, business reference librarians promote on-demand, subject-specific sessions, allowing students to schedule orientation sessions when the research need arises. MBA students are most interested in retrieving relevant data, analysis, and other types of information. Lesson plans are irrelevant, as students' immediate research needs drive the content of the session. It is important to focus on their specific research need, with less emphasis on the "how" of research.

Similarly, the journalism librarian has responded to the deadline-driven nature of journalism students' work by providing project-focused instruction. The Journalism Library supports the Graduate School of Journalism, which offers three degrees: the MS in journalism; the PhD in communications; and new in 2005, the MA in journalism, which affords students with some journalism experience the opportunity to spend a year developing in-depth knowledge within a subject area, while writing journalistic pieces focused on the subject area of choice. The journalism librarian supports all journalism programs by offering classroom instruction as part of orientation programs, as well as by faculty or student request. The new MA program posed an unusual situation because its students already possess general journalistic research skills but require guidance in using the subject-specific research resources that will enrich their reporting and writing.

To meet student needs of social work students in the most customizable and flexible way possible, the Social Work Library has forgone traditionally scheduled reference hours in favor of an on-call consultative model, centered on providing-high quality, user-driven research consultations. The Social Work Library serves the research needs of more than nine hundred MS and PhD students enrolled at the Columbia University School of Social Work. Due to the nature of the two-year social work master's program, students are assigned to a field placement three days a week, limiting the time they are on campus to receive library instruction and reference assistance; therefore, much of the focus of the Social Work Library's instruction program is on student-initiated one-on-one research consultations. The articulated role of social work education on students' development of interpersonal, collaborative, and advocacy skills creates a particularly captive audience of students who are very receptive to this approach.

Based on our observations throughout our years of working with students in business, journalism, and social work, we have realized that the needs of graduate professional students differ greatly from those of their peers in more traditional graduate academic programs. We have the unique advantage of having libraries physically located within the respective schools, meaning that we are more visible to the schools' administrations; so our role in providing instruction and research guidance is also more visible. Professional students' information-seeking behaviors and expectations of library services are therefore often based on their need for efficiency and convenience rather than a need to be exhaustive in their research for the sake of scholarship. In the case of business, journalism, and social work, we have designed flexible reference and instruction programs that are easily customizable to meet the specific needs of our students. Case studies of each of these programs are presented here.

Case Study I: Business
Kathleen M. Dreyer

Analysis of the Learning Situation
Four MBA students, working in a group for a specific assignment, requested an on-demand library session. The session lasted one hour and focused on finding company and industry information for an airline.

Information Literacy Standards
(Note: A complete list of ACRL *Information Literacy Competency Standards for Higher Education* [Chicago: ACRL, 2000] appears as appendix A.)

MBA students are mostly interested in getting information quickly and efficiently. This on-demand session addressed the following Information Literacy Competency Standard for Higher Education: Standard Two: "The information literate student accesses needed information effectively and efficiently" and Standard Four: "The information literate student, individually or as a member of a group, uses information effectively to accomplish a specific purpose."[1]

Lesson Plan
Because the on-demand session focused on a specific assignment, the students learned how to use the information to complete the assignment or research. Information on companies is extensive, and the students discovered through our interaction how to evaluate the various sources and then apply the relevant information to their coursework. I did not employ a formal lesson plan outline; though a handout on company research was given. The students asked questions during the session; the answers to these questions formed the bulk of the session's content.

Description of the Instruction Session: What Actually Happened?

To begin the session, I asked which type of information the group needed about the company: financial statements, analyst reports, or newspaper articles, and how much detail or historical data they wanted. In this case, the students needed all the information available on the company.

I started with the database Factiva, demonstrating how to find articles on an airline. First, I entered the name of the airline in the search box and did not limit the search. This search retrieved thousands of articles, many not useful at all. I then demonstrated to the students how to limit their search to the headline and lead paragraph of the article, and to limit their search to just a subset of the database. This search yielded fewer articles with a higher degree of relevance. This helped the students understand the importance of limiting their searches.

Next, I covered several databases for finding financial information on a company and discussed how to download the data to a spreadsheet. Most company databases are simple to search, as they only require the user to enter a ticker symbol or company name. However, I covered several company databases and discussed the different information that could be found in each. For example, the database EdgarScan has company filings but does not have earnings estimates. Industry information on the airline industry was also covered. In this case, we looked at the S&P Industry Profile for the airline industry.

During the session, the students asked many questions, such as how to find analysts' reports, market share, and earnings estimates. Sources for competitor information and industry ratios also were discussed. These questions made the session interesting for both the students and myself and gave me a chance to interact with the students and really understand their research needs. By not having a formal lesson plan to follow, I was able to focus the session on the information the students really needed.

Case Study II: Journalism
Deborah Y. Wassertzug

Analysis of the Learning Situation

When the new Journalism MA program began in fall 2005, I marketed subject-specific library instruction to faculty coordinators of the four subject areas that constitute the program: arts and culture; economics and business; politics and government; and science. All faculty responded positively, and I held four sessions within the first month of the school year. This case study focuses on the session held for the students in the arts and culture concentration.

Students in the MA program enjoy more time to spend with their topics, but as journalists, they are interested in getting to the heart of the issue as quickly as feasible. My instinct, therefore, was to design as open-ended a session as possible, allowing for ample time for questions from students.

Information Literacy Standards

(Note: A complete list of ACRL *Information Literacy Competency Standards for Higher Education* [Chicago: ACRL, 2000] appears as appendix A.)

Given the information-seeking habits of journalists, the ACRL Information Literacy Competency Standard that applies most naturally to the learning situation is Standard Two: "The information literate student accesses needed information effectively and efficiently."[2] This standard encompasses both the presentation of intellectual content and that of more technical concerns of relevance (e.g., which Web browser to use, how to extract content from the database, etc.).

Lesson Plan

Instruction sessions, particularly in busy professional programs such as the Journalism School, afford an excellent opportunity to offer useful research tips, to introduce general ideas about information-seeking behavior, and to conduct general library outreach. But a structured lesson plan will invariably fail because it does not allow for student questions, or for higher (or lower!) levels of interest in a particular resource on the part of the students.

Prior to the session, I met with the faculty coordinator for arts and culture. She briefly described her students' story pitches, by way of providing a general idea of where their interests lay. At the meeting, I suggested that I would show them some basic databases that are potentially useful for all the topics mentioned and then show more specialized tools for specific disciplines, depending on the students' interest level.

For this session, I had the luxury of offering more detailed explanations on particular resources and, depending on the pace of the session, a chance to demonstrate more specialized resources. Because I was not necessarily familiar with all the resources relevant to each subject concentration, my preparation time was longer than usual. I conducted my own investigation of subject-specific resources and also consulted with subject-specialist colleagues.

Description of the Instruction Session: What Actually Happened?

Six students from the arts and culture concentration, along with their professor, attended my ninety-minute session. I prepared a handout that included my name and contact information, the URL for the library's

Web site, and a selective listing of five general interest databases with significant secondary source material related to arts and culture, as well as suggestions of campus libraries with relevant collections. To keep the handout succinct, I did not include databases with primary source material, opting to show them to the students based on their areas of interest.

I began the session by showing basic navigational techniques for the library Web site (because it is never safe to assume that students are aware the Web site exists) emphasizing that the library catalog and many other services can be accessed through it. Given the group's interest in the arts, I noted the catalog's ability to limit searches by format (such as films or sound recordings).

Next, I walked the students through the selected databases listed on the handout, pointing out ways to search for materials of interest (for example, book reviews). Many students were somewhat familiar with ProQuest Research Library, but when a sample search turned up a result with no full-text availability on ProQuest, I had the opportunity to demonstrate Columbia's e-Link utility, which performs a catalog search and locates the article online via another database. The group was astonished and pleased to learn of this utility. It is interesting to note that when presenting instruction to journalists, the salient details of the session may be these types of tools, which, though not subject specific, facilitate their fast retrieval of information. When they were familiar with e-Link, electronic resources heavy on abstracting and indexing, but containing less full text, did not seem as counterintuitive because they now knew where to click to find out whether the article was available online.

I presented JSTOR to the students as a good source for scholarly journal articles. JSTOR seemed familiar to the students from their course-related readings, but they were not aware of its search and browse capabilities. I knew that at least one of the students was interested in a music-related topic, so I demonstrated the browse feature of the database and clicked on the music category to show the many journal titles available there.

When I had covered a select number of databases, I gave brief virtual tours of libraries on campus of interest to students concentrating in arts and culture. The students expressed interest in one aspect or another of each library's collection. Although not all the information imparted about each library would necessarily be retained, I felt it important to make the students aware of the many collections available for them at Columbia's libraries. Often students in a professional program such as journalism feel "cloistered" in their own department and are reluctant to explore the wider university's resources. This mind-set is particularly counterproductive for the MA students, who are expected to avail themselves of the entire university's offerings.

At this point in the session, an hour had passed. I had shown the resources listed on the handout and answered the students' many questions about them. Because we were scheduled for a ninety-minute session, I recommended that we look at some of the specialized databases of primary source material in the arts (such as art images and sound recordings). The students and the professor alike found this segment of the session to be the most interesting, and it was not difficult to spend another thirty minutes demonstrating how to access digital versions of Mozart sonatas, slides of masterworks in visual art, and historical maps of New York. At the end of the session, I encouraged the students to contact me with any questions or to schedule a research consultation.

Case Study III: Social Work
Alysse D. Jordan

Analysis of the Learning Situation
The School of Social Work course, Human Behavior in the Social Environment (HBSE), is a required course for all social work students. To satisfy the requirements of the course, students must do a thorough literature review and compile an annotated bibliography pertaining to a particular social or behavioral phenomenon from a developmental life course perspective. The final paper includes an executive summary of the document that describes the overall substantive content of the bibliography, a critical analysis of the literature, and recommended future directions.

Because this is the first intensive research assignment they receive at the Columbia University School of Social Work (CUSSW), many students feel uncertain about their research skills and ability to navigate library resources in order to approach the assignment in a systematic way. Students often schedule a research consultation as a first step in the research process. A significant number of the requests I receive for research consultations are related to the HBSE assignment.

Information Literacy Standards
(Note: A complete list of ACRL *Information Literacy Competency Standards for Higher Education* [Chicago: ACRL, 2000] appears as appendix A.)

Social work graduate education is generally divided into a theoretical (classroom) component and a practical (field placement) component. Because their time spent on campus is relatively limited, students tend to focus research efforts on accessing appropriate information as quickly as possible and on accomplishing a specific purpose, with little interest in or time to delve into the more esoteric aspects of library research.

Therefore, in developing a framework for research consultations with master's-level social work students, taking ACRL's Information Literacy Competency Standards into account, it is clear that the emphasis should be placed on addressing Standard Two: "The information literate student accesses needed information effectively and efficiently."[3] Generally speaking, however, from my perspective as well as that of the student, the consultation takes place with the following desirable outcomes in mind:

- Identifies keywords, synonyms, and related terms for the information needed
- Constructs a search strategy using appropriate commands for the information retrieval system selected
- Uses specialized online or in-person services available at the institution to retrieve information needed
- Assesses the quantity, quality, and relevance of the search results to determine whether alternative information retrieval systems or investigative methods should be utilized
- Identifies gaps in the information retrieved and determines if the search strategy should be revised
- Repeats the search using the revised strategy as necessary.

Lesson Plan

Research consultations with social work students generally last from thirty minutes to one hour. During a consultation, I typically assist a student with the process of choosing a topic, articulating a research question, searching for relevant literature, and finally, identifying and critically assessing key resources needed to complete an assignment.

I conscientiously do not employ a standard lesson plan when conducting a one-on-one research consultation, as the agenda is set by the student, and often dictated by a specific assignment, as in the case illustrated here.

Description of the Instruction Session: What Actually Happened?

A first-year student in the social work master's program scheduled an appointment to discuss her annotated bibliography assignment for the HBSE course, indicating that she would like to focus on the effects of fetal drug exposure across the lifespan. During my consultation with this student, it was clear that she was not completely sure about her topic, and she mentioned that she was having trouble locating relevant articles.

When I asked this student where she had searched thus far, she indicated that she had only used Google and CLIO (Columbia's online catalog), using the keywords, Fetal Drug Exposure Across the Lifespan. I explained the difference between controlled vocabulary and natural language, and introduced her to the online databases available through the library's Web site. I recommended that she begin searching for journal articles in PsycINFO. Upon connecting to the PsycINFO database, I explained the interface briefly, pointing out the thesaurus and basic limits, such as English Language and Publication Year. Before launching a search, I explained the concept of using Boolean operators and truncation symbols to perform more efficient database searches. This made sense to her, and she composed an appropriate keyword search, which resulted in a large results set.

This student was pleased with the results, as this was quite a bit more than she was able to locate on her own. However, as we scrolled through the first page of results, it appeared that locating relevant articles might still be a challenge. I suggested that often, finding one relevant article and looking at the complete reference can be a very helpful way of coming up with further search terms and that an article's cited references will often point to similar readings.

I then suggested that a reasonable way to limit a large set of results, particularly for this assignment, might be to limit her search to longitudinal studies by clicking on "More Limits." Although she was pleased with my demonstration of this search technique, the results were not exactly what she was hoping for. I suggested that she might want to start thinking about modifying the search, to which she agreed, and typed in a revised search, which resulted in a smaller, but more focused, set of results. At this point, we had spent forty-five minutes together and she needed to get to her next class. She asked if I had any further suggestions, at which point I recommended that she also search ERIC, Social Work Abstracts, and Sociological Abstracts to access literature on the topic from multiple perspectives. She thanked me and said that she wished she had known about these resources sooner, adding that she would definitely encourage fellow students to schedule a research consultation.

Reflection on the Instruction Session: Lessons Learned

Most business students come to the library familiar with the types of data they are looking for, so they are usually most concerned with efficiently locating and easily manipulating the information that they find, given the multiple options available for data retrieval. Feedback given by the business students after their session indicated that the students derived a better understanding of useful resources for company and industry research. On-demand sessions are also very helpful to business reference librarians, as they provide insight into the research needs of our patrons. The sessions also afford an excellent opportunity to interact with the students, and to discuss and promote library resources.

The busy schedules of journalism students are not conducive to regular classroom visits, and unlike business, their work is less frequently group based. Sessions such as the one described illustrate the value of target-marketing sessions, with a very specific focus, to faculty. When the professor is involved in shaping the content of the session, and she herself invites students to attend, success is more guaranteed than when I approach the students directly. Unlike the business students, journalism students' interests tend to shift frequently, based on their assignments.

At the Social Work Library, research consultations, which blur the lines between instruction and reference, have become the prevalent form of interaction with users, with several advantages worthy of mention. First, consultations in the Social Work Library are scheduled at a time convenient for the student, unlike traditional reference desk hours or group instruction sessions, which are based on availability of library staff. Second, as there is no set script that determines the path the consultation will take, the research consultation is among the few truly "user-driven" services reference librarians can provide. Finally, the student receives the undivided attention of the librarian, who devotes a significant amount of time to addressing the needs of the student in a personalized, meaningful way, exactly the kind of collaborative interaction that social work students are encouraged to strive for in the classroom, and ultimately, the workplace.

The case studies described illustrate the success of merging reference and instruction into discrete consultations. These consultations meet the unique needs of our students as we provide targeted sessions that address their immediate information need and they learn how to use the library to do their research in the process.

Whether we are meeting students' needs through on-demand instruction for groups of students, leading sessions designed with faculty input, or conducting research consultations with individual students, instruction to our users is ultimately served by something common to all three libraries: in-depth knowledge of our users' information needs and information-seeking styles, knowledge that is continually enhanced by the instructional opportunities we provide.

Notes

1. Association of College and Research Libraries, *Information Literacy Competency Standards for Higher Education* (Chicago: ACRL, 2000). Available online from http://www.ala.org/ala/acrl/acrlstandards/inform ationliteracycompetency.htm.

2. Ibid.

3. Ibid.

Teaching Resources

Company and Industry Research Handout
Kathleen M. Dreyer

CORPORATE FILINGS WITH THE SEC
Bloomberg
Online database providing current and historical financial quotes, business newswires, and descriptive information, research and statistics on over 52,000 companies worldwide.

EdgarScan
An excellent Internet resource provided by PricewaterhouseCoopers, EdgarScan is an interface to the United States Securities and Exchange Commission Electronic Data Gathering, Analysis and Retrieval (SEC EDGAR) database.

Thomson Research
Thomson Research contains real-time and historical SEC EDGAR filings, scanned images of company annual reports and foreign exchange filings.

STOCK PRICES
Bloomberg

Datastream
Large database of statistical time series covering stocks, bonds, commodities and economic data for numerous countries, along with company profiles. See the notebook at the workstation for instructions. Coverage varies by dataset.

Factiva
Full-text database providing timely and detailed facts, figures and analyses of companies, industries and financial markets. Includes industry and trade publications, news sources, and company and market data. Coverage varies by source.

Thomson ONE Banker
Thomson ONE Banker provides access to financial data on public companies, as well as merger and acquisition information and market data. Users can search and screen across databases to identify companies that meet your specific investment criteria as well as conduct peer analysis

FINANCIAL & OPERATING INFORMATION
Bloomberg
OSIRIS
OSIRIS is a comprehensive database of listed corporates, banks and insurance companies around the world.

Thomson ONE Banker
ANALYSTS' REPORTS
Investext
Contains full-text research reports from over 600 investment banks, brokerages, and other third party researchers. The reports cover U.S. and international companies and are updated daily.

Reuters Research On-Demand
Contains full-text research reports from over 600 investment banks, brokerages, and other third party researchers. The reports cover U.S. and international companies and are updated daily.

Journalism Session Handout
Arts & Culture Resources for Journalism MA Students
Deborah Wassertzug

The following are selected resources available via Columbia University Libraries for your research. Access them via Library Web at **http://www. columbia.edu/cu/lweb/**

ProQuest: Contains several thousand periodical titles, spanning newspapers and magazines, to trade publications and scholarly journals. **TIP:** If the full text of an article isn't available in ProQuest, click the **e-Link** icon to see if Columbia has access via another source.

JSTOR: A full-text repository of over 600 scholarly journals, with emphasis on historical access. A wide range of journal titles in the arts and humanities are represented.

ProQuest Historical Newspapers: A database composed of scanned microfilm backfiles of a number of US newspapers (including the *New York Times, Wall Street Journal, Los Angeles Times, Chicago Tribune*, and more). Emphasis on historical access rather than recent issues.

Factiva: Best known as a business database, Factiva is the closest competitor to LexisNexis and provides better access to newspapers, magazines, and journals than LexisNexis Academic does, and also better broadcast transcript coverage (good for locating interviews).

Readers' Guide Full Text and Readers' Guide Retrospective: This index database covers popular magazines that may not be included in ProQuest or other sources. **TIP:** If the full text of an article isn't available in ProQuest, click the **e-Link** icon to see if Columbia has access via another source.

Columbia Libraries to Visit:

Avery Architectural & Fine Arts Library: Books and periodicals in architecture, historic preservation, art history, painting, sculpture, graphic arts, decorative arts, city planning, real estate, and archaeology. Mostly a noncirculating collection.

Butler Library: Home to Columbia's collections in the humanities and history, it also houses: Butler Media Center, which has films available to be screened on site (only faculty may borrow); the Oral History Research Office; and the Rare Book and Manuscript Library.

Barnard College Library: A smaller library includes the Dance collection, the Barnard Media Center, as well as a Zine Collection (primarily focused on Women's Studies).

Music & Arts Library: Extensive print collections include books on music, musical scores, and a non-circulating collection of tens of thousands of recordings of both Western and non-Western music. Facilities are available for listening to recordings in all formats.

Information Literacy Competency Standards for Higher Education

Approved by the Board of Directors of the
Association of College and Research Libraries on January 18, 2000

Information Literacy Defined

Information literacy is a set of abilities requiring individuals to "recognize when information is needed and have the ability to locate, evaluate, and use effectively the needed information."[1] Information literacy also is increasingly important in the contemporary environment of rapid technological change and proliferating information resources. Because of the escalating complexity of this environment, individuals are faced with diverse, abundant information choices—in their academic studies, in the workplace, and in their personal lives. Information is available through libraries, community resources, special interest organizations, media, and the Internet—and increasingly, information comes to individuals in unfiltered formats, raising questions about its authenticity, validity, and reliability. In addition, information is available through multiple media, including graphical, aural, and textual, and these pose new challenges for individuals in evaluating and understanding it. The uncertain quality and expanding quantity of information pose large challenges for society. The sheer abundance of information will not in itself create a more informed citizenry without a complementary cluster of abilities necessary to use information effectively.

Information literacy forms the basis for lifelong learning. It is common to all disciplines, to all learning environments, and to all levels of education. It enables learners to master content and extend their investigations, become more self-directed, and assume greater control over their own learning. An information literate individual is able to:
- Determine the extent of information needed
- Access the needed information effectively and efficiently
- Evaluate information and its sources critically

- Incorporate selected information into one's knowledge base
- Use information effectively to accomplish a specific purpose
- Understand the economic, legal, and social issues surrounding the use of information, and access and use information ethically and legally

Information Literacy and Information Technology

Information literacy is related to information technology skills, but has broader implications for the individual, the educational system, and for society. Information technology skills enable an individual to use computers, software applications, databases, and other technologies to achieve a wide variety of academic, work-related, and personal goals. Information literate individuals necessarily develop some technology skills.

Information literacy, while showing significant overlap with information technology skills, is a distinct and broader area of competence. Increasingly, information technology skills are interwoven with, and support, information literacy. A 1999 report from the National Research Council promotes the concept of "fluency" with information technology and delineates several distinctions useful in understanding relationships among information literacy, computer literacy, and broader technological competence. The report notes that "computer literacy" is concerned with rote learning of specific hardware and software applications, while "fluency with technology" focuses on understanding the underlying concepts of technology and applying problem-solving and critical thinking to using technology. The report also discusses differences between information technology fluency and information literacy as it is understood in K-12 and higher education. Among these are information literacy's focus on content, communication, analysis, information searching, and evaluation; whereas information technology "fluency" focuses on a deep understanding of technology and graduated, increasingly skilled use of it.[2]

"Fluency" with information technology may require more intellectual abilities than the rote learning of software and hardware associated with "computer literacy", but the focus is still on the technology itself. Information literacy, on the other hand, is an intellectual framework for understanding, finding, evaluating, and using information—activities which may be accomplished in part by fluency with information technology, in part by sound investigative methods, but most important, through critical discernment and reasoning. Information literacy initiates, sustains, and extends lifelong learning through abilities which may use technologies but are ultimately independent of them.

Information Literacy and Higher Education

Developing lifelong learners is central to the mission of higher education institutions. By ensuring that individuals have the intellectual abilities of reasoning and critical thinking, and by helping them construct a framework for learning how to learn, colleges and universities provide the foundation for continued growth throughout their careers, as well as in their roles as informed citizens and members of communities. Information literacy is a key component of, and contributor to, lifelong learning. Information literacy competency extends learning beyond formal classroom settings and provides practice with self-directed investigations as individuals move into internships, first professional positions, and increasing responsibilities in all arenas of life. Because information literacy augments students' competency with evaluating, managing, and using information, it is now considered by several regional and discipline-based accreditation associations as a key outcome for college students.[3]

For students not on traditional campuses, information resources are often available through networks and other channels, and distributed learning technologies permit teaching and learning to occur when the teacher and the student are not in the same place at the same time. The challenge for those promoting information literacy in distance education courses is to develop a comparable range of experiences in learning about information resources as are offered on traditional campuses. Information literacy competencies for distance learning students should be comparable to those for "on campus" students.

Incorporating information literacy across curricula, in all programs and services, and throughout the administrative life of the university, requires the collaborative efforts of faculty, librarians, and administrators. Through lectures and by leading discussions, faculty establish the context for learning. Faculty also inspire students to explore the unknown, offer guidance on how best to fulfill information needs, and monitor students' progress. Academic librarians coordinate the evaluation and selection of intellectual resources for programs and services; organize, and maintain collections and many points of access to information; and provide instruction to students and faculty who seek information. Administrators create opportunities for collaboration and staff development among faculty, librarians, and other professionals who initiate information literacy programs, lead in planning and budgeting for those programs, and provide ongoing resources to sustain them.

Information Literacy and Pedagogy

The Boyer Commission Report, *Reinventing Undergraduate Education*, recommends strategies that require the student to engage actively in "framing of a significant question or set of questions, the research or creative exploration to find answers, and the communications skills to convey the results..."[4] Courses structured in such a way create student-centered learning environments where inquiry is the norm, problem solving becomes the focus, and thinking critically is part of the process. Such learning environments require information literacy competencies.

Gaining skills in information literacy multiplies the opportunities for students' self-directed learning, as they become engaged in using a wide variety of information sources to expand their knowledge, ask informed questions, and sharpen their critical thinking for still further self-directed learning. Achieving competency in information literacy requires an understanding that this cluster of abilities is not extraneous to the curriculum but is woven into the curriculum's content, structure, and sequence. This curricular integration also affords many possibilities for furthering the influence and impact of such student-centered teaching methods as problem-based learning, evidence-based learning, and inquiry learning. Guided by faculty and others in problem-based approaches, students reason about course content at a deeper level than is possible through the exclusive use of lectures and textbooks. To take fullest advantage of problem-based learning, students must often use thinking skills requiring them to become skilled users of information sources in many locations and formats, thereby increasing their responsibility for their own learning.

To obtain the information they seek for their investigations, individuals have many options. One is to utilize an information retrieval system, such as may be found in a library or in databases accessible by computer from any location. Another option is to select an appropriate investigative method for observing phenomena directly. For example, physicians, archaeologists, and astronomers frequently depend upon physical examination to detect the presence of particular phenomena. In addition, mathematicians, chemists, and physicists often utilize technologies such as statistical software or simulators to create artificial conditions in which to observe and analyze the interaction of phenomena. As students progress through their undergraduate years and graduate programs, they need to have repeated opportunities for seeking, evaluating, and managing information gathered from multiple sources and discipline-specific research methods.

Use of the Standards

Information Literacy Competency Standards for Higher Education provides a framework for assessing the information literate individual. It also extends the work of the American Association of School Librarians Task Force on Information Literacy Standards, thereby providing higher education an opportunity to articulate its information literacy competencies with those of K-12 so that a continuum of expectations develops for students at all levels. The competencies presented here outline the process by which faculty, librarians and others pinpoint specific indicators that identify a student as information literate.

Students also will find the competencies useful, because they provide students with a framework for gaining control over how they interact with information in their environment. It will help to sensitize them to the need to develop a metacognitive approach to learning, making them conscious of the explicit actions required for gathering, analyzing, and using information. All students are expected to demonstrate all of the competencies described in this document, but not everyone will demonstrate them to the same level of proficiency or at the same speed.

Furthermore, some disciplines may place greater emphasis on the mastery of competencies at certain points in the process, and therefore certain competencies would receive greater weight than others in any rubric for measurement. Many of the competencies are likely to be performed recursively, in that the reflective and evaluative aspects included within each standard will require the student to return to an earlier point in the process, revise the information-seeking approach, and repeat the same steps.

To implement the standards fully, an institution should first review its mission and educational goals to determine how information literacy would improve learning and enhance the institution's effectiveness. To facilitate acceptance of the concept, faculty and staff development is also crucial.

Information Literacy and Assessment

In the following competencies, there are five standards and twenty-two performance indicators. The standards focus upon the needs of students in higher education at all levels. The standards also list a range of outcomes for assessing student progress toward information literacy. These outcomes serve as guidelines for faculty, librarians, and others in developing local methods for measuring student learning in the context of an institution's unique mission. In addition to assessing all students' basic information literacy skills, faculty and librarians should also work together to develop assessment instruments and strategies in the context of particular disciplines, as information literacy manifests itself in the specific understanding of the knowledge creation, scholarly activity, and publication processes found in those disciplines.

In implementing these standards, institutions need to recognize that different levels of thinking skills are associated with various learning outcomes—and therefore different instruments or methods are essential to assess those outcomes. For example, both "higher order" and "lower order" thinking skills, based on Bloom's Taxonomy of Educational Objectives, are evident throughout the outcomes detailed in this document. It is strongly suggested that assessment methods appropriate to the thinking skills associated with each outcome be identified as an integral part of the institution's implementation plan.

For example, the following outcomes illustrate "higher order" and "lower order" thinking skills:

"Lower Order" thinking skill:
Outcome 2.2.a. Identifies keywords, synonyms, and related terms for the information needed.

"Higher Order" thinking skill:
Outcome 3.3.b. Extends initial synthesis, when possible, to a higher level of abstraction to construct new hypotheses that may required additional information.

Faculty, librarians, and others will find that discussing assessment methods collaboratively is a very productive exercise in planning a systematic, comprehensive information literacy program. This assessment program should reach all students, pinpoint areas for further program development, and consolidate learning goals already achieved. It also should make explicit to the institution's constituencies how information literacy contributes to producing educated students and citizens.

Notes
1. American Library Association. *Presidential Committee on Information Literacy. Final Report.* (Chicago: American Library Association, 1989.) http://www.ala.org/ala/acrl/acrlpubs/whitepapers/presidential.htm
2. National Research Council. Commission on Physical Sciences, Mathematics, and Applications. Committee on Information Technology Literacy, Computer Science and Telecommunications Board. *Being Fluent with Information Technology.* Publication. (Washington, D.C.: National Academy Press, 1999) http://www.nap.edu/books/030906399X/html/
3. Several key accrediting agencies concerned with information literacy are: The Middle States Commission on Higher Education (MSCHE), the Western Association of Schools and College (WASC), and the Southern Association of Colleges and Schools (SACS).
4. Boyer Commission on Educating Undergraduates in the Research University. *Reinventing Undergraduate Education: A Blueprint for America's Research Universities.* http://naples.cc.sunysb.edu/Pres/boyer.nsf/

Standards, Performance Indicators, and Outcomes

Standard One
The information literate student determines the nature and extent of the information needed.

Performance Indicators:
1. The information literate student defines and articulates the need for information.

Outcomes Include:
   a. Confers with instructors and participates in class discussions, peer workgroups, and electronic discussions to identify a research topic, or other information need
   b. Develops a thesis statement and formulates questions based on the information need
   c. Explores general information sources to increase familiarity with the topic
   d. Defines or modifies the information need to achieve a manageable focus
   e. Identifies key concepts and terms that describe the information need
   f. Recognizes that existing information can be combined with original thought, experimentation, and/or analysis to produce new information

2. The information literate student identifies a variety of types and formats of potential sources for information.

Outcomes Include:
   a. Knows how information is formally and informally produced, organized, and disseminated
   b. Recognizes that knowledge can be organized into disciplines that influence the way information is accessed
   c. Identifies the value and differences of potential resources in a variety of formats (e.g., multimedia, database, website, data set, audio/visual, book)
   d. Identifies the purpose and audience of potential resources (e.g., popular vs. scholarly, current vs. historical)
   e. Differentiates between primary and secondary sources, recognizing how their use and importance vary with each discipline

    f. Realizes that information may need to be constructed with raw data from primary sources

3. The information literate student considers the costs and benefits of acquiring the needed information.

Outcomes Include:
    a. Determines the availability of needed information and makes decisions on broadening the information seeking process beyond local resources (e.g., interlibrary loan; using resources at other locations; obtaining images, videos, text, or sound)
    b. Considers the feasibility of acquiring a new language or skill (e.g., foreign or discipline-based) in order to gather needed information and to understand its context
    c. Defines a realistic overall plan and timeline to acquire the needed information

4. The information literate student reevaluates the nature and extent of the information need.

Outcomes Include:
    a. Reviews the initial information need to clarify, revise, or refine the question
    b. Describes criteria used to make information decisions and choices

Standard Two
The information literate student accesses needed information effectively and efficiently.

Performance Indicators:
1. The information literate student selects the most appropriate investigative methods or information retrieval systems for accessing the needed information.

Outcomes Include:
    a. Identifies appropriate investigative methods (e.g., laboratory experiment, simulation, fieldwork)
    b. Investigates benefits and applicability of various investigative methods
    c. Investigates the scope, content, and organization of information retrieval systems
    d. Selects efficient and effective approaches for accessing the

information needed from the investigative method or information retrieval system

2. The information literate student constructs and implements effectively-designed search strategies.

Outcomes Include:
   a. Develops a research plan appropriate to the investigative method
   b. Identifies keywords, synonyms and related terms for the information needed
   c. Selects controlled vocabulary specific to the discipline or information retrieval source
   d. Constructs a search strategy using appropriate commands for the information retrieval system selected (e.g., Boolean operators, truncation, and proximity for search engines; internal organizers such as indexes for books)
   e. Implements the search strategy in various information retrieval systems using different user interfaces and search engines, with different command languages, protocols, and search parameters
   f. Implements the search using investigative protocols appropriate to the discipline

3. The information literate student retrieves information online or in person using a variety of methods.

Outcomes Include:
   a. Uses various search systems to retrieve information in a variety of formats
   b. Uses various classification schemes and other systems (e.g., call number systems or indexes) to locate information resources within the library or to identify specific sites for physical exploration
   c. Uses specialized online or in person services available at the institution to retrieve information needed (e.g., interlibrary loan/ document delivery, professional associations, institutional research offices, community resources, experts and practitioners)
   d. Uses surveys, letters, interviews, and other forms of inquiry to retrieve primary information

4. The information literate student refines the search strategy if necessary.

Outcomes Include:
   a. Assesses the quantity, quality, and relevance of the search results

to determine whether alternative information retrieval systems or investigative methods should be utilized

    b. Identifies gaps in the information retrieved and determines if the search strategy should be revised

    c. Repeats the search using the revised strategy as necessary

5. The information literate student extracts, records, and manages the information and its sources.

Outcomes Include:

    a. Selects among various technologies the most appropriate one for the task of extracting the needed information (e.g., copy/paste software functions, photocopier, scanner, audio/visual equipment, or exploratory instruments)

    b. Creates a system for organizing the information

    c. Differentiates between the types of sources cited and understands the elements and correct syntax of a citation for a wide range of resources

    d. Records all pertinent citation information for future reference

    e. Uses various technologies to manage the information selected and organized

Standard Three
The information literate student evaluates information and its sources critically and incorporates selected information into his or her knowledge base and value system.

Performance Indicators:
1. The information literate student summarizes the main ideas to be extracted from the information gathered.

Outcomes Include:

    a. Reads the text and selects main ideas

    b. Restates textual concepts in his/her own words and selects data accurately

    c. Identifies verbatim material that can be then appropriately quoted

2. The information literate student articulates and applies initial criteria for evaluating both the information and its sources.

Outcomes Include:

    a. Examines and compares information from various sources in order to evaluate reliability, validity, accuracy, authority, timeliness, and point of view or bias

b. Analyzes the structure and logic of supporting arguments or methods
c. Recognizes prejudice, deception, or manipulation
d. Recognizes the cultural, physical, or other context within which the information was created and understands the impact of context on interpreting the information

3. The information literate student synthesizes main ideas to construct new concepts.

Outcomes Include:
a. Recognizes interrelationships among concepts and combines them into potentially useful primary statements with supporting evidence
b. Extends initial synthesis, when possible, at a higher level of abstraction to construct new hypotheses that may require additional information
c. Utilizes computer and other technologies (e.g. spreadsheets, databases, multimedia, and audio or visual equipment) for studying the interaction of ideas and other phenomena

4. The information literate student compares new knowledge with prior knowledge to determine the value added, contradictions, or other unique characteristics of the information.

Outcomes Include:
a. Determines whether information satisfies the research or other information need
b. Uses consciously selected criteria to determine whether the information contradicts or verifies information used from other sources
c. Draws conclusions based upon information gathered
d. Tests theories with discipline-appropriate techniques (e.g., simulators, experiments)
e. Determines probable accuracy by questioning the source of the data, the limitations of the information gathering tools or strategies, and the reasonableness of the conclusions
f. Integrates new information with previous information or knowledge
g. Selects information that provides evidence for the topic

5. The information literate student determines whether the new knowledge has an impact on the individual's value system and takes steps to reconcile differences.

Outcomes Include:
  a. Investigates differing viewpoints encountered in the literature
  b. Determines whether to incorporate or reject viewpoints encountered

6. The information literate student validates understanding and interpretation of the information through discourse with other individuals, subject-area experts, and/or practitioners.

Outcomes Include:
  a. Participates in classroom and other discussions
  b. Participates in class-sponsored electronic communication forums designed to encourage discourse on the topic (e.g., e-mail, bulletin boards, chat rooms)
  c. Seeks expert opinion through a variety of mechanisms (e.g., interviews, e-mail, listservs)

7. The information literate student determines whether the initial query should be revised.

Outcomes Include:
  a. Determines if original information need has been satisfied or if additional information is needed
  b. Reviews search strategy and incorporates additional concepts as necessary
  c. Reviews information retrieval sources used and expands to include others as needed

Standard Four
The information literate student, individually or as a member of a group, uses information effectively to accomplish a specific purpose.

Performance Indicators:
1. The information literate student applies new and prior information to the planning and creation of a particular product or performance.

Outcomes Include:
  a. Organizes the content in a manner that supports the purposes and format of the product or performance (e.g. outlines, drafts, storyboards)
  b. Articulates knowledge and skills transferred from prior experiences to planning and creating the product or performance
  c. Integrates the new and prior information, including quotations

and paraphrasings, in a manner that supports the purposes of the product or performance
  d. Manipulates digital text, images, and data, as needed, transferring them from their original locations and formats to a new context

2. The information literate student revises the development process for the product or performance.

Outcomes Include:
  a. Maintains a journal or log of activities related to the information seeking, evaluating, and communicating process
  b. Reflects on past successes, failures, and alternative strategies

3. The information literate student communicates the product or performance effectively to others.
Outcomes Include:
  a. Chooses a communication medium and format that best supports the purposes of the product or performance and the intended audience
  b. Uses a range of information technology applications in creating the product or performance
  c. Incorporates principles of design and communication
  d. Communicates clearly and with a style that supports the purposes of the intended audience

Standard Five
The information literate student understands many of the economic, legal, and social issues surrounding the use of information and accesses and uses information ethically and legally.

Performance Indicators:
1. The information literate student understands many of the ethical, legal and socio-economic issues surrounding information and information technology.

Outcomes Include:
  a. Identifies and discusses issues related to privacy and security in both the print and electronic environments
  b. Identifies and discusses issues related to free vs. fee-based access to information
  c. Identifies and discusses issues related to censorship and freedom of speech

    d. Demonstrates an understanding of intellectual property, copyright, and fair use of copyrighted material

2. The information literate student follows laws, regulations, institutional policies, and etiquette related to the access and use of information resources.

Outcomes Include:
    a. Participates in electronic discussions following accepted practices (e.g. "Netiquette")
    b. Uses approved passwords and other forms of ID for access to information resources
    c. Complies with institutional policies on access to information resources
    d. Preserves the integrity of information resources, equipment, systems and facilities
    e. Legally obtains, stores, and disseminates text, data, images, or sounds
    f. Demonstrates an understanding of what constitutes plagiarism and does not represent work attributable to others as his/her own
    g. Demonstrates an understanding of institutional policies related to human subjects research

3. The information literate student acknowledges the use of information sources in communicating the product or performance.

Outcomes Include:
    a. Selects an appropriate documentation style and uses it consistently to cite sources
    b. Posts permission granted notices, as needed, for copyrighted material

Contributors

Editors

Douglas Cook, DEd, is distance and grants librarian and professor at Shippensburg University of Pennsylvania. He received his MLS from the University of Maryland and his doctorate from the Pennsylvania State University. He is the 2005–2006 Chair of the ACRL, Education and Behavioral Sciences Section (EBSS). He has recently been elected as a member-at-large of the Governing Board of the Associated College Libraries of Central Pennsylvania (ACLCP), a regional academic library professional development organization. He has had three book chapters published, including "Creating Connections: A Review of the Literature," in *The Collaborative Imperative: Librarians and Faculty Working Together in the Information Universe*, eds. Richard Raspa and Dane Ward, (Chicago: ACRL, 2000). His most recent article was "A Pennsylvania Library Collaborative Celebrates Its Past and Plans for Its Future: A Forty-year Commitment to People, Service and Collection Development," with Steven McKinzie and the ACLCP Fortieth Anniversary Planning Committee, *Against the Grain* 17, no. 5 (2005). He may be contacted by e-mail at dlcook@ship.edu.

Tasha Cooper is reference librarian at Syracuse University Library, previously having served as reference and educational services librarian at the George T. Harrell Library, Penn State College of Medicine, Milton S. Hershey Medical Center, and assistant instructional services librarian at the John G. Snowden Memorial Library, Lycoming College. Tasha is a member of the Instruction Section, and Education and Behavioral Sciences Section of the ACRL. She has an MLS from Syracuse University and an MEd in higher education from Pennsylvania State University. She may be contacted by e-mail at nacoop01@syr.edu.

Authors

Susan Ariew is the research and collections librarian for education at the University of South Florida (USF), where she teaches LIS 2005, Library and Internet Research Skills, a three-credit-hour undergraduate class in information literacy. She is a new member of the USF Tampa Library faculty coming from Virginia Tech where she worked for ten years as college librarian for education and human development. Much of the work Susan did at Virginia Tech included instruction sessions with graduate students enrolled in master's and PhD programs in education or human development. In addition to her work as an academic librarian at Virginia Tech, Susan also worked at the University of Illinois at Urbana-Champaign and at the Center for Research Libraries in Chicago. She also spent several years teaching English, writing, and composition at the high school and collegiate levels. Her research and publication interests include academic librarians' status, collaborative relationships between librarians and academic faculty, diversity resources for teachers, and assessment tools for evaluating library instruction and student learning. She may be contacted by e-mail at sariew@lib.usf.edu.

Laura Barrett is the undergraduate services librarian at the Odegaard Undergraduate Library, University of Washington (UW), where she coordinates information literacy instruction. She also is the psychology subject librarian for the UW Libraries' Seattle campus. Laura has recently facilitated and participated in discussions about libraries and civic engagement, at both the ALA and the ACRL conferences. Laura earned her master's of science in information at the University of Michigan School of Information. She may be contacted by e-mail at barrettl@u.washington. edu.

Navaz Peshotan Bhavnagri, PhD, is an associate professor of early childhood education in the Teacher Education Division, College of Education, Wayne State University, Detroit, Michigan. She received her doctorate from the University of Illinois, and has more than forty years of experience in university teaching. For the past fifteen years, she has collaborated with librarians when teaching a graduate course that focuses on library and empirical research methods. She is author and coauthor of several articles and chapters, including numerous articles on research methods, and served as an editor of a special issue of *Childhood Education*. She serves as a reviewer for three research journals. She may be contacted by e-mail at aa4214@wayne.edu.

Veronica Bielat is a public services librarian and liaison to the College of Education at Wayne State University, Detroit, Michigan. She received her MLIS from Wayne State University. She is also an adjunct faculty member of the Library and Information Science Program at Wayne State University, and annually co-teaches a course titled Instructional Methods for Librarians. Veronica and Navaz Peshotan Bhavnagri recently published an article entitled "Faculty–Librarian Collaboration to Teach Research Skills: Electronic Symbiosis" in *Reference Librarian*, 89/90 (2005). She may be contacted by e-mail at ag6887@wayne.edu.

Jennifer D. Brown is outreach services librarian and assistant professor of library science at the University of Alaska Southeast, William A. Egan Library. Her responsibilities include library support of UAS distance students. She received her MLIS from the University of Hawaii at Manoa, Library and Information Science Program in December 2001. Along with an "in press" article coauthored with Thomas Duke, Jennifer cowrote "Educating Instruction Librarians: A Model for Library and Information Science Education" (2001), *Research Strategies*, 18, no. 4 (2001): 253–64 (with Yvonne N. Meulemans). She may be contacted by e-mail at jennifer.brown@uas.alaska.edu.

Patti Schifter Caravello is director of the UCLA Library's Information Literacy Program and librarian for anthropology, archaeology, and sociology at the UCLA Charles E. Young Research Library. Her responsibilities include instruction, collection development, department liaison, reference and consultation. Patti directs the librarywide initiative that provides UCLA librarians resources and leadership for enhancing information literacy efforts on campus. She is currently a member of the ACRL Anthropology and Sociology Section's Information Literacy Committee, which is developing discipline-specific IL standards. She may be contacted by e-mail at patti@library.ucla.edu.

Melissa Cast is the education librarian for the University of Nebraska at Omaha where she has coordinated many of the library's information literacy activities. She currently serves on the Executive Council of the Education and Behavioral Sciences Section of ACRL as a member-at-large. Melissa has an MLS from the School of Library and Information Sciences, University of Missouri-Columbia. She may be contacted by e-mail at mcast@mail.unomaha.edu.

Chantana Charoenpanitkul is government documents/GIS librarian at the Ezra Lehman Memorial Library, Shippensburg University of Pennsylvania. Before coming to Shippensburg, she headed the Retrospective Cataloging/Collection Maintenance Unit in the Catalog Department at Ellis Library, University of Missouri-Columbia. A native of Thailand, she earned an MA in art history from MS University of Baroda, India. Prior to her library profession, she was an assistant professor in art and art history at Rajapadthr University and an adjunct professor at Chulalongkorn University. She received her MALS and has completed the required coursework toward a PhD in art history at the University of Missouri-Columbia. She may be contacted by e-mail at chchar@ship.edu.

Collette D. Childers is the education librarian and Curriculum Materials Center coordinator in the Pollak Library at California State University, Fullerton. She provides reference assistance and library instruction for the College of Education's teacher preparation, master's, and EdD programs. She may be contacted by e-mail at cchilders@fullerton.edu.

Christopher Cox is assistant director of libraries at the University of Wisconsin, Eau Claire's McIntyre Library. His responsibilities include supervision of the student employment program and development of the library's strategic plan. Forever intrigued by technology and its application to library instruction, Chris has written on diverse technological topics such as streaming media and course management systems. His work has been published in *College & Research Libraries News* and *Computers in Libraries*. He also serves as editor of *Internet Reference Services Quarterly*, as column editor for *College and Undergraduate Libraries*, and he is a frequent reviewer for *Choice Magazine*. He is a proud member of ALA and ACRL, and serves on various committees, including the AASL/ACRL Interdivisional Committee on Information Literacy. He may be contacted by e-mail at coxcn@uwec.edu.

Alice L. Daugherty is an instructional and reference librarian at Louisiana State University. She holds an MLIS from Wayne State University. Alice is the current chair of ALA's New Members Round Table Local Arrangements Committee and the Coordinator for the Louisiana Library Association's User Education Interest Group. Her research interests include assessment, instructional design, and library anxiety. She may be contacted by e-mail at adaugher@lsu.edu.

Kathleen M. Dreyer is the electronic services and reference librarian at the Thomas J. Watson Library of Business & Economics, Columbia University. Before coming to Columbia, Kathleen was a reference librarian at the Lippincott Library at the University of Pennsylvania. She has an MLIS from Drexel University. Kathleen has worked with business and economics students for more than five years. She may be contacted by e-mail at kd2145@columbia.edu.

Thomas Scott Duke, PhD, is assistant professor of education at the University of Alaska Southeast, where he teaches courses in special education, multicultural education, and classroom research and coordinates the Special Education Teacher Endorsement Program. He earned his PhD in special education at the University of Hawaii at Manoa. His publications include "Problematizing Collaboration: A Critical Review of the Empirical Literature on Teaching Teams," *Teacher Education & Special Education*, 27, no. 3 (2004): 126–36; "Hidden, Invisible, Marginalized, Ignored: A Critical Review of the Professional and Empirical Literature (or Lack Thereof) on Gay and Lesbian Teachers in the United States" (In press), *Journal of Gay and Lesbian Issues in Education*; and "Librarian and Faculty Collaborative Instruction: A Phenomenological Self-study" (In press), *Research Strategies* (coauthored with Jennifer Brown). He may be contacted by e-mail at thomas.duke@uas.alaska.edu.

Allison Faix received her MLIS from the University of Pittsburgh in 1999. She is currently the reference/interlibrary loan librarian at Coastal Carolina University in Conway, South Carolina, where she oversees the Interlibrary Loan Department, serves as reference coordinator, and teaches information literacy sessions. She may be contacted by e-mail at afaix@coastal.edu.

Mary Feeney is the librarian for journalism, library science, and business at the University of Arizona Library. She has an MA in information resources and library science from the University of Arizona. During graduate school, she completed an internship in the News Library at National Public Radio (NPR), which led to her interest in working with journalism students. She has presented on using portfolios for assessment of library science students and copresented on mentoring. Her publications include articles on library services for distance students, organizing resources in a federated searching tool, and teaching business research to engineering students. She may be contacted by e-mail at feeneym@u.library.arizona. edu.

Cynthia Gibbon is a reference and instruction librarian at Gettysburg College's Musselman Library. She holds an MLIS from the University of Pittsburgh and a master of liberal arts from Western Maryland College (now McDaniel College). She and Jennifer Leigh of the management department of Gettysburg College have collaborated on an article currently under review and a presentation slated for the 2006 Academy of Management conference. She may be contacted by e-mail at cgibbon@gettysburg.edu.

Jennifer Hughes received her MLIS from the University of South Carolina in 2004. She is currently the access services librarian at Coastal Carolina University in Conway, South Carolina, where she oversees the circulation department, provides reference services, and teaches information literacy sessions. She may be contacted by e-mail at jhughes@coastal.edu.

Janet McNeil Hurlbert is associate dean and director of library services at Lycoming College in Williamsport, Pennsylvania. One of her fields of interest is student research and she continues to be active in the information literacy/library instruction program at her library. Her MA degree in library science is from the University of Denver. She has authored and coauthored numerous articles and book chapters, including an article appearing in the *Journal of College and Research Libraries* that was included in the ALA Instructional Round Table's "Top Twenty" list for 2003. She may be contacted by e-mail at hurlbjan@lycoming.edu.

Alysse D. Jordan is the social work librarian at Columbia University. She holds an MILS from the University of Michigan and has been working in academic libraries since 1993. She was selected to participate in the Minnesota Institute for Early-Career Librarians in 1998 and the Association of Research Libraries Leadership and Career Development Program in 2003–2004. She contributed chapters to *Diversity in Libraries: Academic Residency Programs* (Greenwood Press, 2001) and *Multiracial America: A Resource Guide on the History and Literature of Interracial Issues* (Scarecrow Press, 2005). She may be contacted by e-mail at aj204@columbia.edu.

Sara K. Kearns is an assistant professor and instruction coordinator for Kansas State University Libraries. Sara holds an MLS from the Catholic University of America. She is author of the following publication: "Marketing Library Service Assessment," *Technical Services Quarterly* 22, no. 2 (2004): 49–61. She may be contacted by e-mail at skearns@ksu.edu.

Steven C. Koehn, PhD, is assistant professor of communication at Lycoming College, Williamsport, Pennsylvania, and chair of the Department of Communication. His doctorate in instructional communication is from West Virginia University. He holds a master's in broadcast management from Pepperdine University and a BA in communication/film from Virginia Tech University. He may be contacted by e-mail at koehn@lycoming.edu.

Corinne Laverty, PhD, is head of the Education Library at Queen's University, Kingston, Canada. She develops and teaches workshops for students and faculty on information literacy, innovative teaching and learning resources, and resource-based learning. Cory's research interests focus on student development of information literacy in online courses and best practices for the integration of educational technologies in university classrooms. Her degrees include a BM from Queen's University, a BEd from the University of London, England, an MM and an MLIS from the University of Western Ontario, Canada, and a PhD in Information Science, University of Wales, United Kingdom. She may be contacted by e-mail at lavertyc@post.queensu.ca.

Jennifer S. A. Leigh, PhD, is assistant professor of management at Gettysburg College, where she teaches courses on social issues in management, work-based learning, and organizational behavior. Her research interests include interorganizational relationships, corporate citizenship, and management pedagogy. She holds a PhD in management from Boston College, an MA in whole systems design from Antioch University Seattle, and a BA in history with a concentration in women's studies from Swarthmore College. She may be contacted by e-mail at jleigh@gettysburg. edu.

Patricia O'Brien Libutti, PhD, currently owns a consulting business, Creative Information Solutions. Past positions include social sciences/ education librarian, Rutgers, the State University of New Jersey; Cybrarian, ThinkQuest; education librarian, Fordham University, Lincoln Center, NYC; adjunct, Educational Technology and Humanities Reference; and K–12 educator, art. Her PhD dissertation in educational psychology explored facilitation of curiosity and creativity. Her publications over the past decade have focused on the instructional roles of librarians in technology-rich scenarios. She has contributed numerous chapters to books, and edited three books published by ACRL: *Digital Resources and Librarians: Case Studies in Innovation, Invention, and Implementation*, published in 2004; *Librarians as Learners; Librarians as Teachers: The Diffusion of Internet Expertise in Academic Libraries*, in 1999; and in 1995, the inspiration for this book, with coeditor Bonnie Gratch-Lindauer, *Teaching Information Retrieval and Evaluation Skills to Educators: A Casebook of Applications*. Tricia chaired the Education and Behavioral Sciences Section, ACRL (1995–1996). and was chair of the Education Division, Special Libraries Association (2004–2005). She may be contacted by e-mail at libutti@gmail. com.

Barbara P. Norelli is the social sciences and instructional services librarian at Scribner Library of Skidmore College, Saratoga Springs, New York. She received her BA and MLS from University at Albany (SUNY). Prior to joining the Skidmore Library faculty, she held a variety of positions at Albany Law School, including associate law librarian and head of public services, and was head of reference at Santa Clara University's Heafey Law

Library in California. As chair of the ACRL Law & Political Science Section (LPSS) Education Task Force, she is helping to develop discipline-specific information literacy standards for political science. Barbara's most recent article, "Setting the Record Straight: How Online Database Providers Are Handling Plagiarism and Fabrication Issues," was published in the March 2005 issue of *College & Research Libraries*. Nominated by the Management and Business Department faculty, Barbara received the President's Award in recognition of her exemplary commitment to the educational mission and progressive spirit of Skidmore College on May 27, 2004. She may be contacted by e-mail at bnorelli@skidmore.edu.

David M. Oldenkamp is the international studies librarian at Indiana University, Bloomington's Herman B. Wells Library. Before coming to Indiana, he was the social sciences reference librarian at Muhlenberg College, which is where this case study originated. David received his MLS and MA in international relations from Syracuse University. Special thanks go to Christopher W. Herrick, PhD, whose International Law and Organization class brings out the best in students and librarians. David may be contacted by e-mail at doldenka@indiana.edu.

Justina O. Osa, EdD, is the education and behavioral sciences librarian, at the Pennsylvania State University, University Libraries, University Park. Her research and professional presentation foci include: finding ways to enable all students to learn and succeed in school; determining how to effectively and efficiently present concepts and curricular topics to heterogeneous classrooms; studying the relationship between student language proficiency and academic achievement; and examining areas where the library could assist students in their academic achievement. She is a member of the Board of Examiners, National Council for the Accreditation of Teacher Education (NCATE). She is active in professional associations and serves as member, chair, and cochair in several professional committees and task forces. She also served on the IFLA Boat Library Feasibility Study Project in Africa. She may be contacted by e-mail at joo2@psu.edu.

Suzan Parker is the reference and instruction coordinator and the social sciences subject librarian at the co-located campus of the University of Washington, Bothell, and Cascadia Community College. Most recently, she has presented on the developmental and contextual nature of information literacy at the League for Innovation in the Community College and at the Pacific Northwest Higher Education Teaching & Learning conferences. She earned her MLIS from the University of Washington Information School. She may be contacted by e-mail at sparker@uwb.edu

Rebecca Pasco, PhD, is an associate professor in the college of education and coordinator of the Library Science Education Programs at the University of Nebraska, Omaha. Her experience in school, public, and academic libraries supports her writing and research on issues related to library science, which include information literacy, technology and instruction, distance education, critical theory, and youth services. Rebecca holds an MLS and a PhD from the School of Library and Information Management at Emporia State University. She may be contacted by e-mail at rpasco@mail.unomaha.edu.

Brenda Reed is public services librarian of the Education Library at Queen's University, Kingston, Canada. She works in the areas of reference and instruction. Her interests focus on the development of classroom teaching strategies through the use of inspirational materials, especially children's literature, and exploring ways to enhance online professional development of school librarians. Brenda holds a BEd, ME, and an MLIS from the University of Western Ontario, Canada, and an MEd from Queen's University. She may be contacted by e-mail at reedb@post.queensu.ca.

Christine G. Renne, PhD, is a professor in the Elementary and Bilingual Education Department at California State University, Fullerton. She teaches in the credential, master's, and EdD programs, primarily in the areas of curriculum and instruction, and mathematics. She may be contacted by e-mail at crenne@fullerton.edu.

Aaron K. Shrimplin is the electronic information services librarian at Miami University Libraries. He is part of a three-person team responsible for the libraries' Web site and is a subject specialist for political science, law, and international studies. He also manages the libraries' Electronic Data Center (EDC) with Jen-chien Yu. He has published articles in *IASSIST Quarterly* with Jen-chien Yu; *Library Collections, Acquisitions, and Technical Services*; *Performance Measurement & Metric*; and *College and Research Library News*. He may be contacted by e-mail at aaron@lib.muohio.edu.

Ryan L. Sittler is reference/instruction librarian at the Ezra Lehman Memorial Library, Shippensburg University of Pennsylvania. Previously, he was a member of the staff at the Yocum Library, Reading Area Community College. Ryan holds an MSLS from Clarion University of Pennsylvania and is currently pursuing an MSIT at Bloomsburg University of Pennsylvania. He is a recipient of an H.W. Wilson Scholarship in 2005. His previous publication, "Distance Education and Computer-based Services: The Opportunities and Challenges for Small Academic Libraries" appeared in the spring 2005 issue of *Bookmobile and Outreach Services.* He may be contacted by e-mail at rlsittler@aol.com.

Jane A. Smith is assistant professor and education reference librarian at Texas A&M University, College Station. She earned her bachelor's in elementary education from the University of Texas at Austin and her MLS from Texas Woman's University. She has been a library media specialist in a public elementary school, as well as a public schoolteacher. She may be contacted by e-mail at janeasmith@tamu.edu.

Marcia G. Stockham holds an MA in library science from the University of Missouri-Columbia. She is an associate professor and education librarian for Kansas State University Libraries. She is coauthor of several publications, including, with Elizabeth Turtle and Eric Hansen, "KANAnswer: A Collaborative Statewide Virtual Reference Pilot Project," *Reference Librarian* 38, no. 79/80 (Nov. 2003): 257–66; and with Elizabeth Turtle, "Providing Off-campus Library Services by 'Team': An Assessment," *Journal of Library Administration* 41, no. 3/4 (2004): 443–57. She may be contacted by e-mail at stockham@ksu.edu.

Lolly Templeton, EdD, is an associate professor and early childhood program director at Westfield State College in Westfield, Massachusetts. Her research interests include early childhood curriculum, course-embedded information literacy instruction, mentoring, educational technology, and Professional Development School partnerships. Lolly cowrote an article with Signia Warner, "Incorporating Information Literacy into Teacher Education," *Academic Exchange Quarterly* 6, no. 4 (2002): 71–76, and they have presented aspects of their collaborative work at annual meetings of the American Education Research Association in Chicago (2003) and San Diego (2004). Lolly received her BA and EdD from the University of Massachusetts, Amherst, and her MEd from Westfield State College. She may be contacted by e-mail at ltempleton@wsc.ma.edu.

Signia Warner, EdD, is senior librarian and director of Ely Library's Education Resources Center at Westfield State College in Westfield, Massachusetts. She works collaboratively with Lolly Templeton and other faculty and students to embed information literacy instruction in the content of education coursework. Signia cowrote an article with Lolly Templeton, "Incorporating Information Literacy into Teacher Education," *Academic Exchange Quarterly* 6, no. 4 (2002): 71–76, and they have presented aspects of their collaborative work at annual meetings of the American Education

Research Association in Chicago (2003) and San Diego (2004). Signia teaches graduate and undergraduate courses for the Education Department as an adjunct professor in the Division of Graduate and Continuing Education. She received her BA from the University of California, Santa Cruz, her MLS from the State University of New York, Albany, and her EdD from the University of Massachusetts, Amherst. She may be contacted by e-mail at swarner@wsc.ma.edu.

Deborah Y. Wassertzug holds an MLS from the University of Maryland, College Park. She has been the journalism librarian at Columbia since 1998. She coordinates Columbia's chat reference service, Ask Us Now. She began her career in the Research Library Residency Program at the University of Michigan. She has given talks on virtual reference and other topics throughout the New York metropolitan area. She may be contacted by e-mail at dw242@columbia.edu.

Janelle Wertzberger is director of reference and instruction at Gettysburg College in Gettysburg, Pennsylvania. She has published and presented on information literacy in the biology curriculum and librarian liaison programs, and is currently working on a book chapter about using "clickers" (personal response devices) in information literacy instruction. She holds an MLIS from the University of Texas at Austin and an MA in English from the University of Florida. She may be contacted by e-mail at jwertzbe@gettysburg.edu.

Karin E. Westman, PhD, is an associate professor of English at Kansas State University, where she teaches courses on modern and contemporary British literature and women's literature. She holds a PhD from Vanderbilt University. In addition to other publications, she is author of the following: "Generation, Not Regeneration: Screening Out Class, Gender, and Cultural Change in the Film of Regeneration" in *Critical Perspectives on Pat Barker*, ed. Margaretta Jolly, Sharon Monteith, Ron Paul, and Nahem Yousaf (Columbia, SC: University of South Carolina Press, 2005), 162–74; "For Her Generation the Newspaper was a Book'": Media, Mediation, and Oscillation in Virginia Woolf's Between the Acts," *Journal of Modern Literature* 29, no. 2 (forthcoming, 2006); with Naomi Wood, "Preservice Teachers, Technology, and Information Literacy" in *Proceedings of SITE 2002, 13th International Conference*, vol. 3, ed. Dee Anna Willis, Jerry Price, and Niki Davis, (Norfolk, VA: Association for the Advancement of Computing in Education, 2002): 1826–30; and *Pat Barker's Regeneration: A Reader's Guide* (New York: Continuum, 2001). She may be contacted by e-mail at westmank@ksu.edu.

Grace Xu is the social work librarian at the University of Southern California (USC). She is responsible for reference, instruction, collection development, and outreach at the Randall Information Center, a research lab at the School of Social Work. Prior to this, she was the social science librarian and instructional technology specialist at the Norlin Library, University of Colorado at Boulder. A graduate of the University of Illinois at Urbana-Champaign, Xu has two MS degrees, one in library and information science (2001), and the other in journalism (2002). She may be contacted by e-mail at gracex@usc.edu.

Jen-chien Yu has been an electronic information services librarian/data specialist at Miami University Libraries since 2001. She develops Web-based services and applications, with a focus on applications for numeric data users and instructional outreach to first-year students. She is involved in the development of E-learn, a Web-based instruction for first-year students funded by an Ohio Board of Regents Grant. She teaches Introduction to Information Studies in the Digital Age, a semester-long course in locating and creating information in a variety of digital formats. She recently copresented a paper titled "The DDI and Its Internet Interface: Integrating Survey Data Information" at the International Conference on Digital Archive Technologies, in Taipei, Taiwan. She may be contacted by e-mail at jyu@lib.muohio.edu.